A Man by Any Other Name

SERIES EDITORS

Stephen Berry
University of Georgia

Amy Murrell Taylor
University of Kentucky

ADVISORY BOARD

Edward L. Ayers
University of Richmond
Catherine Clinton
University of Texas at San Antonio
J. Matthew Gallman
University of Florida
Elizabeth Leonard
Colby College

James Marten
Marquette University
Scott Nelson
University of Georgia
Daniel E. Sutherland
University of Arkansas
Elizabeth Varon
University of Virginia

A Man by Any Other Name

William Clarke Quantrill and the Search for American Manhood

BY JOSEPH M. BEILEIN JR.

The University of Georgia Press
Athens

© 2023 by the University of Georgia Press
Athens, Georgia 30602
www.ugapress.org
All rights reserved
Set in 9.75/13.5 Baskerville 10 Pro Regular
by Kaelin Chappell Broaddus

Most University of Georgia Press titles are
available from popular e-book vendors.

Printed digitally

Library of Congress Cataloging-in-Publication Data

Names: Beilein, Joseph M., Jr., author.
Title: A man by any other name : William Clarke Quantrill and the search for American
    manhood / by Joseph M. Beilein, Jr.
Other titles: William Clarke Quantrill and the search for American manhood
Description: Athens : The University of Georgia Press, [2023] | Series: Uncivil wars |
    Includes bibliographical references and index.
Identifiers: LCCN 2022058900 | ISBN 9780820364513 (hardback) | ISBN 9780820364520
    (paperback) | ISBN 9780820364537 (epub) | ISBN 9780820364544 (pdf)
Subjects: LCSH: Quantrill, William Clarke, 1837–1865. | West (U.S.)—History—Civil War,
    1861–1865—Underground movements. | United States—History—Civil War, 1861–1865—
    Underground movements. | Masculinity—United States—History—19th century. |
    Guerrillas—Missouri—Biography. | Soldiers—Missouri—Biography.
Classification: LCC E470.45.Q3 .B45 2023 | DDC 973.7/86092 [B]—dc23/eng/20221207
LC record available at https://lccn.loc.gov/2022058900

For Rachel

CONTENTS

Illustrations and Maps ix

Preface xi

Introduction. Prey 1

SCHOOLMASTER. 1837–1856

Chapter 1. Student 21

Chapter 2. Teacher 36

Chapter 3. Dunce 45

FRONTIERSMAN. 1857–1860

Chapter 4. Roustabout 55

Chapter 5. Hunter 68

Chapter 6. Jailbird 86

CONFIDENCE MAN. 1860–1861

Chapter 7. Charley Hart 93

Chapter 8. Detective 105

Chapter 9. Overseer 118

WARRIOR. 1861–1862

Chapter 10. Killer 127

Chapter 11. Captain 137

Chapter 12. Partisan Ranger 152

CHIEFTAIN. 1863–1864

    Chapter 13. Colonel 159

    Chapter 14. Gambler 173

WANDERER. 1864–1865

    Chapter 15. Outcast 189

    Chapter 16. Vagabond 195

    Chapter 17. Quarry 204

    Acknowledgments 211

    Notes 215

    Bibliography 243

    Index 257

ILLUSTRATIONS AND MAPS

ILLUSTRATIONS

Portrait of William Clarke Quantrill   6

Powder horn   74

Census page for Charles Hart   101

Presentation of mythical black flag   141

MAPS

Quantrill in Kentucky, 1865   14

Travels across the Plains and Mountains,
Summer 1858–Summer 1859   62

Missouri-Kansas Border Region, 1857–1860   112

Bushwhackers' Zones of Activity   168

Retreat to Texas   182

PREFACE

William Clarke Quantrill stood in the parlor of the crowded boardinghouse in Aubrey, Kansas, amid a maelstrom of wickedness. Simultaneously calm and commanding, he occupied the center of gravity around which the guerrillas of western Missouri and their violence swirled. The bushwhackers in his immediate orbit gestured with revolvers and pushed frightened men across the parlor as they cursed and shouted demands. Quantrill and his raiders had thundered into Aubrey at dawn on March 7, 1862, and caught most of the men still asleep in their beds. The guerrillas used raids like this one to keep borderland Unionists and the U.S. Army off balance, a sensation that the discombobulated guests of the local boardinghouse could confirm. Many of them were barely able to dress and gather their senses before bushwhackers burst into their rooms and swept them up into a whirlwind of chaos.[1]

The presence of the bushwhacker chief particularly disturbed one guest. Abraham Ellis, who slouched in the corner of the parlor, wiped blood from his eyes and looked through the jumble of bodies at Quantrill. "He [Quantrill] had a mustache and side whiskers and both had a red tinge and at that time he had assumed the appearance and countenance of a desperado," but Ellis immediately recognized the young man he had known as a friend before the war. Ellis remembered traveling for business over the winter of 1859–1860 and calling on Quantrill, whom he fondly recalled as "an interesting well-educated man." Quantrill's letters from those days reveal him to be thoughtful and introspective—a lover of romantic poetry, especially Lord Byron and Thomas Campbell. He wrote about flowers and birds in a way that suggested his own poetic sensibilities, something that a lover of verse like Ellis probably appreciated. On the night of the visit, Ellis and Quantrill shared a bed, a common occurrence on the frontier. As it was undoubtedly cold, the bedfellows huddled close under heavy quilts, lingering in cozy conversation "until after 2 p.m." the next day.[2]

Between that moment of intimacy and their meeting in Aubrey, the world had turned upside down. After Lincoln was elected in November 1860, eleven slave states seceded, and North and South went to war. Ellis joined the Union army in 1861 as a lieutenant at age forty-six and served as a quartermaster for a Kansas unit. He heard rumors that his youthful friend Quantrill had become a jayhawker who liberated slaves, then a horse thief and cattle rustler, and finally a traitor, joining up with the proslavery Missourians when the war broke out.[3]

Ellis's mind returned to the present chaos of the parlor just as Quantrill met his gaze. "Why, Ellis is that you?" As his old friend came to his side, Ellis told Quantrill that he had been awakened around dawn by shouts from outside the boardinghouse, and he had wandered to the second-floor window for a look. While peering down at the horsemen in the street, he had been shot "in the center of the forehead where the brains of most men are supposed to be located." The impact of the bullet had knocked him to the ground. The next thing he knew, a couple of bushwhackers had robbed him of his money, and he had somehow ended up downstairs with the rest of the guests of the boardinghouse. Sitting there, face to face, listening to Ellis recount his traumatic morning, Quantrill confessed that he was the one who had shot Ellis, and that he "was damned sorry for it as [Ellis] was one of the Kansas men he did not want to hurt." Quantrill found a bowl of water and a washcloth, knelt down, cleaned the blood from Ellis's face, and gently bandaged his wound.[4]

Ellis lived the rest of his life with conflicted feelings about Quantrill. He knew that Quantrill wore the face of "a desperately bad man, a highway robber of the darkest shade," but he sensed that a different man lived behind the piratical mask. He could not shake the sense that the man who had put a bullet in his head "was not entirely a demon." Quantrill was also the man who had carefully bandaged him and who "could be pleasant at times." As Ellis remembered, "He talked kindly to me . . . after he recognized me." "Ellis's thoughts remained at war with themselves, battling over which memory of Quantrill was authentic: the clean-shaven, kind young man or the mustachioed bushwhacker. He probably stayed awake many nights wrestling over the true identity of his friend turned assailant.[5]

Like Ellis, this book ponders what kind of man Quantrill really was. For many readers, Quantrill is totally unknown. Others might know him as the leader of Confederate guerrillas in Missouri and the architect of the infamous raid on Lawrence, Kansas, in 1863. Some may recall him as the forefather of postwar outlaws like the James and Younger Gang. A few might remember reading or hearing his name in books or films, a cultural reference, a single word symbolizing the savagery of the warfare that raged along the border, or a point of pride for fictional characters like Rooster Cogburn, who talks fondly of his time riding with Quantrill in *True Grit*. These allusions aside, Quantrill remains a mystery.[6]

Despite his enigmatic quality, Quantrill shared a trait with many other men who came of age in the mid-nineteenth century. He was hyperconscious of manliness, both his own and others'. He constantly measured his achievements and skills against those of other men. He talked, lamented, joked, and boasted about being a man. Spending most of his adult life among other men in one manly world or another, on the teamster trail or in army and mining camps, in boardinghouses or on hunts on the plains, and finally in the brushy haunts of the guerrillas, Quantrill became fluent in the language of manliness. He learned how to survive in the wild, practiced horsemanship and shooting until he could best nearly anyone, came to see the power of violence and the value of martial prowess, and ultimately carried himself as a man's man. Talking the talk and walking the walk, Quantrill possessed an abundance of charisma that he used throughout his life to ingratiate himself with groups of strangers—both men and women, but mostly men.[7]

For all his practiced masculinity, Quantrill was a changeling. Ellis remembered Quantrill as easily shiftable—a boon companion, a jayhawker, a thief, a border ruffian, and ultimately a Confederate raider—a man who seemed to inhabit the forms of nearly every type of white man along the border during this time. Seemingly everyman, he did not fit any single category of manhood. Readers are likely familiar with some of the distinctive forms of nineteenth-century manhood brought to life by historians and writers: the southern planter, yeoman farmer, northern gentleman, urban street tough, and western hunter. Quantrill was reminiscent of all these types of white men, but he refused to settle into any one of these identities, instead spending most of his time living in the spaces between them.[8]

Transformation defined his persona, and Quantrill was not alone in this respect. He represented a growing number of men who came of age in the middle decades of the nineteenth century, men who saw change—internal and external—as the essential ingredient to survival and achievement in the rapidly evolving country. While scholars and some history buffs are familiar with white and Black men who shifted, adapted, and disguised themselves—go-ahead men, runaway slaves, and confidence men to name a few—these men tend to live on the margins of the history of that era. In reality, though, Quantrill and others like him hardly existed at the fringes, but rather lived as fully dynamic figures at the very center of things. These changelings cut through the assumptions of their immediate social worlds, sparking and driving the action and destabilizing otherwise static communities.[9]

Although Quantrill's metamorphoses make sincere study of him challenging, here they will offer a new way of seeing him. Taking his transformations seriously, this book explores each change of occupation and the corresponding alteration of his appearance as part of an honest, if misguided, effort to improve himself or his situation. A series of impressions of Quantrill in the various characters he embodied portrays him at different periods in his life when he lived as a teacher, hunter, confidence man, and killer. Some of these impressions—the ones based on a large pile of records—are rich in color and texture, while others are more like sketches, rough outlines of the man as he moved through some lightly documented parts of his life. The overall path these portraits chart is chronological with some overlap. Taken together, a collage of the many Quantrills comes into focus, a composite rendering of him, a face of many faces that might or might not have been like the one that lingered in Ellis's mind.

These impressions offer windows not only into his persona but also into his politics. For Quantrill, ideology tracked closely with identity, and his performance as a man should be understood as inherently political. As he changed and became a new type of man, so, too, did his view of the world, especially during the antebellum years. He occasionally articulated his views in the abstract, intellectual terms used by politicians and historians—proslavery, antislavery, free soil, abolitionism, and so on. More often, Quantrill's politics were unspoken, visceral, and felt, a reality that might frustrate political junkies looking for constant, explicit tracking of his political orientation from one day to the next.

These readers might serve themselves better by viewing Quantrill holistically and making close study of the way he presented himself, with a keen eye for actions or things that could appear prosaic but in fact spoke a great deal about where a man stood on the issues like a wink or a strut, a particular book, a mustache or beard, a Bowie knife, or a colorful shirt. Whatever he thought about slavery and freedom, manliness and whiteness, inarticulate vibrations originating from the same inner place as the impulses to dress, act, and speak in certain ways told him how he felt about these issues and they can tell us too.

A journey through Quantrill's personas takes us to the fringes of historiography and geography. For some time now, scholars have asserted that guerrilla warfare should not be viewed as a "sideshow" to the traditional narrative of the Civil War, with a few historians even pushing the guerrillas, partisans, and bushwhackers into the spotlight of the main stage, where they stand awkwardly out of place. Without minimizing the importance of the guerrilla conflict, *A Man by Any Other Name* takes a different approach: rather than yank Quantrill and his raiders to the center of the national drama, this book asks readers to follow the path away from the familiar mainstream icons and events and down into the densely wooded freak show of the guerrilla war. In this context, the authentic Quantrill and his war are better understood.[10]

Quantrill's biography is also a story of the American West. By tracking Quantrill out to the uncharted frontier of antebellum America and back to the settlements, this book suggests that his experiences on the plains and in the western mountains shaped him into a bushwhacker chief and influenced the way his men fought. This assertion, that the guerrilla movement of western Missouri is better understood as a conflict defined by westernness, follows the lead of a growing number of scholars who have reframed our understanding of the Civil War so that the influence of the West on the cause, conduct, and outcome of the fighting can more readily be seen.[11]

Although we have Ellis's impressions of his final "interview" with the infamous guerrilla, Quantrill's own perspective on the interface is harder to know. It is tempting to picture the faces of Ellis and Quantrill as they sat inches apart, friends turned enemies, one man veiled in ghastly horror and the other sporting the guise of a killer, as a reflection of man's duality, a classical tragedy viewed through a Freudian lens. There is something to that vision in this bloody corner of the Civil War—brother against brother, father against son, and all that. However, the little evidence that does exist of Quantrill's reaction to the meeting suggests that he did not see it in this way. Instead, when he looked on his friend's mutilated face, now clean and bandaged, he thought the whole affair humorous. After apologizing about shooting Ellis in the head, he noted that it was not a good shot but "a *damned* good shot." In the tradition of Old Southwest humor, Quantrill probably did not smile at his joke, but he might have winked, a subtle reminder that his war was a carnival, and violence occasionally served as punch line to cosmic jest.[12]

After Quantrill and his men rode away from Aubrey, a doctor removed the bullet from Ellis's head along with pieces of his skull. Later, someone, perhaps the doctor, sent the fragments of Ellis's cranium to the Army and Navy Medical Museum for examination and memorialization. They were not just evidence of a miracle but relics imbued with patriotism and the heroic cause of the Union. Pilgrims in search of proof of national triumph might visit Ellis's skull bones and other horrific oddities created by the destructive violence of the war, including an infamous general's right leg.[13]

Despite his astounding survival, Ellis did not fully recover. He struggled to perform a full day's work, and as he grew old, his personality changed dramatically, becoming increasingly moody and abrasive. What's more, the hole in Ellis's head never fully closed. The children around Elk City where he lived revered him and called him "Uncle Abe," but around the state of Kansas and across the border in Missouri, people knew him as "Bullet Hole Ellis." He was a walking, talking embodiment of the violence and victimhood created by guerrilla warfare along the border, an ambulatory reminder of the destruction of the Civil War and the scars it left on the people. Ellis was a reminder of Quantrill and all that he brought with him—death, friendship, poetry, fire, sincerity, humor, and disguises. One of these masks he bestowed on Ellis; it was a mask his onetime friend could not remove, and one that permanently marked him as a participant in the border war's deadly masquerade. Anyone who pursued Quantrill into the tangled, shadowy brush of the borderlands was wise to remember that things were rarely what they seemed, hunters quickly became prey, and only a fool took things at face value.[14]

A Man by Any Other Name

INTRODUCTION: *Prey*

A band of Confederate guerrillas slept peacefully on the morning of May 10, 1865, in a Kentucky hayloft. Curled up or stretched out, the bushwhackers were dressed in odd combinations of military uniforms and civilian garments. Their clothes were dyed in the full spectrum of hues from bright colors to quiet shades of brown. Some wore guerrilla shirts—antebellum hunting shirts embroidered with colorful flowers made for them by their women—rested plumed hats on their faces, and used blue Union jackets as blankets or pillows. Pistols lay here and there on the floor beside their owners. More than one guerrilla had fallen asleep with his revolvers holstered uncomfortably in his belt, however, and a few men even gripped the handles of their guns as they dreamed. This harlequin clutch of dozing killers made for quite the sight. Equally peculiar and ominous, they must have looked like a troop of bloody circus riders, worn out from their endless performance in some deadly sideshow.

To envision them now is to picture rest for the weary. It was a moment of unearned comfort. It was the calm before the storm. Like one of their palm-worn riding gloves resting on the rough-hewn planks, it was a gauntlet laid before the god of war.[1]

For the last few days, Union militiamen had chased these guerrillas to and fro across the Bluegrass, and they were dead tired. Finally shaking their pursuers and sensing rain, they rode to the farm of James H. Wakefield, a friend and supporter, where most of them retired to the barn in search of shelter from the heavy clouds overhead. For many of the other men who fought in the Civil War, the tempest was subsiding, and some measure of peace was entering their lives. Robert E. Lee and his Army of Northern Virginia had surrendered a month earlier, surrenders by other armies and partisans had occurred throughout April, and the very same day that the guerrillas fell asleep in Wakefield's barn, President Andrew Johnson proclaimed armed resistance in the South was "*virtually* at an end." These slumbering bushwhackers, then, embodied the war's lingering reality.[2]

In the dry fodder of Wakefield's barn where the men made their beds, they slept deeply under the rhythm of the raindrops falling on the roof above. The pitter-patter relaxed their minds. Some men dreamed, others snored, and a few likely made the small, inarticulate noises that all men, killers or not, make when exhausted and finally succumbing to sleep. In the dark, infinite space of the unconscious, time trickled past and the rain grew louder and it thundered and in their dreams the men might have heard the beating hooves of horsemen riding in the sky.[3]

That same morning, Edwin Terrell and twenty manhunters rode their horses up the road to Taylorsville, Kentucky, in the rain. Terrell was a twenty-year-old killer and the best counterguerrilla in the Union Department of Kentucky. Since January, he and his band had prowled central Kentucky hunting the most notable Confederate guerrillas and gunning them down one after another. For weeks now, though, these hired guns had looked unsuccessfully for a Missouri bushwhacker—William Clarke Quantrill—and they were used up. The column slowed and stopped before a roadside blacksmith's shop, and as the riders lifted the brims of their soaked hats, they watched a Black man come out and talk to Terrell. After a brief back and forth, the blacksmith pointed down a lane that ran off the road. Without a word, the men began to check over their pistols and carbines, and some hopped down to adjust their tack.[4]

Almstead Jacobs, the African American blacksmith, was a pivotal figure in this story, but he is often overlooked. Like an actor in a silent film, Jacobs was in the frame briefly—just long enough to act out that dramatic gesture—and then the story cuts away without any lines attributed to him. There was more to this man, though, than his fleeting moment in the spotlight. By 1865, he was an accomplished blacksmith. He was thirty years old and married to a twenty-five-year-old woman named Adeline. Together they had a one-year-old girl—Annie. At this point in the war, it might be assumed that the Jacobs family and all Black men, women, and children were free, but Kentucky did not abolish slavery during the war, and it was estimated that more than half of the enslaved population in the state remained in bondage at this late juncture. Some slaveholders held on to their human property until December 1865 when the Thirteenth Amendment became law. Whether his wife and daughter were a part of this group is unknown. Jacobs, though, was free, and based on his actions, he felt it his duty to help free others. When he saw Terrell and his Union guerrillas come riding up the road, Jacobs set his hammer and tongs aside, took off his gloves, and walked away from the furnace and out into the cool rain. In so doing, he risked everything: his shop, his freedom, his life, and the lives of his wife and child. Nevertheless, he stood in the mud talking to the boyish killer about what he had seen that morning.[5]

Terrell told his men that the Black man had counted twenty-one horsemen riding past his shop a couple of hours before noon. The guerrilla hunters knew they could trust Jacobs. Black men and women, enslaved and free, provided counterinsurgents like Terrell and his men with reliable intelligence when they were able to. They were the only people the guerrilla hunters could count on in a turncoat war. White folks, Terrell and his men included, often said one thing and did another. In that way every white person—Union or Confederate, man or woman, fighter or supporter—was a guerrilla.[6]

At another word from Terrell the creep toward the kill began. The guerrilla hunters headed down the lane by twos—setting a walking pace at first. The perspective of one of the hunters, John Langford, who, like most of the others, was a native-born Kentuckian and a Unionist, offers the best view of the action. Years after the war, Langford wrote about his experience, creating one of the few surviving documents detailing the action. He recalled that as his horse walked on down the gentle slope, he saw the roof of a large house and then spotted a barn, all while he was on the lookout for men, keenly aware that an ambush might await them.[7]

Langford rode on vigilantly and saw more of the house and the barn as the trees on either side of the lane opened up. Terrell, Langford, and some of the other lead riders saw a couple of men in the yard and quite a few horses. As each hunter recognized the prey, he loosened his grip on his reins. There was a flurry of heels and spurs, and hands to pistols or carbines. The hunters' horses went from a canter to a gallop to a sprint, and as they came thundering down on the unsuspecting bushwhackers, one of the men standing outside the barn yelled, "Here they come!"[8]

4 INTRODUCTION

Guerrillas came tumbling, running, and jumping out of the barn. Jolted out of their sleep, they must have been disconcerted. They panicked—grabbing for pistols, looking for a way out of the barn, running for their mounts, and swiveling their heads around to catch a glimpse of the enemy.[9]

Terrell's men broke in individual pursuit. Most of the bushwhackers had already mounted their rested horses and fled to the tree line. Langford saw a stray man struggle to get up on a wheeling and rearing horse. After a moment, the blundering horseman let go of the mount and took off for the woods on foot. Easy prey. Langford spurred his horse toward the fleeing bushwhacker, and as his horse had nearly overtaken the runner, he pulled his mount to the left and straightened his right arm, swung it downward, and put a charge into the man's back. Down he went.[10]

Langford did not mention how he felt after blasting a hole in the back of this man. It is hard to imagine that he felt much besides the electric energy of adrenaline at that situation, with pistol balls snapping through the air and horses flying here and there across the field. After riding past the downed man, Langford found his attention drawn to the hunters ahead of him who pursued the last couple of desperate guerrillas. He urged his mount on, following the action, but it was over before he could get in on either kill.[11]

Langford trotted back to the man he put down, reined up, hopped off his horse, and walked toward his prey. The man was facedown but still moving—writhing, really—so Langford flipped him over. He saw that his victim was alive but that he was struggling to move. A few other hunters leaped down from their mounts. Langford took the wounded man's revolvers and rifled his pockets for money and souvenirs as another scavenger pulled off the man's boots. In different circumstances, they would have executed the wounded man, but they desperately needed intelligence. A couple of hunters went to the Wakefield house for a quilt. They picked the man up—a heap of groaning deadweight—hauled him into the house, and laid him in the lounge.[12]

After a moment or two, Terrell barged into the room. Pushing past Wakefield, Langford, and the others, he looked at the bleeding and twisted figure for a moment. Terrell asked the wounded man whether he was Quantrill or whether he rode with Quantrill. Catching his breath, the wounded prisoner replied in a soft, melodious voice, "No. I'm Captain Clarke, Fourth Missouri Cavalry." Although Terrell certainly recognized the name as that of another Confederate raider ripping up the countryside that spring, he realized that he had again missed Quantrill and burst into a tantrum—a terrifying spectacle. Terrell became unhinged like a child who had lost his senses: he began smashing up the furniture in Wakefield's house, threatening to kill the farmer and his family and burn everything to the ground. Terrell exploded into room after room until the old farmer eased his frustrations by giving him some money and a demijohn of whiskey. His palm and liver greased, the hunter in chief relaxed a bit.[13]

After Terrell cooled down, the wounded man asked him whether he might be left at the Wakefield house to die. On guard against a trick, Terrell initially refused. However, when he realized that the wounded man was paralyzed below his arms, he agreed, making Clarke swear an oath that he would remain there until he died or was retrieved. Terrell told Wakefield that he would be held accountable for the prisoner.[14]

Terrell had to take Clarke at his word. The head assassin did not know Quantrill from Adam. He had no idea what his prized quarry looked like. He never glimpsed a likeness of the man and had nothing more than a rough description of him. It was thought within the U.S. Army that Quantrill was "a spare built man with sandy hair and light complexion"—the picture of nearly *any* white man and therefore almost *every* white man.[15]

Even today Quantrill evades easy identification. Over the last 150 years Quantrill's biographers—men who might be said to know him well—have tried to put a face on this infamous man, but a perusal of the covers and pages of their books suggests that there is no consensus on his appearance. There are three photographs of three *different* men. There is an etching of Quantrill in a Confederate uniform that he never wore. There is the image of him with a handlebar mustache graffitied onto his upper lip so that he resembles every villain who ever tied a damsel to train tracks. Finally, there is a hand-drawn portrait of Quantrill that must have looked something like him, because his men paraded it around at their postwar reunions. Referring to this portrait, a woman who knew Quantrill well and was rumored to be his bride noted, "The usual picture one sees of him scarcely looks like him." Even if any of these images offer a blurry rendering of Quantrill, the presence of so many dubious portraits leaves us in doubt.[16]

William Clarke Quantrill as he appears in the front of John Newman Edwards's *Noted Guerrillas* (1877). Based on a likeness of Quantrill, the drawing offers a blurry, vague image of the guerrilla chief. Kate Clarke, Quantrill's close companion, thought this portrait barely looked like him. Adding another layer of misidentification to his subject, Edwards believed Quantrill's name was Charles William Quantrell. (Edwards, *Noted Guerrillas*)

These journalists, scholars, and writers—John N. Edwards, William E. Connelley, Albert Castel, Edward Leslie, Paul R. Petersen, and others—hunted Quantrill, all of them thinking they bagged their prey. They displayed a picture of their man like a proud hunter might decorate his mantle with a trophy kill. Taken together, though, these biographers became Quantrill's unwitting accomplices, helping him hide in plain sight for many generations after his death. Paging through these different portrayals of the bushwhacker, it is difficult to know which one is the real bushwhacking chieftain and which one is a pretender. In this small sense, we can empathize with Terrell, who went blindly after this faceless death dealer in those uncertain and bloody days of 1865.[17]

To be sure, Quantrill was as slippery as they came. Beyond his lack of a good likeness, very few people could attest to knowing the bushwhacker. Only the men and women who participated in the guerrilla movement of western Missouri and a few other people knew him. By design, fighters in the guerrilla war often cloaked their identities by wearing blue Union uniforms. Additionally, Quantrill cultivated a mysterious persona, and he seemed to be everywhere at once. While his base of activity was known to be western Missouri, it was rumored that he traveled south to Texas and across the country to Richmond, Virginia, at different junctures in the war. Hypervigilant U.S. officers and overeager newspapermen reported Quantrill sightings across the Middle West, claiming that he was responsible for a raid here, was arrested there, or was shot down somewhere else. By the spring of 1865, Quantrill had been reported killed or captured many times, with each report proven wrong after the bushwhacker was heard from elsewhere. Even as Terrell and his men hunted him in Kentucky, some Union officers thought he was still raising hell back in Missouri.[18]

There is no way to be certain what Terrell knew about Quantrill. Everyone had heard about the brutal raid Quantrill led on Lawrence, Kansas, in August 1863—it was pasted over a full page in the September 5 issue of *Harper's Weekly*. In Lawrence, raiders from Missouri killed around 180 men and boys, most unarmed, and burned dozens of homes, shops, and barns. This attack made Quantrill infamous. The Union Provost Marshals, a group of officers who maintained order among the civilian population and became an intelligence agency that hunted guerrillas and spies, started a file on Quantrill at some point. Either the contents of that file were misplaced, or a light-fingered government bureaucrat relocated them to his personal collection. Thus it is difficult to know the extent of the U.S. Army's intelligence on Quantrill or how much of it Terrell was able to access.[19]

Whatever the army gathered on Quantrill, the infamous bushwhacker interested the newspapers. The Charles City, Iowa, *Republican Intelligencer* ran a story entitled "Who Quantrile Is" that exposed "Quantrile" as "no less than the celebrated thief, forger and bigamist, known as Dr. J. B. Hayne." This scoundrel certainly possessed the resume of a man who did the things Quantrill was accused of doing. Intriguingly, the *Republican Intelligencer* reported, "His [Quantrile's/Hayne's] likeness is in the Rogue's Gallery at the Cent. Station, N.Y." Frustratingly, the editor of the Charles City paper did not reveal how he knew this, nor did he print the portrait. The story described Dr. J. B. Hayne as a jailbird who changed his name and took the exam to become a major of a regiment—Union or Confederate, the *Republican Intelligencer* did not bother to divulge—but "his knowledge in military tactics was exceedingly limited." This bit probably furrowed the brows of a few readers who had heard about Quantrill's battlefield successes. Despite this inconsistency, the article ended in a flourish: "He has been guilty of all the vile crimes ever recorded against a human being. . . . He brought ruin upon many families. . . . He was an expert forger, and a cold-blooded murderer, and a debauchee of the worst kind. This monstrosity of human nature is known as Quantrile."[20]

Terrell might not have been the type of man who read the news or saw the wild stories about Quantrill or Quantrile. He was young—so young that it is hard to imagine him keeping up with current events beyond his immediate deadly environment. Moreover, some stories depicted Terrell as a simple brute. He supposedly killed his commanding officer, and he gunned down unarmed men. One time, when an alleged guerrilla who had just surrendered was shaking hands with one of his captors, Terrell walked up and shot the prisoner full of holes. According to these tales, Terrell was a thug in riding boots.[21]

Or maybe not. Guerrilla scholar Matthew C. Hulbert depicts Terrell as something more than a murderous boy, asserting that this orphan who was pulled into a violent world at a formative age was a prodigy killer. He says that in hunting the guerrillas, Terrell "actively strove to change the rules of the game—or, better still, the rules of engagement—to suit his own particular skillset and to maximize the reward it would allow him to accumulate in wartime." Hulbert's Terrell sounds like that famous western gunfighter Billy the Kid. He was young and deadly, but he was also smart—an innovator and contract-killing entrepreneur.[22]

If Terrell did read the papers, which some ambitious and intelligent killers were known to do—again, William H. Bonney comes to mind—he likely read a surprising story about Quantrill that was circulating at the time. "A great many stories have been started concerning the former character, conduct, and exploits of this noted rascal," began a November 28, 1863, column about him in the *Independent* of Oskaloosa, Kansas. No doubt the *Independent* surprised some of its readers when it revealed, "Quantrell came from a town in Ohio, called Canal Dover, in Tuscarawas county. His father's name is Thomas H. Quantrell, a man of good standing in society." The younger Quantrill eventually left home and went westward in search of new opportunities like so many boys of his generation. If readers were not surprised to learn that this savage Confederate guerrilla was in fact a northerner from a good household, they were certainly jolted when they read that right before the war Quantrill had "taught school near Stanton, [Kansas,] and gave general satisfaction." An upright Yankee schoolmaster turned proslavery murderous Visigoth—the story seemed to be pure fiction.[23]

But it was the truth. In 1909, William E. Connelley confirmed these facts about Quantrill's antebellum life. In writing his remarkable, case-making *Quantrill and the Border Wars*, Connelley collected the most extensive pile of documents related to the guerrilla chieftain up to that point. He interviewed dozens—maybe hundreds—of men and women from Kansas and elsewhere who participated in Bleeding Kansas and the Civil War. He even developed a relationship with one of Quantrill's men—William H. Gregg—from whom he gleaned intimate information. Although Connelley's stance was adamantly anti-Quantrill to the point of misleading his readers, *Quantrill and the Border Wars* establishes an outline of the infamous bushwhacker's life: he was born in Ohio in 1837, he resided in Kansas and taught school there, he lived at various places and traveled across the Great Plains and the Rocky Mountains. Then, when the war came, this northern-born schoolmaster crossed over and took sides with slaveholding Missourians.[24]

For over one hundred years, scholars, journalists, and writers have more or less agreed with the basic facts of Quantrill's case. The disagreement falls along the old battle lines of the Civil War. Connelley and Quantrill biographer Albert Castel both wrote histories that reject the popular themes of reunification and Lost Cause ideals. As a professional historian, Castel produced the superior work, but his interpretation follows closely Connelley's one-dimensional depiction of Quantrill as a vile man, a traitor, and the embodiment of an evil particular to proslavery antagonists. The other camp includes Confederate cavalryman and unreconstructed rebel John N. Edwards, who wrote the first history of the border war in 1877, and Paul E. Petersen, a modern-day biographer and in-house historian for a pro-Quantrill website. They both insist on Quantrill's nobility. In their versions of the narrative, Quantrill and his adopted southern brethren were victims of an overreaching Federal government and violent, unhinged abolitionists who did not understand the southern "way of life" or slavery. Theirs is a story steeped in Lost Cause mythology.[25]

It seems that neither side of this long-running historiographical fight will ever surrender. Like rival bands of guerrillas pursuing each other generation after generation at the dark fringes of Civil War history, one side takes a shot, maybe scores a hit, and is long gone before much of a response can be made. Then sometime later a potshot comes whizzing back. The skirmish has gone like this for the last 150 years, and it will presumably continue for the foreseeable future.[26]

What this protracted refighting of the Civil War on the border loses is Quantrill *the man*. For all its merit, the morally righteous and academically grounded narrative that Connelley and Castel present still lacks some of the nuance of the human experience. Edwards and Petersen refuse to acknowledge the context or even some of the facts of Quantrill's life and the larger Civil War. Somehow, Quantrill's story serves both sides well as a symbol: For the progressive, pro-Union side, he is the perfect bad guy. For the unreconstructed and neo-Confederates, his story can be used to deflect assertions that the war was centered on slavery. Without creating a false equivalency between these two positions—Connelley and Castel are absolutely on the right side of history—both sides nevertheless use Quantrill as an avatar for their "cause."[27]

Terrell knew he was not chasing a symbol but a very real gunman. Whether he thought he was on the trail of a teacher turned raider or a depraved medical man and forger or someone else altogether, Terrell trusted that he would know the bushwhacker when he saw him. Like other young rogues, Terrell was fueled by unfounded confidence, a belief that he could see around corners and peek behind the veil. With conviction, then, he walked out of the Wakefield house after his interrogation of Captain Clarke and told his guerrilla hunters that Quantrill had escaped. The hunters set about reloading and charging cylinders and watering and feeding their horses. They mounted up again and rode into the brush on the lookout for a man they had never seen.[28]

On their way through Wakefield's yard, Terrell, Langford, and the others trotted past the bodies of two dead guerrillas. These men were killed because they had tried to save Clarke. One of them was shot close to Clarke but was able to ride on before falling from his horse. The second Samaritan-bushwhacker tarried too long, and the hunters caught up to him when his horse became mired in a muddy creek near the tree line. While his horse wallowed, he was surrounded and gunned down. These men, Dick Glasscock and Clarke Hockensmith, were both veteran guerrillas whose fates prove the hypothesis that no good deed goes unpunished.[29]

The guerrilla hunters followed scattered trails here and there. It was the practice of Missouri guerrillas to escape in different directions, making their own path through the bush until they separated from their pursuers and reunited at a predetermined place. This highly effective tactic made it nearly impossible for Union troopers to catch the guerrillas and made the pursuit of the guerrillas deadly. A few greenhorn captains made the mistake of breaking up their own forces in pursuit of dispersed bushwhackers, only to see these smaller parties get swallowed up by a much larger reunited band of guerrillas.[30]

Despite his age, Terrell was no novice. He was too smart to send smaller groups along the dozens of trails left by the guerrillas. Instead, his band parsed the trails together and followed them as best they could around and around the countryside without ever seeing a partisan. They were safe but without success in finding Quantrill.[31]

Being confronted by scattered trails, faint signs here and there, and few indications of direction or destination must have evoked frustration, intrigue, and even paranoia among the guerrilla hunters, sensations that are familiar enough to a scholar who decides to pursue Quantrill through the archives. Tracking him from one box of documents to the next at the University of Kansas and the Denver Public Library can feel like a snipe hunt. There are some straightforward documents, including letters from the guerrillas' victims and transcribed notes from interviews. However, other records mystify more than they clarify. A slip of paper with an unanswered question about a murder, a letter from an old bushwhacker with a few provocative lines surrounded by illegible script, notes scribbled on the back of an envelope and inexplicably scratched out—the list of enigmatic evidence goes on and on.[32]

Quantrill also cut paths through collections that are familiar to all historians of the Civil War like the *Official Records*, the Provost Marshals' records, and the U.S. Census. Even in these sources, there are unexpected twists that make the trail go cold time and again. An otherwise lucid historian might start mumbling to himself. Worse, he might find himself scrolling down one of the many conspiratorial threads that exists below the surface level of the internet as he comes to grips with the fact that Quantrill anticipated this postmortem chase, that in life he intentionally left false signs, hid his tracks, and buried seeds of doubt in records he knew would live on. Stalking this old bushwhacker takes a toll on one's spirits and sanity.[33]

Maybe Terrell began to feel a bit mad as he rode in circles through the woods. Exactly how long they were out there searching for Quantrill after their raid on the Wakefield farm is contested. Years after the war, James Wakefield recalled that Terrell and his company left the wounded man at his home for two nights. Wakefield's account rings true. He did not have a reason for lying about the amount of time that Clarke lay bleeding on his sofa, although it is possible that his memory slipped. Langford was adamant that he and his comrades were only away from the Wakefield place for one day before they made the circuit back to the beginning of their journey. "I am not mistaken," he protested. "Glasscock and Hockensmith might have been there two nights," but he was sure Terrell and his men only spent a day chasing their tails. Perhaps Langford was embarrassed to admit that this group of supposedly expert guerrilla hunters came back empty handed after two full days in the brush. One day does not sound quite as bad.[34]

There was something more at stake for Langford. After two days of chasing shadows, Terrell and company returned to the site of the original ambush and were probably surprised to find Clarke alive and still there. Langford insisted, "Every feature of that tragedy is as distinct in my mind as it was on that rainy May morning twenty three years ago." He was probably referring to May 10, but perhaps he meant the day after that, or even two days after the initial attack. Langford's point, though, was that he remembered it all *very well*. "And even now it requires but little imagination for me to hear again the words of the wounded man," Langford recalled, "as he said with pathos:—'Boys you have got Quantrill at last.'"[35]

William Clarke Quantrill in the flesh—there he was, or what was left of him. He probably did not look like much curled up and pale on Wakefield's sofa with the hunters huddled around him, pushing and poking their heads in to get a look. In the full verve of life, though, Quantrill's image seared itself into the memory of everyone who saw him. The women and men who left descriptions of Quantrill said he was taller than the average man, standing about five feet, ten inches tall, with a straight back, a strong frame, and a confident walk. His face was pleasant looking with mostly proportional features that included a roman nose. Quantrill's hair was reportedly somewhere between sandy blond and tow colored, while his mustache and patchy beard were reddish brown. His eyes were truly memorable. Quantrill's iridescent blueish-gray eyes seemed to penetrate and look inside a person, generating a magnetism that either drew people closer or repulsed them in ways they could not articulate. Bad or good, he was unforgettable.[36]

Given the accounts of Quantrill's striking appearance, it is a bit surprising that Terrell was not more suspicious, but apparently this wunderkind of deception and assassination could not read this particular rogue. Terrell did not have a likeness to go by or much of a description, but there were clues. It does not take much of a leap to get from Captain *Clarke* to William *Clarke* Quantrill, although it was possible that Terrell was unaware of Quantrill's full name. More obvious, though, was the fact that both of these bushwhackers were from Missouri. Yet Terrell had looked at the wounded man with those electric eyes and let him go.[37]

Perhaps Quantrill was the bushwhacker beau ideal, a figure capable of transformation and deceit on a level exceeding what Terrell could comprehend. Quantrill's adoption of the alias Captain Clarke, Fourth Missouri Cavalry suggested something canny about his approach to manliness. He was like a strolling actor who went from settlement to settlement playing different roles in the taverns and tents that served as the theaters of antebellum America. With a change of hairstyle, new clothes, and a willingness to act the part, Quantrill was able to become one type of man or another. Quantrill was a teacher who became a farmer and then a western adventurer; he was a northerner who became a westerner who became a southerner; he was a Confederate guerrilla who passed as a Union cavalry captain. His most fundamental identity was that of the changeling, a man who saw the costumes and masks and understood that every man was playing a part.[38]

Terrell, though, also shapeshifted. While much of his life remains a mystery, it was believed that Terrell began the war in the Confederate army. He was rumored to have killed his commander while he was fighting for the Confederacy. Perhaps in fleeing the inevitable death sentence, he joined the U.S. military. He eventually became a guerrilla hunter and adopted the bushwhackers' tactics. Terrell's men did not dress like the Union soldiers they were. Instead, they wore the same outfits as some of the guerrillas—civilian clothes and sometimes garb that was flamboyant in its colors and stitching. If anyone was going to see Quantrill's mask, it would have been a man who also lived a masquerade. In the end, though, it took the bushwhacker giving himself up for Terrell to see who lay before him.[39]

After Quantrill's admission, the hunters converted a spring wagon into an ambulance. They loaded it with straw and pillows to minimize the bumping and jarring during the ride up the country roads to Louisville, where they were going to present their catch to the department commander, General John M. Palmer. In looking after the condition of the wagon bed, there was a great concern for the comfort of Quantrill. Perhaps it was a show of gratitude for keeping his word and staying put, or maybe the hunters wanted to make sure he lived long enough for the public spectacle of a trial and the inevitable hanging. It is also possible that the bushwhacker's charm disarmed his captors. Whatever the case, Quantrill was as comfortable as possible as the wagon creaked and bounced up the rutted lane away from Wakefield's house.[40]

The parade of hunters and the wagon with their prize slowly pro-

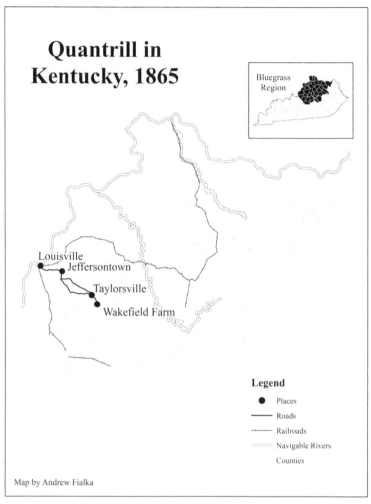

William Clarke Quantrill spent his last months in Kentucky. He led a company of Missouri bushwhackers to the Bluegrass State to link up with a Confederate army and surrender as soldiers. If they did otherwise, they would almost certainly be executed as outlaws, a status assigned to Confederate guerrillas by Union army commanders earlier in the war. From January until May 1865, Quantrill and his men harassed Unionists and Union soldiers, but they never found a Confederate command to join. This map illustrates the location of the ambush at the Wakefield farm and traces the route the guerrilla hunters marched with their wounded captive to Louisville.

ceeded, stopping twice before reaching headquarters. Langford recalled, "[At Taylorsville] we got a Doctor to draw Quantrils [*sic*] water." At Jeffersontown—a suburb of Louisville—Terrell decided to stay the night. Again, he made doctors examine his captive, and they confirmed the diagnosis of paralysis.[41]

The next morning Terrell arranged his men around the wagon so that they would arrive at headquarters looking the part of conquering heroes. However rough and fearsome, the hunters and their mounts must have looked sharp after the rare night of sleep and some good food. As the victors paraded down the dirt road and then the cobblestone streets of Louisville, their big thoroughbreds danced and whinnied, snorted and snapped their teeth at other horses. Although Quantrill lay in the middle of the escort, there is no way to know how many people in the gathering crowds knew the identity of the prisoner. Even so, Langford and a few of the others probably boasted about their trophy. After trotting through town, they made their way to the Military Prison hospital, where they moved the captive to a cot and put him in the care of the Sisters of Charity, an order of Catholic nuns.[42]

The city soon learned about Quantrill's arrival. On May 14, he *Louisville Daily Courier* reported, "Quantrill the notorious Kansas guerrilla, arrived in this city yesterday morning about 11 o'clock. He was conveyed in a country wagon . . . and guarded by Terrill's men disguised as guerrillas. . . . All the honor of his capture is due to Captain Terrill and his company." The *Louisville Daily Democrat* told its readers, "Captain Terrill and his company arrived here yesterday from Taylorsville. They brought with them the guerrilla who bears the name of 'Quantrill.'" The next day the *Louisville Daily Union Press* reported, "The noted guerrilla who has been operating in Kentucky under the name of Quantrill, and whose capture we noticed Saturday, is in the Military Prison hospital. There is very little hope of his recovery."[43]

Despite these reports, confusion accompanied the news of Quantrill's demise just as it did every part of his life. Even as he lay immobile, leaking blood and pus, Quantrill still proved cagey, challenging the acceptance of the obvious. The *Daily Courier* reported, "Quantrill has been sailing under the name of Captain Clark and it is supposed by many that it is not the veritable Kansas outlaw." The *Daily Courier*—a pro-Union rag—tried to assure its readers that Terrell had evidence that the wounded prisoner was in fact the same man who had led the raid on Lawrence. On the very same day, the *Daily Democrat* said with thinly veiled optimism, "It is not the Quantrill of Kansas notoriety, for we have been assured that he was at last accounts a colonel in [the] rebel army under Price."[44]

Wherever the newspapers speculated the legendary bushwhacker was, the real Quantrill was lying uncomfortably in the hospital. It was unlikely he had much interaction with others in his final weeks. The U.S. military left his care to the Sisters of Charity, who saw the humanity of all men—the sick, the dying, the hopeless, and even Confederate raiders. One nun in particular, Sister Matilda, took care of Quantrill, although it is unknown exactly how much she attended to him. Given the significance of Louisville as a depot for wounded and sick men from battlefields in the theater, Sister Matilda probably had her hands full.[45]

Clergy also visited Quantrill and other guerrillas. For instance, Kentucky partisans Sue Mundy, whose God-given name was M. Jerome Clark, and Henry C. Magruder found solace in religious men. Father Talbott came to Sue Mundy on the morning of Mundy's execution. The priest told Mundy that he/she was to be hanged that afternoon, then they prayed together, and the gender-bending bushwhacker was baptized into the church. Magruder, too, admitted his sins to a local priest, perhaps Talbott or maybe another one, who took down every word of the extensive confession.[46]

At the end of his life Quantrill became a Catholic. His conversion was overseen by Father Powers, and there is little doubt that as a new convert, the guerrilla was offered an opportunity to confess his sins and receive forgiveness. Quantrill recalled his sins—leaving his mother, perhaps an incident in Illinois, maybe an awkward moment under a shared blanket on the frontier, guilt over the deaths of friends and maybe even enemies, or any number of other things. In his Irish brogue, Father Powers told Quantrill that he was forgiven in the eyes of God.[47]

Whatever God might have thought of Quantrill, a few southerners honored Quantrill's prowess with a gift. The *Daily Union Press* reported that, not long after he arrived in Louisville, "he was found to be in possession of a beautiful bouquet, to which was attached a card bearing the following inscription: 'Compliments of Miss Maggie Frederick and Sallie Lovell to Mr. Quantrill.'" Flummoxed, the Unionist newspaper editorialized, "[The bouquet] was presented to the distinguished bandit, we suppose, as a testimonial to his valor. A strange way some people have of showing their loyalty."[48]

Presuming that the newspaper report was accurate, and that Quantrill did in fact receive a bouquet, the wounded man probably appreciated the nosegay. Like so many other nineteenth-century men, Quantrill sought recognition of his prowess, and now he held a beautiful spray, a consolation for a lifetime of effort. His final skirmish was a failure—he did not put out pickets, he let himself fall asleep, he did not prepare his horse for battle—but these flowers marked him as a warrior. He passed many tests, survived an unknown number of fights, achieved victories, and won fame as a chieftain.[49]

As Quantrill looked on the bouquet he probably saw some of the virtues he tried to embody during his lifetime. In those days, women and men believed there was a language of flowers, with each variety representing an emotion or idea. Like the guerrilla shirts stitched with different flowers that Quantrill and his men wore, this bouquet either contained a message from the person who made it or said something specific about its recipient. Monkshood represented chivalry; trefoils symbolized revenge; chrysanthemums, roses, woodbines, and many other flowers expressed one kind of love or another. Even dandelions held a specific meaning. They were known as rustic oracles and indicated prophecy or a warning. We can only speculate which flowers were included in this bouquet, but it probably contained a message full of ideas, emotions, and personal qualities that made Quantrill think.[50]

Quantrill eventually closed his eyes and dreamed, but the scenes that flashed through his mind cannot be known. If he was anything like other dying Civil War soldiers, Quantrill thought of his mother, other people he loved, and his boyhood home. Perhaps he retraced his circuitous quest to become a man. Beginning with his origins in Ohio and moving through his days of early manhood in the West, his mind might have charted the trail that eventually led him to this hospital bed in which he lay rotting—an instructive path not only for the dying bushwhacker reflecting on his life, but also for anyone interested in the essence of Quantrill. Eventually, after a month of falling in and out of consciousness, Quantrill breathed his last on June 6, 1865. He finally found the slumber that he had sought in Wakefield's hayloft, but instead of a flowery guerrilla shirt covering him, Quantrill clutched a bouquet of wilted flowers to his chest, the only thing to mask the stench.[51]

Schoolmaster
1837–1856

CHAPTER 1: *Student*

William Clarke Quantrill took his first breath of air on the last day of July 1837. In late 1836, Caroline Cornelia and Thomas Henry Quantrill arrived in Canal Dover in a horse-drawn buggy. This strong-willed young woman and her husband—a promising craftsman—were married in October 1836 in Chambersburg, Pennsylvania, and their first child was conceived not long after. While Caroline was pregnant, the young couple picked up and moved to Ohio to raise their family, unaware that their son would grow up to be one of the most infamous men of the nineteenth century. But William was not born the man he would become.[1]

Instead, like other boys born in nineteenth century America, William transitioned from boyhood to manhood through a pedagogical process. Shaped by the people around him and the institutions that structured his community, his education was sometimes intentional. but more often than not, it was inexact and accidental. It took place at home, inside the walls of the schoolhouse, and outside on the muddy streets of antebellum America. Some of the lessons were obvious and explicit, but many were implicit, seeping into William's mind in sub-conscious ways.[2]

To further complicate things, as any teacher knows, students do not retain lessons the same way (or at all). William learned how to be a man by mimicking, listening, reading, and doing. However, what he retained was dependent on his personality. In other words, the man he became was not a direct reflection of his curriculum; he was the result of refraction—perception altered and deflected by his intellect and emotions. Only by fully immersing ourselves in William's childhood can we feel his feelings, reconstruct his way of seeing, and piece together the puzzle of the way in which he became a man.[3]

William proved to be a sensitive boy. A newspaper story that ran in the Kentucky's *Louisville Courier-Journal* in 1888, half a century after his birth and decades after the war that made him infamous, offered the most intimate, if fleeting, glimpse of the child. The article quoted an interview with his mother, who remembered, "His disposition was always, up to the last I saw of him, of a retiring nature." Caroline Quantrill asserted, "He was never known to be quarrelsome, and his instincts seemed all to be of the nature of a girl more than those of a young man." She further recalled, "He had a ready smile and a warm heart." The journalist who interviewed William's mother also gained access to some of his antebellum correspondence and observed something about his penmanship that he thought worth mentioning—Quantrill possessed "handwriting resembling a woman's." In addition to talking to Caroline Quantrill, the newspaperman also interviewed a few of William's former guerrillas, and they remembered that their chieftain's "voice was a very peculiar and charming one. It was sonorous, very far reaching: musical, and in no way sharp."[4]

A retiring nature, a warm heart, a musical, peculiar voice, a woman's penmanship—these qualities do not seem to fit the persona of a piratical marauder. Rather, as a child, William seemed more like a Victorian angel, a domestic cherub, rosy cheeked and perched on his father's knee or quietly playing on the floor like those children depicted in *Godey's* or *Harper's*. He was the embodiment of the softer qualities of human nature.[5]

Put another way, William sounded effeminate. His disposition, mannerisms, voice, and handwriting, all taken together, make it difficult to imagine him as manly or even boyish. It was perhaps instinctive for his mother to emphasize the best traits of her son. Maybe she attempted to counter his iconic image as a murderous warrior by remembering him to the newspaperman as reserved and peaceful. However, Caroline Quantrill's description of William as *girlish* does not seem like an attempt to polish a tarnished image. It seems to be an authentic recollection of her boy.[6]

Although they did not make any references to his feminine nature, the townspeople more or less agreed with this description. Quantrill's community remembered him as a boy who demonstrated restraint, describing him as gentle and self-possessed. A couple of decades after the war, there were clearly still warm feelings for him in his hometown, as an 1884 history of Tuscarawas County, Ohio, records, "The people about Dover who knew Quantrill in his youth, speak of him only in kindness." In the same passage, the town's denizens described him as "civil and quiet." He was not remembered as some rowdy or a trouble-maker acting out or tormenting his peers. There was nothing that the people of Canal Dover could see in William at a young age that sug-gested his fate as a leader of southern guerrillas.[7]

From his earliest years, William was shaped into a man by his parents and in particular his mother. Little is known about Caroline Quantrill's early life. She was born in Somerset County, Pennsylvania, in 1819, but her family moved to Chambersburg not long after her birth. She was below average height, with "golden hair, blue eyes of the most intelli-gent expression, [and] a round face that must once have been beauti-ful." Apparently, her famous son resembled her more than he did his father. Caroline was a good wife and mother who kept her household in order. She and Thomas Quantrill had eight children in all, but four of the babies died within a year of their births. Despite the toll of these deaths, Caroline pressed on, taking care of her husband and children and providing for her household after her husband's death.[8]

Her postwar excursions to discover what happened to her oldest son provide evidence that she was assertive and strong. Beginning in the 1880s, sometimes with one of William's boyhood friends as a compan-ion, Caroline traveled around the country from Kentucky to western Missouri. She talked to William's former comrades and listened to sto-ries of his wartime deeds. Caroline often stayed away from her home in Ohio for weeks or months—an uncommon amount of travel for a nineteenth-century woman in her fifties and sixties.[9]

Caroline imprinted herself on William's personality. Like other middle-class mothers, she used love, guilt, and encouragement to shape her children's consciences as they grew up and left her home. As the oldest, William probably felt more of this affection—positive and negative—than the other children. Reading William's letters to his mother, it was as if he heard his mother's voice inside his head. He was in constant dialogue with her. She was there in his mind, interjecting into his internal monologue. Caroline was his conscience. It was as if William already knew—or imagined he knew—what Caroline's response would be to the news he reported.[10]

William's letters to his mother suggest that she was the love of his youth. More than any other person, Caroline remained a presence in his life and story even after he departed it. Even at a distance, she seemed to be his closest confidant during the antebellum years. William and his mother had a complicated relationship. In his correspondence, he spoke about how much he loved her, missed her, and wanted to return to Canal Dover to see her and live in the comfort of her house. However, in contrast, he also lashed out at her—sometimes at the same time as he confessed that he missed her. He threatened to withhold future letters home until she put a letter in the mail for him. It was quite possible that Caroline reached out to William but that her letters were lost, or that they reached one of his temporary homes after he moved on. But his anger showed that he suspected neglect rather than postal mishap. He was incapable of fully understanding, dealing with, or articulating some of his feelings for the woman who birthed him, raised him, and tried to maintain a bond with him over a chasm of time and space that began to widen when he initially left home for Illinois.[11]

Still, William shared his feelings with Caroline almost as freely as he might write them in a journal. He knew that some of his correspondence would be shared, but he prefaced other parts as confessions, and he specifically told her to keep some things to herself. He did not tell his mother everything. There were events and people he wanted to tell her about but could not, and there was always the chance that a letter might be intercepted and opened, or that it might fall into the hands of some unintended reader after Caroline read it. William thus withheld damaging information. Still, he seemed beholden to her judgment and her approval. Mostly, his missives showed the ways in which the chains of affection welded to his psyche in his childhood clung to him hundreds and thousands of miles from home and after years apart.[12]

William's letters home also reveal the type of man Caroline raised. Analyzing his correspondence for the lessons his mother taught him is an imprecise process, but a couple of themes show something about the psychic link between mother and son. Specifically, the content of William's confessions, which were intended for Caroline's eyes, might offer a glimpse into the things he thought were important to her. At different times, he informed his mother that he was not living the way he should. William told her, "I have done wrong in going away at all; this I will acknowledge," and "I have been quite foolish in my notions of the last three or four years," while "roving around seeking a fortune." He admitted, "I have been striving and working really without any end in view. And now since I am satisfied that such a course must end in nothing, it must be changed, and that soon or it will be too late." After each admission he promised to change, that he would "turn over a new leaf," that because it was a leap year (1860), he would take his "leap with the year and then keep moving with it," and that after sowing his wild oats, it would be "time to begin harvesting." As the many metaphors suggest, he could only achieve the change he desired by engaging in steady, honest labor. Caroline seemed wary of get-rich-quick schemes and easy paths to fortune.[13]

William and his mother were deeply attached, but his father also worked to pound and shape him into a masculine form. Born in 1813 in Hagerstown, Maryland, Thomas H. Quantrill came of age at a time when boys were often apprenticed to learn a trade that would afford them a living. Either he was apprenticed to a local tinner in Hagerstown, or he learned his trade in Chambersburg, Pennsylvania, where he moved at some point. Like most other apprentices, Thomas Quantrill lived and worked with a master tinsmith who taught him the trade over a four-to-seven-year period. Once he internalized a tinsmith's skill set, Quantrill graduated from his position as an apprentice and became a journeyman. For tinsmiths, the term "journeyman" became a literal one, as many made their living on the road as tinkers, going from house to house and town to town offering to repair any worn or broken household items, such as pots, utensils, or pitchers. Others gained employment in workshops making products out of tin, copper, and the like. It remains unclear how much Thomas traveled or where he sold his skills before he settled in Canal Dover.[14]

Thomas eventually became a master tinsmith. At some point in the 1840s, he established his own shop. By 1850 he was apparently doing well in his business, possessing $2,000 in real estate, although the number of men he employed, if any, is unknown. Looking beyond his own workshop, Thomas set out to write and illustrate a manual for tinsmithing and the trade's various methods of producing a myriad of tin and copper items. The publication of *The Mechanic's Calculator and Tinman's Guide* in 1847 established Thomas Quantrill as an authority, perhaps even *the* authority, in the region's tinsmithing trade. Although Thomas suggested at the outset of the book "that any man of ordinary capacity, understanding the rudiments of arithmetic, will be able to construct *all* the diagrams with ease and facility," he intended the work for other "practical engineers." It is detailed, and it requires mathematical literacy. Nevertheless, Thomas was working to shine a light on a seemingly inaccessible field of production. He wrote, "From an intimate acquaintance with a great number of the trade, he indulges the belief that this effort to promote their interests and facilitate the progress of their mechanical education, will receive a just appreciation. What an immense amount of labor would be saved to mechanics generally if they had free access to books elucidating the theories and principles of their various avocations."[15]

William did not apprentice under his father to become a tinker. By the 1840s, fewer and fewer boys were learning the artisan trades. Beginning in the late 1820s and early 1830s throughout the North, from New England across the Burned-Over District of central New York and into parts of the Old Northwest Territory, a revolution in how people produced and consumed commodities was underway. The so-called market revolution, which began roughly in the 1820s, was built on the factory system that worked to undo the household economy and destroyed the artisanal system through which things were created. Home and work were separated. A few men, the ambitious and connected entrepreneurs, came to own larger workshops that consolidated the local labor force of available tradesmen. But most men ended up working in one of these factories and became members of the increasingly anonymous working class. These changes were facilitated by a new national infrastructure and new roads, bridges, and, most importantly, canals that connected the country, thereby allowing for a flow of people, ideas, and products back and forth from west to east and south to north.[16]

William's hometown of Canal Dover was shaped by the same economic and social changes that were sweeping across the country. In 1820, there were a mere forty-six residents in Dover Township. In 1826, construction began on the Ohio and Erie Canal, which cut down from Lake Erie to the Ohio River and was finished in 1830. The canal turned a modest settlement to a quickly growing hub in eastern Ohio, and it was not long before the town that grew up around the canal came to be known as Canal Dover, an homage to the life-bringing waterway. The population grew by leaps and bounds. By 1840, Dover was the largest township in Tuscarawas County, with 2,247 residents. Within a decade, the population increased by another 1,000. After the 1850 Census and the opening of new western lands, population growth slowed, but during William's boyhood his immediate environs were ever changing.[17]

If William accompanied his father on a walk around town in the late 1840s or early 1850s, they passed an array of businesses and shops. Walking along Front Street, with its view of the boats making their way up the Ohio Canal or down the Tuscarawas River and the men loading and unloading barrels of wheat and crates of shoes, they were aware that they lived in a place connected to the world. This hint of cosmopolitanism was probably reinforced a little bit as William and Thomas Quantrill passed the Liberty Hotel. That fine establishment was there to greet out-of-town travelers as they made their way down the waterways or came across the river and canal in a wagon. William almost certainly waved to Sam Fertig, that stalwart of the tollhouse who collected fares from all those who used the bridge into Canal Dover.[18]

As they turned away from the water and into the town, father and son might walk past the Second Street office of Dr. Brashear—a family friend and the local surgeon—where Thomas maybe inquired about a bothersome cough. After the short consult, they kept on walking, and if they went up Factory Street, William possibly looked in the window of Mr. Kohl's tailor's shop to see the latest fashion. Cutting across the streets this way and that, William and Thomas might also stroll by George Oswald's shoe shop and Mr. Perley's hat store to see what men were wearing on their feet and heads. There were shops out of which emanated a buffet of smells covering the whole range from toxic to fine: the medicinal scents of Mr. Reichenbauch's apothecary shop, the metallic odor of old Cowgill's gunsmithing shop, and the stink of Mr. Hammond's meat market that sold fresh cuts every Monday, Wednesday, and Friday, but always possessed the bloody funk that lingers about a butcher's shop, especially in those hot summer days.[19]

Although William's father was at one time an important part of this local artisanal manufacturing, the changing economy altered his trajectory. Only a few years after the publication of his instructional manual for tinsmithing, Thomas Quantrill began a professional transition. Although he rose to prominence in Dover as a tinsmith and became a community leader in the late 1840s, it was possible that he saw a need to augment his income or even pursue a new career altogether. Perhaps his shop was run out of business or he suffered some other financial crisis, leaving him in need of a new source of revenue to maintain his household. He needed to seek out an opportunity that would last in this new economy.[20]

Thomas won an elected position on the school board, but his political affiliation is unclear. Looking at the decades of the 1840s and 1850s, the election results of Tuscarawas County represent a fairly evenly divided populace. The county elected gubernatorial candidates from the Whig Party in every biennial election from 1840 to 1850. From 1851 until the beginning of the war in 1861, the country went for the gubernatorial candidate from the Locofoco Party once, the Know-Nothing Fusionist Party once, the Democratic Party twice, and the Republican Party twice. Presidential electoral results give us a better picture of Dover Township. In 1844, Dover voted for the Whig Henry Clay by a close margin. Unfortunately, the 1848 election results are missing, but in 1852, 1856, and 1860, Doverites voted for the Democratic candidate. It cannot be determined whether Thomas Quantrill rode the end of the Whiggish wave into office, or whether he was a part of the new groundswell of Democrats to find success at the polls.[21]

The first public school was founded in 1849 in Canal Dover. Thomas was elected principal and superintendent of the school in 1851, and he held these positions until his death in 1854. During his stint as principal and superintendent, Thomas did some teaching, but how much is unknown. Abraham Ellis, who lived in Ohio in the early 1850s and worked to accredit teachers and schools for the state, was familiar with the elder Quantrill's instruction. Ellis recalled that Thomas "was for many years a teacher in the High School," and that in that capacity he had "never heard anything against his character." Even the biographer Connelley, ever seeking to paint a darkened picture of William and his family, felt obliged to remark that Thomas "was a good teacher and was much beloved by his pupils."[22]

Thomas's experience likely formed William's perception of the relationship between labor, money, and masculine identity. Through conversations with his father, discussions between his parents that he inevitably overheard, and his own observations, William learned that men must make enough money to provide for their households. It was one of the things that made a man. Men without means did not rate, and debtors were hardly men at all. William knew that his father worked hard and became a master craftsman and an erudite mechanic who wrote a book. But he also realized that whatever his father's expertise and labor had once been worth, in middle age he needed to take up a new profession to bring in money. It is unclear whether Thomas was embittered by this turn of events, or whether he brought any bitterness home. Regardless, William seemed to acquire the idea that expertise and labor were only as good as the profit they generated.[23]

In addition to the necessity of economic independence, Thomas and Caroline taught William to behave in a manner befitting the expectations of manhood in the 1840s and 1850s North. The same economic trends that led to a change in the way things were produced also ripped apart the social structure of preindustrial America. With home and work separated, a newfound freedom was enjoyed by men of the working and middle classes. Working men were no longer under the watchful eye of their bosses—they now drank where and when they liked. Away from their mothers and wives, men found themselves mixing in barrooms and taverns, occasionally with lewd women. In gambling houses men might bet their wages on cards or other games of chance. With so many temptations, a young man entering this new world needed to be prepared for life in ways that his father did not.[24]

Beginning in the 1820s, reformers like Sylvester Graham developed a philosophy of manhood based on restraint. These individuals believed that excesses of drink, fornication, and gambling took their toll on men, sapping their physical, moral, and intellectual strength. Graham was a well-known antebellum crusader concerned about the sexual health of boys and men. He began his famous *A Lecture to Young Men on Chastity*, originally published in 1834, by insisting, "The wisest and best men of every age, have manifest a deep interest in the welfare of youth; and have considered their intellectual, moral and physical education, character and condition, of the utmost importance to the individual, social and civil welfare of mankind."[25]

Whatever we think of Graham's vanity for placing himself beside the "wisest and best men" of his age, his point was that young people needed to be educated about all parts of life, not just reading, writing, and arithmetic. He knew that boys learned these things one way or another, and it was better that they learn about the dangers of sex from their parents or a stony-faced reformer. In regard to his lesson on sex, Graham's central theme was that it should be avoided. If a boy or young man felt urges, he needed to control them. To keep his loins from running hot, a man should avoid alcohol and coffee. Instead, he should drink fresh water and eat vegetables and bland foods—like a soft, plain brown cracker.[26]

Graham was especially concerned about masturbation, popularizing the idea that it caused insanity. He argued that if a young man failed to apply his foolproof, mood-depressing methods, he could expect to wind up in an institution. Graham provided convincing evidence—an article written by "the distinguished superintendent of the Massachusetts Lunatic Hospital," a certain Dr. Woodward. The good doctor stated, "No cause is more influential in producing insanity, and, in a special manner, perpetuating the disease, than self-pollution." After hearing something like this or being told that their hands might be covered in warts or that they might go blind or that they might simply drop dead, more than a few pubescent boys probably worked to keep their thoughts pure and their hands busy.[27]

Evidence suggests that as an adult, William internalized some of the lessons of restraint pushed by Graham and others. Of the three areas of sin Quantrill was taught to avoid—drinking alcohol, gambling, and pleasuring himself or fornicating outside marriage—we know for sure that at least one of the teachings took. He was a teetotaler. During the war, many of the guerrillas drank, and while he did not mind other men tippling, William abstained. However, he was not as pure when it came to wagering. He gambled often enough that he probably carried a pack of playing cards in his saddlebag, and you can bet he would handicap just about anything you might want to wager on. As far as self-pollution, thankfully the sources omitted any mention either way. It is worth remembering, though, that quite a few people who lived through the Civil War thought William was deranged. Exactly what they thought caused his mind to become troubled, one shudders to think.[28]

At least one source insisted that William was not a well-behaved boy. Frances Beeson (later Frances Beeson Thompson) was a year or two older than William and spent a few years of her youth in Canal Dover. She and William likely attended school together. Years after her childhood and long after the Civil War, she remembered him as a troublemaker and his family as a clan of ne'er-do-wells. It is difficult to know the exact source of Frances's negative recollection, but it seems deeply rooted.[29]

When Connelley went looking for people to share their stories about William Quantrill, Frances Beeson happily obliged. Her tales fit the biographer's negative preconception of the guerrilla and provide the small bit of evidence on which he built his case that William was a bad boy. Beeson told Connelley that William was a hellion who "had to be punished often," that "there was murder in every gleam of his strange glittering eyes," that he ran out on unpaid bills as a young man, and that he attempted to murder her father in his sleep. A few of her recollections were firsthand, and others came from stories that she had heard or that had been passed down through her family. In nearly every case, hers is the only account of an event. There are no other reports to corroborate her tale or to contradict it. Her version of William may be valid, or it may be contrived. What can be said for certain is that her image of the boy runs counter to the other depictions that exist in the record.[30]

Baked within Beeson's claims are hints that she manufactured the stories to fit her own disdain for the Quantrill family. In stark contrast to the other existing accounts that Thomas Quantrill was a good man, Frances Beeson asserted that he was corrupt. Based on Beeson's story, Connelley wrote that Thomas Quantrill's book "was published with money belonging to the school-fund of the village," and that "in some way H. V. Beeson discovered the misuse of the school-funds and called public attention to the matter." As the tale goes, Thomas Quantrill "threatened to kill Beeson . . . He entered Beeson's house with a cocked derringer in his hand." Beeson was drinking cider and was about to dip the end of a hot poker into his mug to warm the cordial, but "when Quantrill entered, Beeson rose suddenly and struck him on the head with a poker before he could shoot, laying him unconscious on the floor with a long gash in his scalp."[31]

Curiously, nothing came of Thomas Quantrill's supposed embezzlement or attempted murder of Beeson. Assuming this occurred around the time of the publication of *The Mechanic's Calculator and Tinman's Guide* in 1847, the more puzzling question remains of why Thomas was made superintendent of the Canal Dover public school system four years after he allegedly pilfered the school fund and tried to cover it up by attempting to murder a man. In contrast, if this event did occur in the late 1840s—or at all—Thomas was not run out of town on a rail, and his children were not burdened with the scorn of the community. Rather, it was the Beeson family who left Canal Dover and moved to Bethlehem, Ohio, where they were residing in 1850. In the census from that year, Harmon V. Beeson is listed as a merchant, but he possessed nothing of value. That toddy-drinking, poker-flailing defender of public funds was broke and later became a debtor.[32]

Whether people believe Frances Beeson's assessment of the Quantrill family and William in particular or they believe the recollections of William's mother and his community, everyone seemed to agree that William was an excellent student. When he was old enough, he attended grammar school. The first schoolhouse in Canal Dover was built in 1827, just on the outskirts of town, but a more permanent brick schoolhouse was constructed on Fourth Street in 1844, right around the time William began his studies. In his first years as a student, he learned to read and write and to do some basic mathematics.[33]

He received a well-rounded education for the time and place. The books taught in the Dover public school were representative of those taught across the North at the time. The list includes Henry Mandeville's *A Course of Reading for Common Schools*, Mathias Green's *An English Grammar*, Richard Green Parker's *Juvenile Philosophy*, Charles Davies's *Arithmetic*, Jesse Olney's *An Elementary Geography*, and Emma Willard's *History of the United States*. As these books demonstrate, the curriculum was designed to teach students literacy, help them master the basics of mathematics, and acquaint them with something of the past and present world, especially the United States.[34]

When William glanced up from his studies, he saw only white faces. No Black children attended the Dover public school. According to the 1850 Census, few African Americans lived in Dover Township or even Tuscarawas County. In William's town, there was one Black household headed by a man named William Willis, a twenty-nine-year-old illiterate barber who was born in Virginia. He lived with his nineteen-year-old wife, Maranda, who was from Maryland, and two other Black men, Wila J. Morris and Jeremiah Nuby, who were also listed as barbers. Only Nuby, who was sixteen, was eligible to attend school, but he was busy cutting hair and shaving faces. Two African American girls also lived in Dover Township, but neither attended school. Ann and Amanda Wineberry—apparently sisters—were twelve and nine respectively. They lived in a household headed by wealthy farmer Basil D. Downey. Although there was nothing recorded about their role in the household, they were probably servants. In Dover, William's world was white. When he did see Black men, women, or children, they were the exception that proved the rule, present only to serve the white people of the town.[35]

Some Black children who lived outside Dover Township in other parts of Tuscarawas County did find their way into a schoolhouse because of a recently changed law. Until 1849, a decades-old law kept Black children out of school in Ohio. An act outlining the establishment of public schools and their funding across the state of Ohio had been passed in 1829. "The school extended equal privileges to all white children," according to *The History of Tuscarawas County, Ohio*, but "those of colored parentage were excluded, and no tax was levied for school purposes upon colored parents." In 1849, "an amendment . . . admitted the children of colored parents" into the public schools. Districts could establish schools for Black children or integrate their schools if they liked. How quickly this legislation took hold across the state is uncertain, but the measure may explain how those Black children in Tuscarawas were able to receive some education in 1850.[36]

The presence and power of whiteness of William's everyday life were given intellectual contours by his history book. The history taught in school confirmed the whiteness of William's world. Many of the assumptions that Americans made (and continue to make) about race are rooted in the history of this country—that is, our interpretation of the past. William learned a history of America in which slavery was abstract and Black Americans were faceless, nameless, and almost nonexistent. This type of history was taught throughout the United States, from New England to the Middle West to the South. According to William's textbook—Willard's *History of the United States*, originally published in 1828 race was not a central part of the American story, at least not the white/Black dynamic that was critical to shaping the country. Although there is some coverage of Native Americans at the outset of the book, slavery, slaveholding, racial identity, and the myriad streams of racism that sprang up in colonial America do not appear in any significant way. Slavery shows up here and there. For instance, the 1844 version of the textbook notes, "A Dutch ship from Africa arriving at Jamestown, a part of her cargo of negroes was purchased by the colony. This was the commencement of negro slavery in the United States." After this not-quite-accurate first mention, African enslavement does not pop up again in the work until discussion of the territorial expansion of the United States after the American Revolution. This whitewashed version of the past combined with the whiteness of Canal Dover to create William Quantrill's ideology.[37]

This unquestioned acceptance of white supremacy was central to the westerner's view of the world. Whether it was the states carved out of the Old Northwest Territory, the Trans-Mississippi West, or the yet-unorganized western territories, the political culture of these places was distinct from that of the North or the South. The part of Ohio in which William was raised was home to people originally from free states to the east, as well as those from slave states. His own parents represented the merger of these two cultures. From the urban North came industry, and from the South came agriculture. Towns and villages often took their form from the New England model, while the strains of manly independence like that so important in the South thrived among the men of the West. The one thing that united these communities was a consensus that the West was a white man's land. Whether they were explicitly for or against slavery or silent on the matter, nearly all westerners seemed to agree that Black men, women, and children were better off living somewhere else.[38]

After graduating from the high school, William became a teacher like his father. Given Thomas's own talent in the classroom, he probably thought his son could become a teacher. As the superintendent of Dover schools, Thomas used his power to hire William on as a teacher. With his experience schooling the town's children, the elder Quantrill could guide his son as he apprenticed in the craft.[39]

In the nineteenth century, it was common practice to hire a recent graduate of the public high school to be the new teacher. For school boards, hiring these teenagers made good sense: These graduates knew the material; as students they had likely developed some experience tutoring younger students and even their peers. Perhaps most importantly, school boards could pay these juvenile schoolmasters and schoolmarms very little. For young teachers, the job provided a bridge from adolescence in their parents' household to their permanent role as adults. Young women ceased teaching when they married and became mothers, and young men often transitioned from teaching to a learned profession such as the law, the ministry, medicine, or business.[40]

Whatever William's long-term plans were, they went off the rails when his father died. Thomas Quantrill suffered from consumption—a term used by nineteenth-century Americans for the disease we know to-day as tuberculosis—and succumbed to it in December 1854. Thomas's death did not mark the end to William's schooling. Instead, when his father was buried in the cemetery at Canal Dover, it merely put to rest the first part of what William needed to learn to become a man. He was now responsible for the rest of his education.[41]

CHAPTER 2: *Teacher*

At eighteen years old, William Clarke Quantrill was overwhelmed with doubt as the weather in northern Illinois became inhospitable. The heavy guilt that he felt after leaving his recently widowed mother further deflated his spirit. On November 17, 1855, with the skies gray, the days shortened, and the wind howling across the prairie, the immature and penniless young man huddled inside his classroom and wrote to his mother, "Well I must tell you one thing & that is that I am tired of the west already, and I do not think I shall stay in it very much longer than I can help, I must stay as long as my school lasts & that is all." After only three months of teaching school in the town of Mendota, William was ready to pack up and take a train back to his hometown of Canal Dover, Ohio. William told his mother, "When I get there again (which will not be long) I will turn over a new leaf entirely. . . . I feel that I have done wrong in going from home & hope you will forgive me." Uneasy about where he was, William was aimlessly enduring, blindly groping through the fog of teenage angst and uncertainty.[1]

Not long after he sent this letter, William disappeared. He absconded from Mendota and his schoolhouse and evaporated from the historical record—the first of several vanishings during his lifetime. He walked away to a place unknowable.[2]

William was still very much a boy when he left home in 1855 at eighteen years old—a student as much as a teacher—but in the nineteenth century he was considered a man. As such, he was expected to rein in his emotions and adopt an ethic of behavior that led to a purpose-driven life. For Americans living in the mid-1800s, there was no exact age *when* a boy became a man. A boy might graduate to manhood with the completion of an apprenticeship. He became a man when he received his inheritance or earned enough money to get married. Sometimes it was as simple as leaving his father's household to make his own way in the world. War, economic turmoil, physical dislocation, plague, drought, or the untimely death of a parent might upset the development of a child and place him in the shoes of an adult earlier than expected. While failure to stand up and become a man would damage his reputation, in those rough-and-tumble days, it could also cost him his life and imperil the survival of his family.[3]

In February 1856 William reemerged in the historical record in Fort Wayne, Indiana—some 250 miles from Mendota—as a changed man. "I suppose you thought I was dead," he began his first letter to his mother in three months. He was teaching again, and his spirits seemed revived. "I have from 35 to 40 schollars every day," he said, adding, "I have got in a good neighborhood, and they say I am the best teacher they ever had. I get 20 dollars a month." This situation was better but not for the obvious reason: he was actually making five dollars a month less at this stop than the amount he had agreed to in Mendota. Rather, William's changed outlook was almost certainly due to a lesson he had absorbed. He informed his mother, "One thing I will tell you this trip I have had has done me more good and I have learned more than I would in three years steady schooling." "What I have learned will be of more benefit to me than any thing I now know of," he continued. William did not care to reveal the nature of this edification. For all its inscrutability, however, William's struggle in Mendota and his apparent salvation in Fort Wayne suggest that his education continued even as he sought to teach others.[4]

❧

In August 1855, William went by rail to Mendota, a town in north central Illinois. While there were other inducements, his father's death seemed to be the primary catalyst for young William's initial westward venture. In addition to losing an important bond that had kept him close to home, he might have felt a duty to provide for his mother and siblings. William likely thought that the best way to do so was to lessen the burden that he placed on Caroline Quantrill as a dependent member of her household, so he moved elsewhere with the idea of sending a few dollars home to her in his letters.

When he left, William went with a friend, fellow teacher Mary Clapp. She was moving to reunite with her parents in Illinois. When she mentioned her move and the possibility of open teaching positions, William likely saw his chance to leave home.[5]

An unmarried young woman and young man traveling together—this was uncommon. Women were thought to be vulnerable, and moving through public spaces could be dangerous, possibly exposing them to a more violent or tawdry world than the one they knew. The experience might impact an impressionable young woman. Traveling hundreds of miles only heightened the threats to an innocent woman. William was there, then, as a protector. Mary Clapp's parents almost certainly permitted him to travel with her; perhaps they even asked him to travel with their daughter. William probably was not courting Mary, or at least he was not seen as a suitor by her parents. He was not a threat to their daughter; he was trusted; he was the escort.

Upon arriving in Mendota, William wrote to his mother, "We are both well except that Mary was looking out the window of the car while we were going along the shore of Lake Michigan when a spark of fire flew in her eye & made it a little sore. But that will be well in a day or so." Besides the rogue ember, the travelers had no trouble. "I have $6 of my money left & maybe next time I write I will send a little along," William related. He told his mother about the landscape, which was "a great deal different from Ohio," saying, "For miles around I can see nothing but tall grass." Commenting on the crops being grown in Illinois, he wrote, "Corn, potatoes, cabbage are plenty." After telling his mother that he was certain he could become the teacher of one of the two schools in the town, he promised, "Next time I will write more."[6]

As a town, Mendota was a lot like Canal Dover. This area of the Illinois prairie went unsettled by white Americans until 1853, when it became the junction point of the Illinois Central and the Chicago, Burlington, and Quincy Railroads. Then the land in Township 36, Range 1 of LaSalle County became a popular destination. First to set up shop was D. D. Giles, who established a general store at the railroad intersection. Once a grid for a town was drawn, clusters of folks arrived: farmers, millers, blacksmiths, carpenters, and all sorts. They named the town Junction—this tribute to the infrastructure that brought the town its prosperity echoed the sentiment of the people of Dover in changing the name of their town to Canal Dover. By the time William arrived, Junction's residents had Indianized the name. The local history recounts, "[The] name was changed to Mendota, which is the Indian name for junction—meaning meeting, or coming together."[7]

The leading citizens of Mendota hired teachers on the cheap. Whether or not it was common to pay teachers so little, William's contract was nothing short of exploitive. By his own account, he signed on to teach for the fall term for twenty-five dollars a month. However, this amount was paid after three months' time, presumably at the end of the term, leaving him to scrape up funds for his room and board for an extended period. William's youth and naivete played a role in his agreement to these terms—he was not the first teacher to sign up for a low-paying job and not the last.[8]

In the surviving letters to his mother, William did not offer details about the schoolhouse or the children he taught. New to the profession, with only a year or so of experience under his belt, he might have struggled, but it is impossible to know exactly what it was like teaching the children of Mendota's farmers, merchants, and craftsmen. In any case, William eventually became a well-liked teacher. From Ohio to Illinois to Indiana and finally Kansas, he merited no complaints against his performance in front of the classroom. Years later, by the time he was teaching his last term in Stanton, Kansas, William was considered very good at his job. In researching his biography, Connelley traveled to Stanton—the tiny community outside Paola—in 1907, and he interviewed more than two dozen men and women who had attended William's schoolhouse in 1859–60. Although it dismayed Connelley, to a person, "they all said he [Quantrill] was a good teacher."[9]

Exactly what William's students meant by "a good teacher" warrants a bit of exploration. When antebellum Americans imagined the stereotypical schoolmaster, many of them likely thought of Washington Irving's officious, ambitious, and abrasive Ichabod Crane, the central character of "The Legend of Sleepy Hollow." The archetypal schoolmaster, as seen in Crane, tended to be authoritarian and a strict disciplinarian; he was violent. Indeed, a birch or hickory rod was the schoolmaster's tool for maintaining order. Recall Irving's description of Crane: "He was a conscientious man, and ever bore in mind the golden maxim, 'spare the rod and spoil the child.'—Ichabod Crane's scholars certainly were not spoiled." In other words, he beat his students, and this was normal behavior for the teacher of the 1800s. Perhaps William was equally violent. If physically enforced discipline was the norm, it is possible that the beatings he issued to his more unruly students were not even considered when his old students rated him.[10]

However, maybe being remembered as a "good teacher" meant that William differed from the stereotypical schoolmaster. Perhaps he was unlike Ichabod Crane or even his father and used affection rather than

40 CHAPTER TWO

the rod to keep his students in line. William's boyhood persona was incongruent with the birch-wielding dictator. In the scant evidence that survives, there is no mention of William being a harsh disciplinarian. If such an assertion could be made, Connelley would have dug it up and printed it.[11]

William, with his "warm heart and ready smile," was an apt fit for the changing face of the teaching profession of the 1850s. He was a man, but a man with gentle traits. While the image of Crane as the archetypal schoolmaster lingered in the collective mind, changes in the teaching profession that had begun in the 1840s suggested that affection was being applied as much as the birch. Across the country the schoolmaster was being joined by the schoolmarm. Young women, like William's friend Mary Clapp, were being brought into schools to teach. School boards felt justified in paying women substantially less than men, which was one reason for hiring them. More important reasons for their employment were the increasing perception that the schoolhouse was an extension of the domestic space over which women now held dominion, and the notion that femininity gave women an innate advantage in educating children. Although women were perceived as weak in body, by the 1850s there was a popular belief across the North that they were morally superior to men and better nurturers.[12]

Whether or not he fit the mold of a teacher, William struggled to survive. With every week, he spent more of the money he had brought with him to Mendota. William began looking outside the schoolhouse for alternative ways to bring in a dollar. "I was sorry to hear that you could not find those Texas papers," he wrote to his mother, imploring her, "I want you to look again for them for if you find them I can make some money this winter." He apparently referred to land grants offered to men who participated in the Texas war for independence. Believing a relative of his had fought in that war, William hoped he might cash in by selling the deeds to a land speculator. Later in the same letter, he pestered Caroline again. "I would like to have those Texas papers very much," he said, and he then suggested, "You had better write grandfather & ask him if he has got them & tell him I can do well with them." William also expressed interest in asking his grandfather to "help [him] a little."[13]

In addition to asking his mother to track down some land-grant papers, William asked her to send copies of his father's book that he might sell. He wrote, "You must be sure to send me those tinners books all of them as soon as you can for those 6 that I brought with me sold in one town & [I] could of sold more if I had them for $2.00 a piece which just paid my board." In this letter, a sense of urgency and perhaps even desperation can be felt in the boy. "I have only $8 dollars now," he confessed, telling his mother again, "Be sure & send them for I can sell 50 in Chicago there are so many tin shops there. If you send them I can send you some money in a week. . . . As soon as you send them books in a week I will send you $20 certain."[14]

William's attention was pulled away from the schoolhouse by the siren song of the woods. "Well I guess I will teach school this winter," he begrudgingly informed his mother. However, whenever William wrote about hunting, his words were bursting with a lively energy. In an October 2, 1855, letter to his boyhood friend Edward T. Kellam back in Dover, Ohio, William reported, "This too is the country for hunting [and] it pays well." He claimed, "A man that understands the business can shoot from 50 to 60 prairie chickens every day [and] get $1.50 per dozen." William also told his friend that he had been to "a place 16 miles from here called inlet pond," where there were "thousands of ducks and geese." About one excursion to the pond, William bragged, "I killed 2 geese and 11 ducks, but the fellow that was with me killed 9 geese and 32 ducks." Toward the close of his letter, he told Edward, "If you was here we would go every day."[15]

William's reference to a "fellow," a man important enough to mention but not important enough to name, hints at a mystery or at least an intriguing vagueness. Several nameless fellows appear throughout the surviving letters that William wrote. More than an epistolary tic, the reoccurrence of these anonymous companions suggests something significant about William and the way that he related to other men. He formed bonds—significant, powerful connections—with other men everywhere he went. William wanted to tell his mother and his hometown friends about these men, but he could not.

This specific fellow made a significant impression on William, whose most cheerful letter from Mendota recounts the hunt and his companion's exploits. Such an association between the pleasure William experienced and the man with whom he shared it cannot be ignored, nor can the fact that William wrote about it to a close friend. Hunting with this fellow was the bright spot of the future guerrilla's time in Illinois. It can only be speculated whether William's hunting partner played a role in the "something" that happened, or whether this man provided instruction on what William called "one good lesson that I would never have learned at home." Regardless, that nameless figure cast a shadow over William's time in Mendota and his exit from that place.[16]

Desperately in need of money and no longer satisfied as a teacher, William seemed near a crisis in his conception of manhood. He had been taught that manhood meant economic independence. Facing the consequences of being without means, he sought land grants, his father's books, anything that might turn a profit. Each letter home was more desperate than the last. Each one signaled an impending doom: the humiliation of destitution and indebtedness. However, a November 1855 letter has a different tone. Telling his "dear Mother" that he had received a package from her including a pair of winter boots, he stated, "[They arrived] a little too late for I had bought me a pair about two or three weeks before." It is strange that a boy without much money should spend the little in his pockets on new boots. It is possible that he was so desperate to keep his feet warm and dry on the walks to and from his schoolhouse that the purchase was a matter of survival. As for those copies of *The Mechanic's Calculator and Tinman's Guide*, William did not sell them. However, he promised Caroline that he would be able to do so soon enough: "The next time I write you may expect some money by express as that is the only safe way to send it." This comment, too, is a bit confusing. The boy needed money, and yet he could not get away to peddle these books, presumably his only available source of extra income. Perhaps he really could not free himself from his duties in the schoolhouse.[17]

His letter took a depressing turn. William told his mother that he was tired of life in Mendota and could not stay in the West much longer. Ever the teacher, he referred to himself as a "dunce" for leaving Canal Dover, remarking, " I could have done just as well at home as out here." Self-loathing fills the remainder of the missive. William felt terrible that his siblings were suffering from ague. He lamented that his mother was taking in boarders to survive. "I have done wrong," he said, and I "hope you will forgive me."[18]

In the late fall of 1855, *something* happened to William. Beyond the challenges mounting before him, a specific event catalyzed the first of several voids in his story. When he reemerged in Fort Wayne, Indiana, in early 1856, William wrote his mother, "I suppose that you think something has happened to me, and you think right." He remained tight-lipped, however, stating, "I think I will not tell you in this letter what it was as this is the first one I have wrote since it happened." William nevertheless reassured Caroline Quantrill about this unspeakable incident: "You will not think so hard of me when you know all." Beyond his mother's response to the ugly or awkward news, he also worried about his grandfather's judgment. "I suppose if Grandfather is there he has scolded me completely," William wrote, "but when he knows all he will think different."[19]

These potential chastisements weighed heavily on Quantrill. He was anxious that the folks back home might think ill of him or turn their backs on him. William closed his letter to his mother from Fort Wayne by declaring, "The next time I will tell you all about what has happened. But I want you to never tell any body else whoever it may be for my sake." Back in Canal Dover, W. W. Scott heard a rumor about his childhood friend William Quantrill: "It is said that he left his school at Mendota in the middle of the term owing to some trouble or scandal."[20]

Because William never articulated exactly what occurred, at least not in his letters, speculation surrounds this part of his life. It is not surprising that stone-casting biographers Connelley and Castel were both sure they knew what happened in Mendota: he killed a man. Given their deductions from reading William's character through the distortion of hindsight, the theory makes perfect sense. Connelley's work calls the boy "a fiend wasteful and reckless of human life," a young man who was endowed with "depravity" and "degeneracy," and who "grew into the gory monster whose baleful shadow falls upon all who share his kindred blood." Castel's account is more succinct, describing William simply as "a juvenile monster." The authors' evidence includes Frances Beeson's stories, the antiquated belief that the Quantrill family tree was full of rascals and therefore evil was genetically imprinted on William's character, and William's own actions much later during the war.[21]

There is a problem with the assertion that William killed a man: there is no evidence that he killed anyone. A murder would have made the news and left a legal record, and it would be mentioned in the histories of LaSalle County—especially if the crime was committed by a man who became a fearsome southern bushwhacker. Moreover, in the wake of the event, William did not act like a man who had murdered someone. He was not concerned about the law tracking him down or some avenging kinsman dirking him in an alleyway.[22]

Perhaps William stole money to pay his room and board. He was, after all, plummeting toward destitution. He wrote often about money—how much was in his billfold, how much he needed, and how much he hoped to make. A mind so fixated on profit might justify taking someone else's funds. Again, though, there is no evidence of such a theft. Yet a crime like petty larceny was less likely to be printed in the papers and less likely to find its way into the local history, so it is possible that William was accused of theft. After all, he did have a new pair of boots.

Other explanations might have caused the abrupt departure from Mendota under the shadow of a "scandal." Speculation about these other possibilities is dangerous—especially about such an iconic figure—sending us tumbling down a slippery slope. As a teacher not much older than his students, a naive, effeminate young man out on his own for the first time, a boy in desperate need of money, William might have found himself in a number of tawdry situations. The details of this scandal may never see the light of day. That said, it whispers volumes that William kept quiet, and that his childhood friend who heard the rumors refused to divulge them. Whatever "happened to" William—whether it was scandalous, murderous, or larcenous—created the immense weight of guilt and shame that sent him running from Mendota.[23]

In November 1855, William gathered up his things and headed down the road. Like most good students, he blamed himself for his failings and whatever it was that happened to him. It was just as likely, though, that his teachers and the lessons they taught him were the cause of his trouble. No matter whose sins he was carrying as he walked away from Mendota, William was a boy struggling to find himself as a man; a more common story in American history is difficult to find.[24]

CHAPTER 3: *Dunce*

As the disgraced William trudged down the road away from Mendota, a different scandal was reverberating across America. "A WOMAN HANGED," declared the lede of a short report in the January 19, 1856, edition of the *Daily American Organ* of Washington, D.C. Papers across the country carried similar headlines for the story about "a colored woman, named Celia, [who] was hanged on the 21st ult., at Fulton, Missouri, for the murder of Robert Newsome, whose slave she was, in June last." Perhaps anticipating skepticism among some of its readers, the *American Organ* assured them, "The evening preceding her execution she made a full confession of her guilt." Reading between the lines, many Americans—North and South—probably guessed that Celia's story was significantly more harrowing and complicated than the brief report of her demise at the gallows.[1]

Celia first appeared in the news around the time William was planning his voyage from Canal Dover to Mendota. A July 5, 1855, story in the Glasgow, Missouri, paper reported, "The Fulton Telegraph gives an account of the murder of Mr. Robert Newson [*sic*] . . . by a negro woman and the subsequent burning of his body." The newspaper recounted that when Newsom, "an old man" who "lived alone," did not turn up for breakfast, a search for him commenced. Without any suspects, the authorities acted predictably: "A negro man was arraigned on suspicion." George, the slave of the murdered man, apparently told his interrogators that "a negro woman named Celia had threatened him." The story breezed right past how or why the woman had threatened George. However, it highlighted Celia's admission, declaring, "Upon being interrogated, the woman confessed that she had killed her master, and burned his body, and told where the parts of the bones could be found. She denied having had any assistance."[2]

45

46 CHAPTER THREE

None of the stories that appeared in the *American Organ*, the *Glasgow Weekly Times*, or other papers mentioned a motive for the murder—they included just enough information to give readers a sense of what had occurred on the Missouri farm during those summer days of 1855. A Black man arrested, a slaveholder murdered and his body burned, reports of a threat, the confession of an enslaved woman: from the outlines of the case it was possible to tease out the larger story and the possible motives.[3]

Celia's life story was not that unusual until she murdered her owner. As historian Melton A. McLaurin recounts, Robert Newsom purchased Celia when she was fourteen years old to serve as his concubine. He raped her for the first time almost immediately after acquiring her in 1850, stopping the wagon on the way back to his farm to do the despicable deed, "and by that act [he] at once established and defined the nature of the relationship between the master and his newly acquired slave." Over the next five years, Newsom continually raped Celia. The psychological torture cannot be imagined. Every day, when the sun went down, she wondered whether Newsom would come lurking through the darkness. This teenage girl closed her eyes each night fearing the embodiment of her degradation—a fat, old man, soft and pink, embittered and entitled, would again fall on top of her, violate her body, and pollute her soul.[4]

Celia bore two children during this period. One was definitely Newsom's, and most likely both of them were. When Celia became pregnant again in February or March 1855, the baby had another possible father, the enslaved man George, with whom she was in a relationship. George could not stand the dynamic between Celia and her owner. He told Celia that "he would have nothing more to do with her if she did not quit the old man." If Celia hoped that George might protect her from Robert, she was disappointed. Of course, as McLaurin points out, for George "to have confronted Newsom directly at this stage to demand that he cease his sexual exploitation of Celia would have been an act that could have cost him his life." Slavery not only dehumanized girls and women through systemic sexual violence, but it also unmade men, withholding from them those core tenets of nineteenth-century masculinity: men's ability to defend their own and retain exclusive access to their sexual partner.[5]

Celia told Newsom to stop coming around, but he did not take this request seriously. That night he lumbered back to her quarters, where he planned to have his way with her in front of their two children. As he opened the door and crossed the threshold, Celia hit Robert upside his head with a log and stunned him. Once the old man was down, she stood over him, and with two hands—strong from work, powerful from mothering—she delivered the death blow. Celia pulled her owner's body into the fire and incinerated him in the hearth he had built for her to prepare his meals. With a log and a roaring fire, three became two.[6]

A few months later, with a noose and a drop, two became one. Newsom's murder and Celia's hanging changed the lives of other members of the extended household. George was sold from Newsom's estate, and Celia's daughters were sold within a year of their mother's execution. The tragic life that these girls were headed toward is easily envisioned as one full of despair, fearful nights, and emotional scarring. Luckily for these two little survivors—and for everyone—the Civil War interrupted the march toward a degrading existence.[7]

Whether or not they knew the specifics of Celia's case, a small but growing number of people were becoming aware of the horrid nature of slavery. Across the North, abolitionists and other reformers, especially middle-class white women, believed that the true evils at the center of the peculiar institution were the sexual assault of Black women and the destruction of the Black family on the auction block. These dehumanizing features made slavery a moral and social problem and more than just an abstract economic or political issue.[8]

While some Americans sharpened their focus on slavery, William seemed ignorant of the issues. He likely knew nothing of Celia's trial, nor did he mention anything about slavery or politics in his letters from this period. In this sense, William existed above the fray, a privilege that he and other people like him possessed. He experienced something in Mendota—exploitation, destitution, abuse, a bawdy scandal—but nothing that took away his freedom. William could walk out on a job, flee the scene of some transgression, and move on to another town and position. He could do so without worry of repercussions except some potential social fallout. Even more to the point, his liberty allowed him to choose whether he learned or cared about an issue like slavery.

In that way, William represented a large portion of the American populace in the 1850s. He was too young to vote at age eighteen, and without the incentive of participation, he did not concern himself with politics, or he was uninformed of the political situation, or both. Most of the men who fought in the Civil War did not participate in the elections that pushed the country toward the conflict because they were also too young to cast ballots. The vast majority of Americans did not engage directly in the electoral process—a statement that seems impossible. Historians of the Civil War era tend to study and highlight the politically active Americans, which has generated a depiction of the mid-nineteenth century as a time when everyone seemed political. However, in the 1856 presidential election, 69.4 percent of adults did not vote because they were women, enslaved, or free people of color in many areas in the North or because they were white men who chose not to participate. In the 1860 presidential election 68.5 percent of adults either were ineligible to vote or stayed home despite having the suffrage. In each of the 1856 and 1860 presidential elections roughly one-fifth of *eligible voters* did not vote.[9]

These last statistics suggest that the United States was a nation populated by a significant number of dunces. With everything on the line, many Americans had better things to do than go to the polls. Some probably did not vote because they had to get a harvest in, were dealing with sickness of some kind, faced a daunting amount of travel to get to the polling place, or were prevented by some other extenuating circumstance. But these justifications do not explain why such a large percentage of eligible voters did not cast ballots at this divisive time. Perhaps more Americans were like William than we might want to believe. They were unaware of or unmoved by—one way or the other—the morality of slavery, the Fugitive Slave Act, popular sovereignty, or any other issues related to the peculiar institution.[10]

William was not engaged in politics, but he certainly read about the Wakarusa War, which broke out in the Kansas Territory at almost the exact time he was fleeing Illinois in November 1855. The Kansas Territory was opened for settlement in 1854 after the passage of the Kansas-Nebraska Act. Stephen Douglas, Democratic senator from Illinois, and Andrew Butler, Democratic senator from South Carolina, proposed the bill to allow the government to sell land in the huge swatch of territory stretching from Missouri's and Iowa's western boundary to the Rocky Mountains after breaking it into two distinct territories: Kansas and Nebraska. Although the Democratic Party was increasingly associated with the interests of slaveholders, Douglas and Butler crafted a bill that seemed like a compromise. Rather than deal with the issue of slavery's extension into these western territories, Douglas and Butler proposed that the settlers of Kansas and Nebraska determine whether the new states would be open to or exclude slavery. This policy is known as popular sovereignty. By dividing the new lands into two territories, the bill implicitly suggested that northerners would move to Nebraska and slaveholders would move to Kansas.[11]

Popular sovereignty actually created a contested territory in Kansas. Proslavery settlers moved there or crossed the border from Missouri to vote in the territorial elections—an act that was legal. Some proslavery men were fire-eating reactionaries who traveled from across the South to do what it took to expand the slaveholding empire of the United States. Others were more moderate, merely wanting more land in which to plant slave-based agriculture. However, antislavery settlers also decided to move to the Kansas Territory in an effort to block the westward expansion of slavery. Within the antislavery coalition, radical abolitionists believed that slavery must end immediately and that Black people should be given equal rights under the law. But there were also conservative Free-Soilers who believed that western lands should be reserved for white men. In their opinion, all Black people, slave or free, should be excluded from the territories.[12]

By late 1855, popular sovereignty had proved to be an ineffectual policy for determining the fate of the territory. After settlers lost faith in electoral politics, some turned to violence to decide whether Kansas would be a slave or free state. Stories of the Wakarusa War filled the papers from December to January. The *New York Herald* reported that the conflict in the hotly contested Kansas Territory began when "a difficulty occurred between a pro-slavery man of the name of Coleman, and a free State man named Dow, in relation to 'a claim;' this resulted in a rencontre, in which Coleman killed Dow." Although the fighting was sparked by this killing over a land claim, the debate over the expansion of slavery and the right of slaveholders to spoil the virgin soil of the Great Plains with their brutal hedonism escalated into the Wakarusa War. In a short period of time, antislavery militants readied themselves in the town of Lawrence, and proslavery settlers and men from Missouri mustered on the Wakarusa River. The *New York Herald* described the proslavery militants as having come "to the Wakarusa camp to fight; they did not ask peace: it was war—war to the knife." The warmongering slavers marched to Lawrence and laid siege to the town.[13]

Even without much bloodshed, the siege was extraordinary. On December 6, one man died in a shoot-out between proslavery militants and antislavery men trying to skirt the cordon around Lawrence. Two days later they called a truce. Despite the small numbers of fighters on each side and the short casualty list, historian Michael E. Woods highlights the significance of the Wakarusa War: "Locally, it was the first time that masses of combatants took the field against each other and they were obviously willing, even eager, to fight. Scuffling at the ballot box had been replaced by large-scale mobilization." Violence ticked upward in 1856 and settled into a partisan conflict. This was Bleeding Kansas.[14]

In May 1856 Massachusetts senator Charles Sumner referred to it as "the crime against Kansas." Sumner, an abolitionist and radical Free-Soil Democrat turned Republican, outlined the crime, the apologies for the crime, and the remedy in a two-day-long speech in Congress. At more than one hundred typeset pages, the speech is known less for Sumner's historical and legal arguments than for his attacks on his fellow senators Stephen Douglas (Ill.) and Andrew Butler (S.C.), both of whom sponsored the Kansas-Nebraska Act. Sumner's verbal assault on Butler was especially vicious. Some of the content was brutal, as were Sumner's insinuations, which elicited verbal and nonverbal responses from his fellow congressmen and the gallery.[15]

"I regret much to miss the elder senator from his seat," Sumner began politely enough, "but the cause against which he has run a tilt with such activity of animosity demands that the opportunity of exposing him should not be lost." The Massachusetts politician mocked Butler, saying, "The senator from South Carolina has read many books of chivalry, and believes himself a chivalrous knight, with sentiments of honor and courage." In particular, Sumner assailed Butler for his stance on one issue: "He has chosen a mistress to whom he has made his vows, and who, though ugly to others is always lovely to him; though polluted in the sight of the world, is chaste in his sight;—I mean the harlot Slavery."[16]

After Sumner attacked Butler's honor, many of their colleagues were worried for Sumner's safety. Everyone in the chamber over those two days knew that Sumner used certain words and said things in a particular tone that could potentially incite violence among the many honor-bound, vain slaveholding men in the chamber. It was as if Sumner was picking a fight, daring someone to bludgeon him or run him through with an Arkansas toothpick. Even Stephen Douglas, one of the targets of Sumner's ire, said during the speech, "That damn fool is going to get himself shot by some other damned fool."[17]

Indeed, the personal insinuation that slaveholders used Black women to fulfill their lust hit close to home. Butler, a wealthy slaveholder with more than eighty slaves in 1850, had not remarried since the death of his second wife in the 1830s. It is possible that he filled the void left by his departed wife with enslaved women on his plantation. However, the 1850 Slave Schedule does not show any mulatto children that might have resulted from these sexual encounters. If Butler did not take an enslaved woman as a "harlot," then Sumner's allusion to sexual relations between slave owners and slaves may explain why Preston Brooks—a representative from Edgefield, South Carolina, and Butler's cousin—became enraged. After Brooks heard the speech, he felt compelled to defend his kinsman's honor; he returned to the Senate a couple of days later with his gutta-percha cane and beat Sumner unconscious. The iconic beating is cited and explored by historians as a case study in honor-driven violence. Exactly whose honor was being defended is not entirely clear. Brooks, like many other southern white men in the chamber over those two days, probably felt the sting of Sumner's words because he had "chosen a mistress" on his own plantation. Although there were no light-skinned slaves on Butler's plantation, according to the 1850 Slave Schedule, Brooks owned a three-year-old mulatto child, likely his own. In listening to "the crime against Kansas," Brooks probably felt as if Sumner knew *something* about him, something he was revealing to the world.[18]

A beating like the one Brooks gave Sumner seems to betray a sense of shame. It is as if all the lashes that enslaved men received for punishment, all the scars, all the pain, were forms of projection. White men like Brooks, Newsom, and the knife-wielding recruits along the Wakarusa lashed out because they resented a small but vocal group of their countrymen who shamed them. After these white men raped Celia, they beat George; after they fathered bastard children on their plantations, they caned a man on the floor of the Senate; after they assaulted some enslaved people on their farms, they grabbed up their guns, hopped on their horses, and rode toward Lawrence. Violence begat shame, and shame begat violence.

As William made his way through northern Illinois and Indiana and worked to bury his own sense of shame deep inside, white men in the

South unsuccessfully tried to hide the despicable thing at the center of slavery. Whether it was Brooks's cane coming down on the scalp of the senator from Massachusetts or Celia's log slamming into Newsom's skull, the violence that punctuated these stories also confirmed what outsiders to the slave system feared—that rape was a prevalent feature of the peculiar institution. Each act of violence lifted a lantern to the oblivion of those dark corners of the slave quarters where men in fine trousers and shirts roughly handled women, girls, and even boys barely clothed in rags. Each blow showed brightly the tears, the blood, the semen, the bile. With each lash, a few more of the Americans who had been blissfully spending their days in the dark became enlightened about the ugly truth of slavery. As their voices rose and were countered by shouts on the other side, the country moved slowly toward war, a war that started along the Wakarusa, a war that would see William fighting side by side with fellows eager to hold on to their birthright as white men—the privilege to venture down to the slave quarters anytime they pleased.

Frontiersman
1857–1860

CHAPTER 4: *Roustabout*

After leaving Mendota under a cloud of scandal, William returned briefly to Canal Dover. He lived under his mother's roof and taught for a few months before looking westward again. William saw an economic opportunity in the newly organized Kansas Territory, a chance to lay claim to cheap, fertile land and set up a farmstead. The idea of moving westward for affordable or even free land was in keeping the Jeffersonian vision for the country. Like his mother and father before him, William was moving west in pursuit of a better life, and in his effort to become a farmer and set down roots, he had the best of intentions.[1]

William's decision to move to Kansas was pivotal. Although he did not know it then, it was his first step on the winding path toward infamy. He was still aloof from the political debates that swirled about the country, and he seemed unconcerned about the increasingly violent form these arguments took in Kansas. Instead, William was motivated by his barely articulate desires as a young man. He demonstrated behaviors that were not uncommon with other men his age. He chafed under the authority of other men, he wanted to get rich with as little effort as possible, and once he was finally away from the supervision of his parents and teachers, he struggled to restrain himself. These impulses moved William, led him into conflict with others, and sent him wandering away from the settled, peaceful life of a farmer and in search of something better or at least different. Like other men in the West, he pursued adventure and wealth but made his way by moving from one job to another, doing anything to earn a dollar.

Early in 1857, William joined a small venture from Canal Dover that included Harmon V. Beeson, his son Richard, and Colonel Henry

Torrey. Beeson and Torrey were debtors who, having failed in Ohio, looked to begin anew somewhere else, and they offered to take William, or Bill, as they called him, with them. The four traveled down the Ohio River, up the Mississippi River to St. Louis, and then finally up the Missouri River. They disembarked at Independence, Missouri, and traveled over land into Kansas. On March 22, 1857, the Beesons, Torrey, and Quantrill reached the plot of land that would become their home on the Marais des Cygnes. The group lived on Torrey's claim and laid claim to two other plots, one owned by Beeson and one that was bought by Bill, perhaps with backing from Torrey.[2]

The lands on either side of the upper Marais des Cygnes were some of the most fertile of eastern Kansas. A French trapper or hunter named the river, calling it the Marsh of the Swans—a name that suggested a wetland as much as a distinct waterway. The river flooded often in the spring and summer months, and some of these floodplains became permanent or semipermanent marshlands. Quite a few creeks flowed into the river near Bill's plot close to Stanton. In these low-lying areas beside the Marais des Cygnes, thick underbrush and thin trees like cottonwoods sprang up close to one another. The area was a refuge for deer, foxes, and a number of other smaller critters. As a man walked away from the river, he found that the land rose before him, the forests featured bigger, older hardwood trees, and the underbrush thinned out considerably. In some of these higher parts of the landscape, the forests gave way to open prairie lands. This diverse environment was well suited to farming. A man could clear the lower more fertile lands beside the river and its many tributary streams and creeks for his crops, then place his house, barn, and other outbuildings closer to the prairie and out of the floodplain. Overall, it was a good location for a farm.[3]

Although the details of the agreement between Bill and Torrey remain murky, it seems that Bill worked as a hired hand to earn some money to pay Torrey back. In a May 16, 1857, letter to his mother, Bill described how he "just finished a hard job of rolling logs at a clearing around [the] cabin," adding, "Yesterday we just finished planting a Ten-acre field of corn on the prairie." After pleading with his mother to sell their belongings in Ohio and come to Kansas, he said, "If we cannot do this I will not stay here longer than fall, for I can make more money in the States at teaching than by hard work here. I am here now as an agent to get a home for us all."[4]

In June 1857, another party from Dover stopped at the Torrey place.

George H. Hildt, a member of this group and a friend of Bill's, kept a diary in which he recorded a brief description of the farm, located northwest of Osawatomie. When they neared the cabin, Hildt said, "[We] saw Torry first. . . . He appeared quite glad to see us and had a great many questions to ask about the Furnace &c Beeson & Bill Q[uantrill] were out after the cattle. they are breaking prairie with three yoke. they all appeared glad to [see] us and were much pleased that we intended to stay with them until tomorrow." "For dinner we had pan cakes [with] molasses," wrote Hildt, and "wild goose berries & side meat and it tasted right good I tell you Wild strawberries grow here in abundance we had quite a feast today." Taking stock of the place, Hildt recorded, "They [Torrey, Quantrill, and the Beesons] live in a cabin about 14 ft square filled up with trunks meal bags bedding pots pans buckets guns tin ware side meat &c." Besides the cramped quarters, the land was promising. Hildt said, "Beeson has a prairie claim I think about as good as any that I have seen Torry owns one of timber as a small portion of prairie Bill Q own[s] one entirely of timber."[5]

Quarters in the Torrey cabin were tight. Their situation was not unlike other living arrangements in nineteenth-century America in which parties of men fashioned some crude refuge from the elements—a trading post, a mining camp, or even a distant army outpost. Torrey, Bill, and the Beesons lived on top of one another. After working all day in the chilling spring rains or in the thick humidity of the hot Kansas summer, the filthy men piled into the house, where their collective stench was enough to overwhelm a man's senses, especially when it came time to bed down.[6]

The context of the sleeping situation contributed to a fantastical postwar mythology. Frances Beeson recounted to Connelley a tale she heard around this time about the older men sleeping together on a mattress and the boys sleeping together on the floor. On cold nights Bill stole the blankets from her brother, Richard. To eliminate this issue, the elder Beeson switched places with his son and slept on the floor with Bill. According to the tale told to Frances by her father or her brother, "By the dim light of the fire [Harmon] saw Bill standing over him in the act of plunging the Mexican dagger into his heart. . . . Torrey was by this time awake, and Beeson told him to make Bill put the dagger back." After the dagger was put away, "Beeson got up and went out of the house. He returned with a good hickory switch or small club which he laid on until Bill cried for mercy."[7]

58   CHAPTER FOUR

This dark and dramatic story about pre-guerrilla Quantrill is compelling and almost believable in a postwar context. After the Confederate surrender, war-weary Kansans scapegoated Bill Quantrill more than anyone or anything else. Though the conflict ended slavery, it also led to the deaths of hundreds of men in Kansas, some killed at home in their beds by guerrillas, as well as the destruction of houses, workshops, barns, and millions of dollars' worth of property. Desperate for an excuse to equate Quantrill with evil, Kansans eagerly swallowed a tale like this one. From the setting during the frontier era of the territory to the observation that the boy intended to use a *Mexican* dagger to commit his bloody crime, the scene describes the origins of a very specific kind of monster: Bill Quantrill was bad to his core, savage, but also cowardly.[8]

Something in this telling seems amiss, though.

Stripped of its drama and removed from the context of postwar reminiscence, this tale does not add up given everything else we know about Bill's early life. He was quiet, shy, even girlish, but here he snapped for want of an extra blanket? Perhaps Harmon Beeson (or his daughter) omitted some provocation, some act that might transform a kid who read and kept to himself into an assassin. If the attack happened at all, withheld wages, an insult, an order ill-received, a whipping like the one described in the story, or an assault of another kind possibly provoked Bill and sent him searching for a knife.[9]

Something else swirls below the words used in this story that makes it challenging to accept as a tale about an attempted murder. Perhaps Frances Beeson's frame of reference for Bill as a wartime killer obscured other important parts of the narrative. After all, as a guerrilla chief he *was* the type of murderer who struck while men were asleep in their beds. Beeson's way of seeing Bill paralleled the views of other Kansans—they knew him to be a killer, so they understood the stories about his antebellum life as a prologue explaining how he became the murderous fiend who haunted their settlements during the Civil War. This tale was the origin story of the villainous Quantrill.

Yet one could hear this story told between men in a tavern or across a campfire as a comic misadventure instead of a horror story. For men accustomed to living and sleeping with one another out on the trail, this tale could allude to an unwelcome sexual advance, something more amorous than murderous. An older boy taking advantage of a younger boy, the two pulling and pushing each other under the cover of a blanket, a boy surprising his unsuspecting bedfellow by an attempted poke with his *dagger*, or a young man trying to defend himself against the unwanted thrusts of an older man—there are too many salacious implications to ignore. Even the conclusion fits better in the context of something embarrassing rather than with a tale of bloody murder. Whipping a boy or young man in this social dynamic was not a punishment for attempted murder.[10]

Whether Bill *poked* Harmon Beeson or tried to kill him, the two did not get on well after that night. In August 1857, Bill told his mother, "I am going to [go in] on a claim in a few weeks, & I will probably leave Mr. Torrey this week," adding, "I think I shall yet try to get a farm." This turn of events tracked with what Bill planned from the beginning. He had meant to go out to the Kansas Territory, work for Torrey and Beeson, and, when he was ready, pay Torrey for the claim on which he backed him. While it seemed that Bill Quantrill was still on good terms with Torrey, he concluded the letter to his mother, "I dont think I shall see the Beesons very often for I am going to do for myself now."[11]

By October, Bill asked Torrey and Beeson to let him out of their agreement. Torrey and Beeson had been withholding the wages Bill earned for working on the Torrey plot and presumably on the Beeson plot. Bill asserted that he was owed ninety dollars, but the two older men sunk most of their money into the various plots of lands they bought, including the one that Torrey was holding for Bill. The local "squatter's court" decided in the young man's favor but determined he was only owed sixty-three dollars. He received half the sum from Torrey. Beeson owed the boy around thirty dollars and either could not pay or refused. Years later, Beeson claimed that Bill had taken his oxen to hold hostage until he received his due wages. Rather than pay Bill, Beeson stalked the youngster until he found him and threatened to murder him unless he returned his oxen. Bill returned the animals, but Beeson never paid the boy the wages he was owed. For decades afterward the Beeson family would tell anyone who would listen—and there were plenty—that Bill was flyblown all the way through.[12]

Bill joined the young men who moved to the area from Dover. George Hildt recorded, "[On] Sunday Nov 1 the prairie on fire all around us & no one but Elick & myself at home. Bill Q who has been with [us] for over a week left for Stanton this [morning] to get his clothes & Charlies guitar." Hildt described the fire as "a magnificeint [*sic*] sight," saying, "The raging flame at every side excited us, & to night as I am writing the horison is light up at every side as if we were surrounded by furnaces and all of them were burning ore." A more superstitious man might have seen some meaning in the twin arrivals of his chum Bill Q and the conflagration that turned the night into day and burned the prairie "in some directions for 10 miles."[13]

While living with the "Dover boys," Bill revealed his first interest in the political situation in Kansas. In a January 22, 1858, letter to W. W. Scott, Bill reported on a recent election in which there were "10,126 votes against the Lecompton swindle & 6000 for it, of which 3000 if not more were illegal." His description of the Lecompton Constitution, a proslavery frame of government proposed in 1857 and put up for a vote on January 4, 1858, as a "swindle" showed him as strongly in the Free-Soil camp at this moment. Bill also called Jim Lane, the infamous Free-Soiler and jayhawker, "as good a man as we have here," explaining, "[Lane's] presence is enough to frighten 100 Missourians." Further affirming his Free-Soil credentials, Bill declared, "It is a pity [the Free Soilers] had not shot every Missourian that was there. The democrats here are the worst men we have for they are all rascals, for no one can be a democrat here without being one; but the day of their death is fast approaching."[14]

In the same letter in which Bill established his Free-Soil principles, he discussed the young women who lived in the Kansas Territory. To his friend Scott, Bill reported, "About the girls I cannot say as much as you could," and then objectified the young women of Kansas in terms familiar among men of the era. He proclaimed, "A man can have his choice for we have all kinds & colors here Black White & Red." Bill also volunteered, "To tell you which I like the best is a mixture of the two latter colors if properly brought up for they are both rich and good looking." The whiteness of a woman made her rich, but it was redness that made her beautiful. Bill also thought these mixed-race women were much better looking than most of the "Dover gals."[15]

Bill's quip about getting to choose from women of "all kinds & colors . . . Black White & Red," reveals his true colors. For Bill, all of these women—or *girls*, as he called them—were there for the taking, things to be acquired. His comment also illustrated his assumptions about the exotic Native American and African American women. Assuming his preference for half-white, half–Native American women was a true reflection of his sexual desire, it conformed to a powerful stereotype of "red" women. Bill's phrasing, that he liked "a mixture of the two latter colors ... for they are both rich and good looking," even sounds like something he heard another man say.[16]

It was not uncommon for men to speak of Native American women in this way during the antebellum period. Female members of the Native populations were there to be conquered along with the territory. Indeed, just as settlers like Bill sought to tame the wild with their guns and plows, they also imagined themselves domesticating the people who inhabited the landscape. These white men saw the sexual autonomy of these "red" women as promiscuity, which further aroused them. They thought Native women knew more than their white counterparts about sexual pleasure. And because many white men did not understand Native American marriage culture, they believed that these women could be seduced without the necessity of a formal—meaning Christian—marriage. Access to them was like access to the land: if a man was willing to take it, it was free.[17]

Bill's omission of an explicit description of Black women did not mean they were free from stereotyping. The opposite was true, and Bill knew that his correspondent, Scott, was aware of the stereotypes associated with each skin color and did not require him to elaborate. By the late 1850s, caricatures of Black women were well established in the minds of white Americans, whether they lived in the South, North, or West. The two dominant stereotypes were the Mammy and the Jezebel. The Mammy was a maternal figure who loved and cared for the white family by which she was enslaved. White southerners, who wished to believe that their slaves loved them and that Black women were a part of their "family, white and black," imagined that some enslaved women who worked in and around the big house as nursemaids, body servants, and cooks were like kind old aunts neutered of any sexual identity. When he wrote to Scott, Bill most likely had the Jezebel in mind, the stereotype of the Black woman as a seductress, an idea that was also a projection of white men and women blaming the rape of Black women on the victims of those assaults.[18]

While living with the Dover boys, Bill helped with the farmwork but mostly found pleasure in the woods, a space that always provided him solace and joy. It was during this time that he likely befriended a hunter and trapper of the classic frontier type named John Bennings—a Missourian by birth who traveled to California and back and spent time

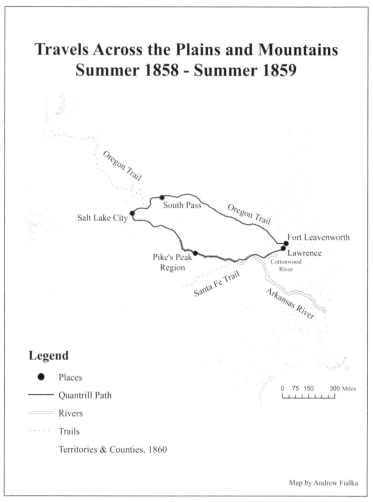

Quantrill joined a supply train that journeyed from Fort Leavenworth to the Utah Territory in 1858. He walked hundreds of miles away from the white settlements of eastern Kansas, following the Oregon Trail and then dipping down toward the Great Salt Lake. After spending time in Salt Lake City and living in the army camp not far from the Mormon capital, Quantrill and some comrades decided to head to Pikes Peak, where gold had been discovered. Their exact route is unknown, but they probably moved east and then southward along a rough path taken by James C. Fremont in 1845–1846 on his way to California. As their route was not nearly as well traveled as the Oregon Trail, Quantrill and his party lost their way in the mountains during a snowstorm. The survivors then made their way into the Pikes Peak region. Quantrill tried his luck at mining for gold for a few months and then rode back toward eastern Kansas with a companion. The two were ambushed by Native Americans along the Cottonwood River. Later, Quantrill proceeded to Lawrence.

nearly everywhere in between. Admiring Bennings's free-moving ways, Bill likely saw him as a role model. The future guerrilla began to spend more time hunting with Bennings and others that fall and into the winter. In his letter to Scott, Bill reported, "Last week I helped to kill a deer & since I have been here I have killed myself 2 antelope & one deer & about 25 Wild Turkeys & geese & before you see me in Ohio I will have killed buffalo." He further noted, "[There] are plenty [of bison] about 100 miles west of us now & those who have killed them say it is fine sport." Bill relished the abundance of wild animals in Kansas, declaring, "This is the place to hunt there is more game to be seen in one day here than in a whole year there [Ohio]."[19]

As he had in Illinois, Bill drifted away from his responsibilities. Unfortunately, a clearer picture of this time cannot be reconstructed from surviving documents. Some suggested that he fell out of favor with the boys from Ohio. Maybe there was some unfortunate late-night confusion like the event at the Torrey cabin, or possibly another unnamed *something* happened. Perhaps the young men away from home for the first time were having too much fun. Maybe the bulk of their efforts was directed at their own immediate pleasure and not toward the work that would sustain them over the long haul, and this shortsightedness led the group to simply deteriorate. It is even possible that Bill just gave up on the farm life. Instead of continuing to plow fields and mend fences, he might have sought adventure and looked westward.[20]

In any case, in the spring or summer of 1858, Bill secured employment that took him to the westernmost reaches of the United States' empire. As a teamster, he joined a wagon train headed to the Utah Territory. The job did not pay much more than a teacher's salary, but it promised to transport Bill to the far West, where he would haul supplies for the small U.S. Army detachment sent there in the summer of 1857 to deal with the Church of Latter-day Saints and provide the rule of law. Rumors swirled about the Mormons' polygamous practices, abuse and kidnapping of women, and threats to non-Mormons with whom they came into contact over the years. They saw Brigham Young, the leader of the church, as especially problematic. After taking office, President James Buchanan determined to remove Young from his post as territorial governor, install a new governor, and appoint other government officials to bring the Mormons into the fold. The army, comprised of both dragoons and infantry, would serve as posse comitatus. By the time Bill hired on to serve as a teamster, the conflict was mostly

64   CHAPTER FOUR

resolved, but the army remained in Utah at Camp Floyd, about fifty miles from Salt Lake City, until 1861.[21]

As a teamster, Bill was likely responsible for at least one team of oxen and a cart. With a quirt in one hand and the reins in the other, he walked alongside the beasts, leading them and occasionally prodding or whipping them onward up the rutted trail. After leaving Fort Leavenworth, Bill walked for a couple of months. Day after day, as the wagon train traveled away from the lush green bottoms and rolling prairies of eastern Kansas, the party traversed the arid, flat, hot plains, where a week might pass between watering places. Somewhere along the way, Bill looked around and believed himself to be navigating a wholly different world. Standing there in the vastness of the great American desert, he probably contemplated his place in the universe.[22]

The wagon train reached South Pass in early September, and its members found themselves caught in the first snowstorm of the season. After the snow stopped the next day, they made their way down the western slope of the Continental Divide. Less than a month later, Bill was in the "Great Salt Lake City," enjoying the new sights, mingling with the religious radicals, and again looking for something to do. There were no other settlements in the high desert like this. It was not borne as a reaction to a gold rush or some other spontaneous phenomenon. Instead, the city was created as a refuge for Young and his followers and placed on the banks of an enormous saline lake, the largest in North America.[23]

Bill and his party likely gawked and made tawdry speculations about the polygamous practices of the Latter-day Saints. Anytime they saw a man with two or more women, they whispered. They fantasized about the bedchambers of these religious radicals, indulging in hushed humor, slaps on the back, and hardy laughs. Bill teased his mother that he might partake in the polygamy of the Mormons, telling her, "I am not thinking of getting married yet, although every man here has from 5 to 8 wives." Perhaps knowing Caroline Quantrill would shudder at the thought of her son marrying so far from home and marrying a Mormon, he implied that he was tempted to tie the knot or knots. Bill explained, "The rich have from 12 to 20 [wives] & Brigham has at present 43." In a letter from January 9, he joked, "I have a notion to marry 4 or 5 women here if I can for here is the only place I will ever have a chance I expect, the Mormons have from 3 to 8 on average."[24]

Searching for a chance to make money, Bill returned to a familiar pattern. On October 15, 1858, he promised to his mother that he would "do what is right . . . [and] try to make a fortune honestly," a task he thought would only take him a year. The exact way he might make his fortune was less clear. "The poorest laborer can command $40 per month [in Salt Lake City]," Bill stated, and he thought he could earn even more. Six weeks later, he told his mother that he was "going to clerk for the Quarter Master in the army at $50 per month."[25]

Despite Bill's promises of responsibility and claims of steady work, the whispered words of a nameless fellow, some charming specter of a man who haunted his correspondence, distracted him. Under the roof of a makeshift tavern or breezy tent, the apparition uttered, "There's gold in them hills." In an October letter, Bill revealed plans to go "in the spring to the Colville gold mines in Canada . . . which they [said] are equal to the California [mines]." Bill claimed that a friend searching for gold there had told him about the veins in Colville, but that this unnamed person had left the area "on account of the Indians." Not unlike the first appearance by the anonymous pal, here, too, an invisible comrade in Bill's correspondence pulled him away from the stable life and toward the dynamic life of the wild. In the meantime, Bill received the job from the quartermaster and then lost it, admitting, "It was all my own fault That [they] threw me out of employment in the dead of winter." He kept his head above water working as a cook, but he tired of Utah and looked to the faraway hills for his fortune.[26]

Bill joined the gold rush to Pikes Peak. Beginning in the summer of 1858, this gold rush, like others, prompted Americans to pack up what could be moved and make their way toward a new place with mineral wealth. Also like other gold rushes, this one, which pulled one hundred thousand men and a few women to the mountains from 1858 to 1861, resulted in very few success stories. Despite the overwhelming odds against striking gold or other mineral deposits, the lure of working hard for a few months, a couple of weeks, or even a day or two to strike it rich overwhelmed the mountain of evidence that suggested joining such a rush would lead to destitution, if not death. With nothing keeping him in the Utah Territory, Bill cast his lot with a company of eighteen other men, all faceless, nameless companions, on their way to the Rocky Mountain goldfields.[27]

Exactly how Bill came to join this particular band of gold-seeking would-be mountaineers remains unknown. Although it is possible that a cooperative created an enterprise like this one, it is more likely that one or two moneyed men backed the venture. These individuals would provide the capital to buy animals and supplies and hire other men to facilitate their journey. Given Bill's limited means, they likely hired him as a laborer, perhaps as a teamster. Even though Bill's descriptions of the journey fail to mention wagons or teams of animals, the company maybe began the trip in Salt Lake City with them and then. Like others, members of the wagon train possibly unhitched the animals and discarded the carts and wagons at higher altitudes and in snowier conditions that made the movement of a wheeled conveyance impossible. In these circumstances, travelers transferred their food and equipment from their wagons to the backs of their beasts, and then led the animals along in a single-file line. As Bill moved through the snow on his pony, he pulled a train of pack animals loaded down with supplies behind him.[28]

The discovery of gold near Pikes Peak was a part of a larger nineteenth-century phenomenon. Beginning with the California gold rush in 1849, these moments of remarkable upheaval, dislocation, migration, and settlement revealed something about the changing nature of American society. Many men—Bill included—felt themselves caught between the Old World and the New World. They had come of age as artisan labor died out as the primary form of production, and kinship no longer served as the glue that bound communities together. Instead, the onrushing wave of capitalism, its factories, and its unskilled labor cut individuals free from the ties that bind and set them loose in pursuit of economic opportunity. There were benefits and problems associated with this new economic worldview. Without access to the independence once afforded by their skill as craftsmen, many men turned to wage labor, or, as its southern critics referred to it, wage slavery. Lacking a clear pathway to a life of respectable means, the discovery of gold at Sutter's Mill, Colville, or Pikes Peak offered a unique opportunity to game the system and gain freedom.[29]

The desire for financial independence helps explain why Bill and his comrades decided to cross a few mountain ranges in the dead of winter. There was also the way in which a journey like this might test the mettle of these men. They, like the thousands of others, did not suddenly go mad or form a suicide pact. Instead, these men set out from a warm, fertile valley toward an icy apocalypse in search of wealth. The prospect of facing mountains, snow, cold, and Indian warriors did not deter them, but only made their quest a proving ground. For Bill to make it from one side of this gauntlet to the other with his life and his scalp would serve as evidence of his manliness. Perhaps his reward would be the riches he apparently thought he was entitled to. The position in the gold-seeking company was also one more job in an endless series of menial employment that demonstrated a pattern of shortsighted decision-making, a blind walk into the unknown, and a march well off the trail he once envisioned for himself.

CHAPTER 5: *Hunter*

In the early months of 1859, Bill Quantrill found himself in the snow. He told his mother, "I have seen some pretty hard & scaly times, both from cold weather & starvation & the Indians & I am one of 7 out of a party of 19 who started from Salt Lake city for the Gold Mines of Pikes Peak." He wrote to his sister Mary, "I was amid snow and desolation in the Rocky Mountains, where nothing was to be seen but snow & sky; no signs of life except in our little company. . . . Some of us strove to be merry, & occasionally would start some song." But these attempts to lift morale were cut short "by some one calling for help to get some poor animal out of the snow." Even as he tried to be cheerful, Bill nevertheless felt the emotional drain of the march across the mountains. As he confessed, "When night came and we were about to lie down to rest, and [had] nothing but the snow to make a bed upon, it was enough to make any one have cool thoughts."[1]

Bill was transformed. He told Mary, who was living in the national capital, "You people of the crowded city can form no idea of what men go through [in the far reaches of the territories]." Quantrill continued, "[Nor can you understand how men] have to struggle to keep from the grasp of grim death, which apparently stares them in the face as they move along." "Grim death" was no literary flourish; he had seen it. There is little doubt that Bill looked into the dying eyes of his comrades as they succumbed to exposure or an Indian bullet during their trek from the camps around the Great Salt Lake in pursuit of gold.[2]

However, when Bill recalled those days, when casualties mounted all around him and chilling ideas crept into his mind, he remembered that when he lay down and huddled closely together with his campmates and drifted to sleep, he did so with "more satisfaction than [he] ever felt *any place else*." Deep in the uncharted wild, where he came face to face with mortality and physical toll, he achieved peace of mind and a clearer sense of self.[3]

In that slog across the mountains, Bill became a man of the frontier. This experience was the most significant one of his young life, shaping his view of the world and influencing his actions during the Civil War. Even though he did not label himself with the terms "frontiers*man*" or "woods*man*," Bill thought of himself as such. More specifically, he most often characterized himself as a hunter, the central archetype in the pantheon of western men. In becoming a hunter, he learned to live in and navigate the brush as he mastered firearms and a horse. Bill also embraced fully the homosocial environment in which men lived without women, depended on one another, and formed emotional and sometimes physical bonds with one another. As he shed much of the mantle of the civilized, restrained man and began to look more like a civilizing man, Bill unwittingly came to inhabit a type of manhood idealized among young men in Missouri's slaveholding society. As he rode down out of those mountains in 1859, he looked every bit the hunter of American reality and myth. He also cut a figure that offered the first vague outline of a bushwhacker.[4]

Although Bill grew into the mold of a hunter in the Rockies, it was in the Ohio woods of his boyhood where the seed of that man first sprouted. Canal Dover, settled only a generation before his birth, was surrounded by rolling hills, creeks, and forests. Nearly everyone who remembered Bill during his youth wrote about him playing in the woods. *The History of Tuscarawas County, Ohio*, emphasizes young Bill's love of nature: "He then resembled other boys in tastes and disposition, was fond of hunting and fishing, and a fine shot with the rifle and always had been civil and quiet." He was a good boy and a boy of the woods.[5]

Bill honed his skill with a firearm in those Ohio woods. Those who knew him in the war remarked on his talent as a marksman. While Bill hunted during the antebellum period with a rifle or shotgun, during the war it was his exploits with a pistol that many remembered, and his skill with one weapon likely translated to another. Early in his memoir of the war, the guerrilla Andrew J. Walker referred to the guerrilla captain as "an expert pistol shot." Quantrill's earliest biographer, John Newman Edwards, who did not know Bill personally but was well acquainted with his comrades, placed the guerrilla chief's marksmanship into a mythical context, saying, "In an organization where skill with a pistol was a passport to leadership, he shot with a revolver as Leather-stocking shot with a rifle." Although Edwards was infamous for his pro-Confederate Lost Cause embellishments and hero worship, his anti-Quantrill rival Connelley conceded that "Quantrill became very expert with the revolver."[6]

For many antebellum men, marksmanship was more than a functional skill; it was a projection of one's inner character. While this indicator of virtue lost some significance in the urban Northeast, where social and economic changes made martial ability less important to manliness, it remained a sign of masculine prowess in the regions in which Bill lived. John Hope Franklin, in his seminal study of violence in the slave states before the Civil War, offers the definitive observation of the relationship between firearms and masculinity, saying, "Not a few Southerners associated good marksmanship with the better attributes of manhood. A young Southerner who wanted to get anywhere would be well-advised to become skilled in the use of arms; at least his fellows would respect him." That Bill learned to shoot well probably helped his entry into the guerrilla ranks during the war and endeared him to his comrades. Bill also served as an early role model; he was *the* pistoleer, a new type of shootist to be imitated.[7]

When Bill moved from Ohio to Illinois, he encountered a man whose skill with a firearm was even better than his own. While the exact identity of this unnamed man is a riddle that will likely never be solved, the hunt took place in the same general area where a much more famous American hunter and icon was living. On those Illinois hunting grounds, Bill Quantrill's tale intertwined with the legend of James Butler "Wild Bill" Hickok. Born on May 27, 1837, Hickok was raised in Homer, Illinois—now Troy Grove—a hamlet a couple of miles south of Mendota. Like Quantrill, Hickok lost his father during his teenage years, and he also spent a great deal of his time tramping about in the woods with a squirrel gun. Around the time that Quantrill moved to town, Hickok took a job pulling mules along the Illinois and Michigan Canal. Exactly how often Hickok returned home or hunted in the area is impossible to know, but there is a small possibility that these two gun-wielding luminaries shared a duck blind.[8]

Connelley, who penned biographies of both Hickok and Quantrill, somehow never drew an explicit connection between the two despite their many similarities. He wrote, "The supreme delight of James Hickok was hunting. He wandered through the bodies of timber skirting the prairie streams of Illinois in search of the small game which remained to his day." Given Hickok's passion for hunting, "he was soon the best hunter in his community. . . . He became the best shot in his part of Illinois." While there was little doubt that both he and Quantrill loved to hunt and were fine marksmen, it is also possible—even likely—that Connelley was influenced by the mythology surrounding these men. By emphasizing their talent with a firearm, the biographer unwittingly contributed to the myth of the western gunslinger.[9]

Whether or not Hickock was the fellow who took Quantrill hunting, their paths moved parallel and came very close to crossing later in life if they did not cross here. In 1855, scared that he had killed a man in a fistfight, Hickok abruptly left northern Illinois for Kansas Territory. He worked as a hired hand there for a little while, breaking the land and putting in a crop. Connelley reported that Hickok was pulled into the border war by 1856 and rode with the jayhawkers. When he was not working the land as a hired hand or helping Jim Lane fight off border ruffians from Missouri, Hickok worked as a teamster transporting goods across the Great Plains, primarily over the Santa Fe Trail. Between all of these jobs, he hunted.[10]

During the Civil War, Hickok and Quantrill fought on opposing sides along the Kansas-Missouri border. However, they occupied similar roles in combat. Quantrill fought as a skilled guerrilla operator, and Hickok served as a talented scout for the Union army. Each man demonstrated a martial ingenuity, a deftness of movement, skill, and sensory observation. They each possessed the necessary combination of dynamism and stoicism required to fight and survive in the brush. Their talent as hunters translated well to the guerrilla warfare of the border region.[11]

Bill Quantrill hunted casually in Illinois, Ohio, and Kansas, but on his trek from Utah to Pikes Peak in early 1859 he came to embody the persona of a professional hunter. Men on similar journeys with fur companies, emigrant wagon trains, or gold prospectors frequently took on new jobs over the course of a journey, and that of professional hunter sat at the top. Bosses gave their hunters freedom to roam, so a man had to be responsible, accountable, and loyal to the company. Wandering off for days or running out on a contract could be catastrophic to a band of men in the wilderness. Physically, a hunter needed superior stamina, vision, scent, strength, and agility, as well as steady hands and quick reflexes. Mentally, a hunter needed to know the landscape, the animals, and the weather. The job required experience. Very few men joined their first expedition as a hunter. Instead, most began work as a boatman or cook and worked their way into the ranks of the hunter.[12]

The hunter's daily experience in a company like this one of gold seekers was different from that of the rest of the group. Well before dawn, the hunter awoke and departed camp. He rode his pony or mule up the trail before veering off the path in search of game. During the winter months a hunter often traveled down the mountain to where animals gathered for food and water. If he discovered a valley or ravine with a flowing stream inhabited by thirsty game, the hunter dismounted and looked for animal signs—scrapes and rubs, droppings, hoof- or pawprints in the snow or mud, or a worn game trail—then found a place to sit and observe the area. Skilled hunters' brains became sensitive to these signs as well as to other factors like the breeze, the sun, and the acoustics of nature. They constantly processed the dynamics of the hunt; they described the hunt as a *feel* for the game. Ever vigilant, a hunter might sit hidden for hours. Alone with his thoughts in the freezing cold, he took no more than a nibble of food and little bit of whiskey or water as he maintained his focus on the potential game. It was grueling.[13]

At any moment, a deer or two might wander to the edge of the stream and give the hunter his chance. Taking careful aim with his powerful Hawken rifle—a heavy .50-caliber rifle designed to withstand the extreme conditions of the Rockies—he squeezed the back trigger until it clicked, setting the front trigger so that he only needed to touch it. With a breath and a gentle squeeze of the hair trigger, the hunter sent the large lead ball ripping through the air toward the flank of a stag. Once the animal had been shot, the hunter might dress it there, pack the meat, fasten it to his horse, and try to catch up with his party, leaving behind a steaming gut pile.[14]

Hunting in the mountains, Bill not only tracked game, but he also stalked a legend. Of the great myths that flowed through the viaducts of the American mind in the nineteenth century, that of the frontier coursed the strongest. A powerful current within the frontier mythology was the idea that it was the duty of white Americans to probe westward, kill animals, live off of the land, fight Indians, cut a life for themselves out of the wilderness, and ultimately civilize the uncivilized. This process purportedly imbued Americans with virtue, creating the basis for the belief that they were exceptional among the white race. For young white men, a submyth offered the possibility of a special role in this process. Epitomized in history by Daniel Boone and in literature by James Fenimore Cooper's Natty Bumppo, the hunter became the vanguard of white progress across the North American continent. In this myth, the man left the white world, went out to the frontier, learned from the Natives and from nature, and then used those lessons to tame the wild, defeat the Indians, and usher along civilization.[15]

Bill's imitation of a woodsman revealed his true quest to become one. Whether it was his unnamed friend in Illinois, or John Bennings, the fellow in Utah, or the hundreds of woodsmen who passed through Kansas and circulated in towns like Salt Lake City and trading posts across the West, Bill spent time among professional hunters, studied them, and learned from them like an apprentice. Mimicking was a fundamental step in the maturation process of any man who set out to learn a trade, and the same held true for hunters. Men were not born hunters, and woodcraft, while informal when compared to the trade organizations of guildsmen in the cities, was nevertheless a skilled form of labor. Before he could break his own paths, Bill followed the trails made by others.[16]

Bill described his physical transformation into a mountain man to his sister. He wore "a complete suit of buckskin; pants, coat, moccasins, a red woolen shirt, a fur cap, a large leather belt in which [was] a large pistol and knife; and then mounted on an Indian pony, with [his] rifle laying across the saddle, ready for use in a moment's warning." As this wild portrait suggests, Bill absorbed the world in which he lived. Just like the woodsmen who came before him, he cloaked himself in the skins of animals of the woods; he rode a wild horse; and he remained ever vigilant, not unlike a predator or prey. "We look rough enough," Bill added, "for we do not shave or cut our hair, and to a person not used to such sights, we look like ruffians." The frontier so imprinted itself on him that he was no longer recognizable as a civilized man.[17]

Bill's powder horn announced his identity as a frontiersman. Dry, accessible gunpowder, was an essential element for the nineteenth-century hunter. Without a bullet encased in gunpowder, hunters kept loose powder handy to pour down the barrel of a rifle or into the cylin-

Given the absence of provenance, it is impossible to know whether this was in fact Quantrill's powder horn. Nevertheless, this excellent example of a horn used by hunters in the 1850s and 1860s is sturdily constructed out of brass. A switch near its end allowed hunters to control how much powder they used to charge their shot. There are loops on either side of the horn so that it can be attached to a chain or a leather thong, fastened to a belt, or worn around the neck. (Courtesy of the Reeves Victorian Home and Carriage House Museum, Dover, Ohio)

ders of a revolver. Originally made of a bull's hollowed-out horns, by the 1800s powder horns came in various materials including leather, copper, and brass. Some had spouts with springs to make sure the right amount of black powder was dispensed each time. A few spouts were equipped with more than one setting to release different amounts of powder to adjust for the shot or the weapon. The local historical society in Dover, Ohio, holds a brass powder horn on which a woodland scene was embossed. With the exception of a couple of minor dents, the artifact is in beautiful condition. Measuring about seven inches long and three and a half inches wide, it fits nicely in a man's palm, sturdy by not too heavy. Regardless of whether this was really Quantrill's horn, it is a fine example of the type of powder horn carried by men in the 1850s.[18]

The deer imprinted on the horn stands in profile below a large tree and beside a bush. This idyllic scene is in keeping with a theme embraced by hunters of yesteryear. The implements of the hunt—horns, rifles, pistols, knives—often featured engraved images of the hunt. Bill's powder horn—if we might entertain the idea that it was in fact his—

simultaneously reflected his pursuit and served as a physical tool for bringing the game down. In that way, the horn was like the hunter who carried it: nature was imprinted on it, but with a little spark and some lead, it made its mark on the wilderness.[19]

≫

In 1859, Bill could not know what the future held for him, but with the luxury of hindsight, his mountain-man persona hints at the origins of flamboyant guerrilla style. The hirsute look of this self-proclaimed ruffian anticipated the bushy beards and curly locks that the guerrillas vainly flaunted. In addition, the hunting shirt Bill wore in the Rockies was a forbearer of the guerrilla shirt. Finally, the pistol that so conspicuously protruded from his belt and the constant desire for more firepower that it symbolized anticipated the Colt Navies that later decorated the waists of the bushwhackers.[20]

Bill's self-portrait recalls—and partially rebuts—the most common origin story of the Missouri bushwhacker. In assessing himself and his band of fellow travelers, he wrote that they were easily mistaken for "ruffians." Within the historical lexicon of Civil War–era Missouri, this term was loaded with meaning. Ruffian, or "border ruffian," typically referred to a proslavery man who crossed over into the Kansas Territory before the war to intimidate voters, harass antislavery settlers, and raid towns and settlements, burning them to the ground and sometimes killing the inhabitants. With little evidence, many historians and Quantrill biographers assert that the border ruffian was the antecedent to the bushwhacker. However, very few so-called border ruffians became guerrillas.[21]

Instead, the stylistic origin of the bushwhacker was not a specific group of antebellum political reactionaries, but rather the frontiersmen that became a common sight in western Missouri and in the Kansas Territory. Bearded, gaudy, and bedecked in hunting shirts, knives, and firearms, they were the opposite of well-kempt men from the cities of the East. These eastern men became increasingly associated with the northern archetype of manhood to which many immigrants to Kansas subscribed.[22]

Although Bill was decidedly western in his outfit, the blade conspicuously strapped at his hip represented the intersection between the martial manhoods of the West and the South, the overlap of the frontiersman and the border ruffian. Since the 1820s, the Bowie knife had served as a necessary tool for the man of the frontier, becoming increasingly popular among southern-born toughs and gentlemen alike. Like the sword on the waist of the knights in Sir Walter Scott's stories, the Bowie knife served as a symbol of assertive and violent masculinity. Historian Jason Phillips tells us that these blade-wielding, status-conscious white men became known as the Bowie-knife gentry. When these proslavery knights flooded into the Kansas Territory from Missouri, Kentucky, Virginia, and a slew of other southern states, looking to secure it as the next slave state, their knives served as a warning and a threat. "When a southern man pulled out his bowie knife," Phillips asserts, "it meant war." Indeed, the Bowie-knife gentry were the true border ruffians—blade-wielding southern filibusters looking to conquer new lands on behalf of the slave South. The large blades tucked in their belts indicated these men's willingness to take Kansas through violence if the political apparatus did not grant them victory. As one of these border ruffians said, they were going to invade the state and "vote at the point of the bowie-knife and revolver."[23]

Although Bill did not yet share the extreme politics of southern white men, he began to identify with an important feature of manhood in the South, where, according to historian Stephen Berry, "boys were supposed to follow a subtly different pattern, one of *civilizing* manhood. Southern men were obliged not merely to affect Civilization but to cause it, the emphasis falling on not merely the composition but the imposition of the self." As Bill spent more time out west, more time honing his martial skills, and more time imposing himself on the environment (even as it inscribed itself on his body), the fraternity of civilizing men became more comfortable to him than the company of civilized men.[24]

Bill's persona and style fit in with that of many men in Missouri. Long before Bill ever set foot in the state, young white men of the border South knew and admired the look of the antebellum frontiersman—and not simply his Bowie knife. Slaveholding Missourians identified as western from the territorial period up until the 1850s. Historian Christopher Phillips contends that it was not until the fighting in the Kansas Territory that "they adopted the cant of Southernness," and even then, westernness was still important to the way that white Missourians saw themselves. Like Bill, Missouri boys who played in the woods in the 1840s and 1850s fantasized about Daniel Boone and his fellow frontiersmen fighting the Indians and the redcoats. Unlike Bill, however, these boys in western Missouri were the direct familial and cultural descendants of the legendary pathbreakers. When Bill arrived and showed his preference for the hunting shirt and woodsman's mane, he was reflecting on his audience a preexisting vision of the warrior ideal. At once he confirmed their values and demonstrated that he fit their mold.[25]

Even as Bill bedecked himself in the knife, pistol, and flamboyant hunting shirt that became important to his identity as a guerrilla chief, he also learned how men bonded when confronted with adversity. Caught for a time in a blizzard, the members of the voyage over the mountains to the goldfields huddled together for warmth. Although Bill did not speak of the exact methods they used to survive the extreme weather, beleaguered travelers surprised by a squall often threw together rude hovels: an overturned wagon, if there was one, buffalo robes, or a tarp was quickly thrown up against the sheets of blinding snow and weighted down or pegged to the ground. Groups of two, three, or more men then got into the shelter and held close to one another to take advantage of their collective warmth, sometimes discarding cold and wet clothing to maximize the heat through skin-to-skin contact. Once they endured the initial brunt of the storm, survivors emerged, dug one another free, searched for animals, gathered wood, and began clearing space for a fire and a proper shelter. Living through such an experience welded men together.[26]

After their harrowing trek, the surviving members of the band made it to Pikes Peak in the spring of 1859. When Bill wrote to his mother about his experience in the goldfields, he reported that he "spent two months in the Gold region [having] [his] own experience . . . There [was] more or less gold scattered over a country about 40 [miles] in width [running] from the mountains east & about 200 [miles] long running with the mountains but not in quantities paying of 1.00 per day in the best diggings." Bill leased mining equipment—a pick, shovel, and pan—and went to work. "I dug out $54.34," he said, adding that as he received that amount over the course of forty-seven days, it "hardly paid . . . board and expenses." With so little payout, the Pikes Peak gold rush was "the Humbug of all Humbugs" in Bill's opinion.[27]

⁊❧

Predictably, Bill quit his claims. As with the other jobs, the day-to-day tedium of mining proved unmanageable. Waking every morning to excavate gold from the earth lost its romance after weeks of minimal results. Bill packed up his things, mounted his pony, and rode east over the plains.

Again, he was accompanied by an unnamed friend riding beside him like a shadow. This fellow might have been a member of the gold-seeking company, maybe even Bill's bedmate. Perhaps he was the adventurer Bill met near Salt Lake City who told him of the Colville mines. Possibly Bill met him in the mining camp near Pikes Peak. Whoever he was, he played the role of the invisible companion, the seemingly ever-present outline of a faceless specter who haunts Bill's correspondence. The nature of these relationships fascinates and intrigues.[28]

Bill was an effeminate boy with a musical voice who never married or fathered any children. He spent a great deal of his early adulthood among other men and preferred the company of men to women. Moreover, Bill's letters contain several mentions of anonymous men, and he shared plenty of beds. An otherwise limited historical record contains many accounts of Bill bedding down with other men. The available documents name six bedmates. Beyond these fellows, he probably shared a bedroll with a few of his fellow travelers across the plains and the mountains, and in the camps in Utah and around Pikes Peak.[29]

Bed sharing was not unusual. Historians of the nineteenth century accept this phenomenon as widespread, the main assumption being that men slept in the same bed with other men because the conditions required it. There were few beds and quilts, and cold frontier nights sent men crawling under the same covers to stay warm. It was not necessarily an indication of any kind of physical intimacy between the two bedmates. Indeed, historian Susan Lee Johnson, author of *Roaring Camp*, a study of the California gold rush and the all-male mining camps, reiterates this point well. "Certainly bed sharing was a common practice," she notes, but she also concedes, "It would be foolhardy to suggest that bed partners commonly shared sexual pleasures."[30]

Johnson warns, however, that "it would also be foolhardy" to think that none of these men sought sexual release or the physical comfort of a close friend. It was, after all, "an era of increased possibilities for same-sex eroticism." Most historians of gender and sexuality agree that sex among men was not uncommon during the early to middle nineteenth century, when sex was still understood to be an act and not an identity. Men were not stigmatized or branded as they would be in the twentieth century. It was not just plausible that a lonely miner, teamster, hunter, or hired hand might lust after a bedmate—it happened.

Just as historians and history buffs caution against dragging some long-dead icon out of the closet, it seems just as wise to not presume that these iconic figures conformed to our modern ideas of sex.[31]

One day, after Bill and his nameless companion set up camp near the Cottonwood River in south-central Kansas Territory, Bill went to hunt. Leaving his campmate behind, presumably to tend to the animals, gather water, and make a fire, he walked through the grass on the lookout for a grazing buffalo, deer, or something smaller—anything to feed himself and his partner. A moment like this, alone in the vastness of the plains, offered Bill an opportunity to reflect on the previous year or two. Goldfields, blinding snow, death, the army camps around the Great Salt Lake, honest Colonel Torrey and that scoundrel Beeson, the hunts and hunting partners, his beloved mother—so many events intertwined with one another, the narrative difficult to explain, even to himself.[32]

He was likely tugging at one of these reminiscences when he heard the shots.

Bill quieted his breath and his mind and listened. There, in the direction of the campsite, he heard more gunfire. An electric jolt engulfed his brain and his blood was pumping and his heart was pushing up into his throat. Before he knew what he was doing he was running. Rifle in hand—loaded and primed—Bill covered more than a mile retracing his steps to the camp over the rolling hills and through clusters of cottonwood trees along the meandering stream.[33]

Just as he came near the encampment, he saw a band of Indians driving their horses away, already too distant for a shot. Or maybe they were just within range, but a shot seemed ill advised. Either way, he slowed down and caught his breath, and when he scanned the ground he found his partner shot to pieces and apparently dead. As he approached his friend, Bill realized that he was still alive, set his rifle aside, and took him in his arms. The travelers were without their mounts or much else and still miles from any white settlements.[34]

When Bill was finally able to write his mother, he recounted the raid, reporting that he had lost his horse and nearly everything else he owned. Worse than that, his partner had been "shot in 3 different places & left for dead." Specifically, Bill had found his comrade "lying on the ground apparently dead but still breathing with difficulty having been shot 3 times." He continued, "His leg [was] broke[n] below the knee [and he was] shot in the thigh with 7 iron slugs & last shot through the body with an arrow which I first thought would kill him." The arrow and Bill's observation that he saw "the Indians driving off our horses" made it clear who the assailants were. Fatefully, "all that saved my head," Bill remembered, "was I was out hunting away from camp."[35]

On those vast plains, looking like the forerunner of the bushwhacker, Bill Quantrill first experienced guerrilla warfare. His camp was bushwhacked, raided at a time when it was least expected. While Bill was away from camp, his companion was probably too busy to be vigilant, and at an opportune moment the warriors struck. They stayed long enough to put down the white man in camp and get what they wanted. Then they were gone. How terrifying. After trekking across the plains once and the mountains twice, Bill was already aware of how vulnerable he and his comrade were, but now he felt the terror of human beings actively exploiting the defenselessness of others. Once his feelings receded into thoughts, he probably reflected on the effectiveness of this attack.

Bill and his companion knew that violence might befall them as they made their way from the goldfields across the plains to eastern parts of the territory. That summer, stories of waylaid bands of argonauts filled the air in towns like Lawrence and Paola in Kansas, as well as St. Joe and Independence in Missouri. Reports of the Kaw, Osage, and Comanche gathering along the southwestern reaches of the territory for their summer buffalo hunts were printed in the papers. White travelers witnessed the Delaware feting their young men before the warriors left to hunt and trap across the plains to the mountains. Other tribes like the Iowa and Cheyenne were rumored to be active as well, making it difficult to know exactly who it was that thundered into Bill's camp. Indeed, warriors from any of these far-ranging tribes could have stumbled on the campsite and seen the ponies there as fair game. Perhaps they believed these white men were trespassing on traditional hunting grounds, or maybe a few young warriors merely wanted some fun at the expense of an unsuspecting paleface.[36]

According to Bill, this raid might have meant the end for his partner if not for a man named Golightly Spybuck. While his account of the violent raid changed over the years, Bill always included the arrival of Spybuck, a Shawnee Indian who was out on the plains that summer with his wife, after the ambush. Whether he heard the shots and came to discover the source of the commotion or he just happened on the waylaid travelers remains unknown. After finding Bill and seeing the condition of his comrade, Spybuck and his wife took the two men in, sheltered them in their wickiup, and took care of them.[37]

Beginning with Connelley, biographers of Quantrill have rejected the existence of this Native American man who supposedly came to his aid in 1859. In *Quantrill and the Border Wars*, Connelley observed, "Spiebuck is said to have told this story often, but the Indian is noted for truthfulness, and there was probably no such man." Connelley, whose social and political views were far more progressive than many of his contemporaries in the late nineteenth and early twentieth centuries, wrote several pieces about the history of Native American tribes and respected indigenous people. He probably found this bond between Quantrill and a Native American elder difficult to reconcile with his preexisting ideas. Connelley so distrusted this part of Quantrill's story that he listed the Indian in his work's index as "Spiebuck, Golightly: *mythical* Shawnee in false story of Quantrill."[38]

Golightly Spybuck most likely did exist, however. There are two entries for the name "Spybuck" in the 1860 Federal Manuscript Census: the "George Spybuck" family and an individual named "J. Spybuck." While J. Spybuck lived in Kansas, he was only thirty-two years old and apparently unmarried, making him too young and single to be Bill's savior. However, George Spybuck was a forty-eight-year-old Indian, born in Ohio in 1812 or 1813 at the very beginning of the War of 1812. His wife was also an Indian, and they had a son and two daughters. During the time the census takers recorded their information, the George Spybuck family was living in Wyandotte Township of Wyandotte County in the Kansas Territory. These Spybucks were listed with a cluster of other Indians living together, perhaps on someone else's land, and not in a household of their own.[39]

It was not uncommon for Native American men and women who found themselves navigating between the red and white worlds to go by two names, one for the whites and one for their own people. For the Indians whose names were recorded in the U.S. Census, it was especially true that European names were likely written down. All of the members of the George Spybuck family were listed by their English names—Mary, James, Margaret, and Virginia—as were other Indians on that page of the census. It is likely that Spybuck was not even a surname in the traditional European sense. Rather, it seems more likely that it was a part of one name given to this man during childhood or young adulthood: Go-Lightly-and-Spy-Buck.[40]

To entertain the existence of Golightly Spybuck is to add another layer to Bill's transformation into a hunter. One major theme in the evolution of a white hunter in history and myth is living with and learning from Native Americans. Such immersion in Indian culture led to mental, spiritual, and physical changes that were often so extreme that these adopted members of Native American households and tribes were no longer recognizable as white. They were called "white Indians." When Bill described himself to his sister as a "ruffian" whom other white people would not recognize as one of their own, he implied that he had gone rough, gone wild, even gone Native.[41]

Moreover, to be taken in by an Indian named Go-Lightly-and-Spy-Buck suggests that Bill was living with a man whose own people deemed him a deerstalker. Whether Spybuck lived up to his name is unknown. What is known is that when Bill told his story he gave this Indian's name again and again. Most Missourians with Bill Quantrill later fought remembered the Indian's name and associated it with their leader. For the man who would become the guerrilla chief, the name Golightly Spybuck carried a significance that needed no translation for men who knew well the myths of the American hunter.[42]

In late July 1859, a haggard Bill walked into the town of Lawrence from the west. Not long after arriving in town, he found paper, ink, and a pen and sat down to write a letter to his mother. This was his first correspondence with her since January, when he had been out in the Utah Territory camped with the army near the Great Salt Lake. After describing his recent trek across the mountains, his failed attempts at panning for gold near Pikes Peak, and the bloody ambush by the Indians, he lamented, "I hardly know what to do at present nor where to go." "You would hardly know me if you were to see me I am so weather beaten & rough looking that every body says I am about 25 years of age," the twenty-two-year-old Bill wrote. The physically drained young man was now overwhelmed with emotion and needed a place of solace, which he hoped to find among the bustling town populated by New Englanders and midwesterners. Instead of the fellow feeling he had grown accustomed to in the mining camps of the mountains and the succor the

Shawnee elder had provided, Bill felt only scorn as he moved among the buttoned-up shopkeepers and clerks along Massachusetts Street. He reported to his mother, "I expect every body thinks & talks hard about [me] but I cannot help it now."[43]

Unlike the mountains or the plains, Lawrence was a town striving to replicate eastern society, and Bill's pathetic appearance alienated him. For those who looked on this ruffian loafing about the streets on that steamy July day simply saw another piece of human refuse, a man wasted by failed get-rich-quick schemes and misguided attempts to master the wilderness. From the perspective of the people of Lawrence, Bill was a man who was apparently lost.[44]

When Bill tramped southward out of Lawrence, his mind was changing. He had just passed through a portal of experience—traumatic events, one after another over the course of little more than a year—that radically altered his development at the exact moment he was moving from boyhood into manhood. As he kicked his way down the road to Osawatomie, his emotions were in a state of flux. The already sensitive and now emotionally vulnerable Bill began to consciously and subconsciously imprint meaning on this struggle. He contrasted his roughness with the tidiness of those Yankee clerks and conflated the harm and pain wreaked by raiding Indians with the scorn of abolitionists.[45]

Over the next year, however, Bill returned to the standards of appearance and behavior expected in the settlements in eastern Kansas. He went back to teaching school in Stanton and gradually found economic stability. He dressed the part, wearing the plain clothes of a schoolmaster. When he taught, he did not speak much about the troubles associated with Bleeding Kansas, but gave the impression to his students that he was in favor of the free-staters. Outside school, he kept to himself.[46]

Students who told Connelley that Quantrill was a good teacher left a few telling observations about their schoolmaster. In those days of sectional strife along the border, Bill looked like the archetypal Yankee schoolmaster, the embodiment of convention, bookishness, and restraint. Roxey Troxel, a thirteen-year-old student during the winter of 1859–1860, remembered that he had "large light-blue eyes, a Roman nose, light complexion, [and] light hair," that he "dressed neatly," and that he "talked for the Free-State side." However, she claimed to have sensed there was something more to her teacher. She remembered Bill's eyes as "peculiar . . . like no other eyes she ever [saw]," and she seemed to hint at something withheld behind the well-appointed facade. Troxel claimed to have picked up on the signal betrayed by the glow of Bill's eyes, or to have felt invisible vibrations emanating outward from her teacher. When she summed up her thoughts on her old teacher, she said that he was "a very quiet man, secretive and peculiar," and that "no one knew how to take him."[47]

Troxel detected incongruence between Bill's outer presentation and his inner self, but she did not speculate as to the nature of this tension. Another student described him in a similar way. Saying that Quantrill "talked for the Free-State side," the pupil added that "he was very quiet . . . dressed neatly, and seemed very particular and careful as to his dress; had peculiar eyes . . . and the upper lids had a queer look." Quiet and particular, peculiar and queer, there seemed to be two Bills. There was the likable schoolmaster, and there was someone else hidden behind his fastidiousness.[48]

As is evident in his correspondence, Bill started to disagree with the politics of his community. He informed his mother, "You have undoubtably heard of the wrongs committed in this territory by the southern people . . . but when one once knows the facts they can easily see that it has been the opposite party that have been the main movers in the troubles & by far the most lawless set of people in the country." Bill believed that northern papers falsely depicted southerners as murderous scoundrels, thus leading the folks back home to see Kansas as a victim of southern ambitions. In contrast, he himself now saw northerners as the antagonists. From his perspective inside the Kansas Territory, Bill believed that Free-Soilers were the instigators of the violence of Bleeding Kansas.[49]

Bill's letters also showed his metamorphosis to be significantly deeper than his political outlook. As his view of the world transcended his immediate surroundings, he stated, "I have seen a little of the world [and] I know how others manage to keep moving in the vast crowd which is moving ahead." He added, "I have seen the means used by different communities to keep body and soul together, I have compared them with each other and find in the end they all amount to the same, with only this difference, that their situations are different, and the ends accomplished are adapted to their situations." Likely thinking about the Mormons, Native Americans, and his own people as he wrote, Bill demonstrated uncommon empathy, and he entertained the idea of living how he pleased.[50]

He reflected on his ordeal in the mountains and balanced these ideas with thoughts about nature and source of happiness. In March, he reported, "The prairie has a carpet of green, variegated with innumerable flowers." However, he told his mother, "As I sit in my schoolroom and contemplate these scenes, in their beauty; I cannot but contrast them with the scenes of a twelve month ago, when all around me was desolation." Whether due to his experience in the wilderness or something else, Bill believed that he did not fit the community in which he lived. He lamented, "I think every thing and every body around me is happy and I alone am miserable." Worse than that, he also concluded, "It seems man is doomed to aspire after happiness; but never in reality to obtain it." Quantrill described what he saw while looking out his window: "The husbandman, the mechanic, the merchant, and all mankind . . . have dreams of the future and building up their prospects on what they seem to see in their future."[51]

While writing these missives Bill made his profound realizations about his time in the mountains. Although he likely longed for a warm schoolhouse, dry clothes, a bath and a shave, and some secure town while wading through chest-high snow with his companions, once he returned and lived in the safety of the normal, straightlaced world, he felt a tension between his authentic self and the man he pretended to be. When he saw the dark reflection of a tired, lonely schoolmaster in the warped windowpane of his schoolhouse, he wanted to exchange the cobbled shoes, trousers, shirt-jack, necktie, and frock coat for riding boots, buckskin, and a brightly colored hunting shirt; he wanted to let his whiskers go unshaved and his hair uncut; and he wanted to flee the walls of the schoolhouse in which he felt imprisoned and alone for the company of men living together in the wild. Bill wanted once more to go on the hunt.

CHAPTER 6: *Jailbird*

In the spring of 1860, near the end of the school term, Bill supposedly faced another unnamed personal calamity. Holland Wheeler, a citizen of Lawrence who knew Bill at the time, "learned that Quantrill was teaching school at or near Paola, and by some misfortune was locked in the calaboose." Soon "some of [Bill's] friends (some really good people), thinking him wronged, let him out." No record exists to reveal exactly what "misfortune" landed Bill in jail. Those who repeated the story either could not recollect it or chose to omit it.[1]

However, some trouble or scandal or misfortune occurred. Throughout Bill's life these occurrences, unmentionable happenings, arose. Perhaps he wandered into the wrong outhouse at an inopportune moment or took an evening stroll through a darkened alley at the exact time some local mischief occurred. Wherever Bill went he was an outsider and easy scapegoat. Still these instances piled up, making it more and more difficult to see them as unique episodes. It seems more likely that the respectable citizens of Mendota and Paola were struck by something about Bill, something in his character or his behavior that cast a shadow over his motivations and actions. When Bill emerged from jail, he walked down one of the many roads that cut through the ever-changing, increasingly settled landscape of the Kansas Territory. As he walked away from yet another town, his shadow grew ever longer until nearly the whole of the land was covered in darkness.[2]

A few months before his stint in jail, Bill sent a nostalgic, reflective letter to his mother. Writing in his schoolhouse, he told her, "I sometimes wish that I was again a scholar. . . . But scholars and companions are all far from me now, and I am left alone to contemplate. It seems to me but a dream, a very little of which I ever realized." Bill seemed determined to make some kind of mark and considered 1860 as good a year as any to do so. "But as this is a leap year," he stated, "I think it advisable for those who intend to turn over a new leaf, to take their leap with the year, and then keep moving with it, and then probably they may have something more than a blank [sheet]." Using yet another metaphor, Bill admitted, "And now that I have sown wild oats so long, I think it is time to begin harvesting; which will only be accomplished by putting in a different crop in different soil." Identifying unrealized dreams, turning over a new leaf, and harvesting a different crop—Bill was ready to change himself.[3]

Immediately following these passages regarding his changing outlook, Bill alluded to the worsening political situation in Kansas, observing, "There is no news here but hard times, and harder still coming, for I see their shadows." Kansans voted in favor of the Wyandotte Constitution, which expressly forbade slavery in the territory, by a two-to-one margin on October 4, 1859. Since Bill's politics had changed and he had become critical of the Free-Soil side, the passage of this new frame of government probably rankled him. Worse, only a couple of weeks after that, John Brown and his party of militant abolitionists raided the U.S. Arsenal at Harpers Ferry, Virginia. News of the raid spread across the nation and back to the Kansas Territory, where Brown had honed his skill as a warrior. If Quantrill was on the fence about his political stance, word of Harpers Ferry drove him firmly into the proslavery camp. In a letter he ranted as follows about the antislavery people of Kansas: "They all sympathize for old J. Brown, who should have been hung years ago, indeed hanging was too good for him. May I never see a more contemptable people than those who sympathize for him. A murderer and a robber, made a martyr of; just think of it."[4]

These events—the Wyandotte Constitution's approval, Brown's raid on Harpers Ferry, and the Kansas's antislavery faction's reaction to the raid—led to the darkness and shadows Bill saw in his mind's eye. He reminded his mother of a line from "Lochiel's Warning" (1801) by the Scottish poet Thomas Campbell: "Coming events cast their shadows before." Indeed, any adult who lived through the late 1850s and 1860 saw some darkness on the horizon. Even so, "I do not fear that my destiny is fixed in this country," Bill assured his mother, "nor do I wish to be compelled to stay in it any longer than possible, for the devil has unlimited sway over this territory."[5]

"Lochiel's Warning" provides a touchstone for Bill's evolving mindset. A wizard in the poem warns the Highland Scots of their impending doom in the 1746 Battle of Culloden. Lochiel, a proud warrior and naysayer, hears the wizard and rebukes the prophet, proclaiming his confidence in his claymore-wielding men, who "are true to the last of their blood and their breath." In the final stanza, Lochiel makes it clear that he and his people have made up their minds to fight regardless of the outcome: "Shall victor exult, or in death be laid low, / With his back to the field, and his feet to the foe! / And leaving in battle no blot on his name, / Look proudly to Heaven from the death-bed of fame."[6]

If Lochiel was real, he ended up gashed and lying dead on the turf. During the historic battle, the Scots threw themselves against the redcoats, who cut them down with musketry and cannon fire. A few Highlanders broke the English line and engaged in intense hand-to-hand fighting with the enemy, but this combat lasted only a few moments before more redcoats joined the fray at that critical place and closed the gap. Historians view the Battle of Culloden as a lost chance at independence for the Scots and the end of the Highland culture and clan structure that ordered Scottish life. In other words, had the fictional Lochiel taken the wizard seriously, he and the others might have lived to fight another day, won their freedom, and perhaps maintained control over the fate of their society.[7]

When Bill read "Lochiel's Warning" in February 1860, he saw cautions around him in the Kansas Territory. More signs materialized in a matter of months. The proslavery Democratic Party held its 1860 convention in the ideological darkness cast by the twin shadows of Bleeding Kansas and the Dred Scott decision. On April 23, Democratic delegates gathered in Charleston, South Carolina, to debate whether to adopt an extreme proslavery platform or a more moderate proslavery stance. The former would endorse the Dred Scott decision and allow slaveholders to take their slaves anywhere in the West, or to northern states that outlawed slavery. The latter would rely on popular sovereignty, allowing the residents of future western territories to decide whether their state entered the Union as slave or free. Stephen A. Douglas, who sponsored the Compromise of 1850 and the Kansas-Nebraska Act, both of which included popular sovereignty as the way of dealing with the slavery question, advocated for popular sovereignty. When it became evident that northern Democrats wanted Douglas as the party's nominee and preferred using popular sovereignty to determine the future of slavery in the West, many southern delegates walked out of the convention. Six weeks later the Democratic Party tried to reunite under a unified platform in Baltimore, Maryland. However, rather than rejoin their northern comrades, the southern delegates who had walked out in Charleston decided to hold their own separate convention. The Democratic Party nominated Douglas and the southern Democrats nominated John C. Breckinridge.[8]

The split in the Democratic Party created an opening for the upstart Republicans in the presidential election of 1860. However, the Republican Party, an antislavery coalition, was trying to get out from under its own dark cloud: Harpers Ferry. John "Osawatomie" Brown's raid on the U.S. Arsenal at Harpers Ferry, Virginia, scared a great number of moderate whites, who worried that the Republican Party sympathized with the ideals and actions of this murderous terrorist. The Democratic Party capitalized on this fear, painting Republicans in a radical light and compounding the anxieties of those wary of a race war. The Republican Party was popular in areas of the country sympathetic to the position that slavery should not expand beyond the current slaveholding states. Even so, in order to win the presidency, Republican candidates needed to assure some percentage of voters in the middle that they were not red-hot disciples of John Brown.

The Republican Party tried to find a candidate for president who was neither too hot nor too cold on slavery. When he announced his campaign in Leavenworth, Kansas Territory, Abraham Lincoln established himself as the type of presidential candidate who favored containing slavery, but not at the cost of law and order. He remarked, "Old John Brown has just been executed for treason against a state. We cannot object, even though he agreed with us in thinking slavery wrong. That cannot excuse violence, bloodshed, and treason. It could avail him nothing that he might think himself right." Lincoln went on, "So, if constitutionally we elect a President, and therefore you undertake to destroy the Union, it will be our duty to deal with you as old John Brown has been dealt with. We shall try to do our duty. We hope and believe that in no section will a majority so act as to render such extreme measures necessary." On May 16, 1860, the Republicans convened to determine their platform for the elections and their candidate for president. Through his own well-positioned stance on slavery and his supporters' savvy, Lincoln became the party's nominee.⁹

During the spring of that election year, the world seemed to hover in a darkened stasis. Wherever Bill went when he left Paola, the uncertain fate of the nation compounded his anxiety over his own personal plight. People on the Kansas-Missouri border, where violence had sporadically flared up since the Wakarusa War, felt the political divisions of the country in ways that other Americans did not quite perceive. In Lawrence and Leavenworth, Paola and Atchison, Kansas City and Independence, men went to sleep with loaded rifles and pistols within arm's reach. A man out on his own in the semiwild stretches between settlements was constantly vigilant. For much of the rest of 1860 Bill roved about, occasionally entering the settlements and mixing with the respectable citizens, but spending much of his time alone skirting the edges of civilization.

As another traveler sat beside his fire in the late summer or fall of 1860, he sensed the presence of a skulker beyond the illumination of his firelight. Nathan Stone, a fifty-nine-year-old hotelkeeper in the abolitionist boomtown of Lawrence, was alone as he traveled to purchase hogs in Miami and Johnson Counties in eastern Kansas Territory. He knew that jayhawkers, ruffians, Delaware, Shawnee, runaways, highwaymen, and scoundrels roamed about in the night. The approaching man did not say "Howdy" or walk into the light but instead stood there, silently sizing up the old man. Stone squinted, straining his eyes against the absence of light, as he tried to make out the shape and demeanor of his nocturnal guest. All he could see against the evening sky was the rough outline of a man. Then the man drifted silently into the oblivion of nighttime. He disappeared like the wilderness around him until he ceased to exist except as something else—a disembodied sound, a haunting memory, or a looming ethereal threat.¹⁰

Confidence Man
1860–1861

CHAPTER 7: *Charley Hart*

"One day, perhaps in June, there came a lone footman across the ferry," recalled Holland Wheeler. Watching from the Whitney House Hotel, a mere stone's throw from the landing, he could see this man as he sauntered into Lawrence in the summer of 1860. Wheeler remembered that "he was dressed with corduroy pants tucked into his boots," and that he wore a "woolen shirt, [and] slouch hat, and carried an oil-cloth grip." The stranger, he said, "was about five feet nine inches in height, bow-legged, weight about 150 or 160 pounds, sandy hair, rather hooked nose, and had a peculiar droop to his eyelids." As Wheeler sat and watched from his perch, the newcomer "walked into the hotel office, deposited the grip, and registered as Charles Hart."[1]

Charles Hart appeared to be one of a few thousand people who had passed through Lawrence since its 1854 founding. In June 1860, the free state's capital boomed with 1,600 residents. Politically active antislavery northerners, many of whom traveled to Kansas with the help of the New England Emigrant Aid Company, made up the majority of the population. The source of this community was the intersection of abolitionism and popular sovereignty, but once people arrived there, they focused on living, thriving, and profiteering. After the abolitionists and their families established the Lawrence, a horde of unattached merchants, speculators, surveyors, physicians, shopkeepers, craftsmen, lawyers, printers, carpenters, and smiths descended on the town to sell their goods, services, and labor.[2]

While in Lawrence, Hart resided at the Whitney House with a crowd of other young footloose fellows—all men on the make. The group included clerks, carpenters, blacksmiths, and surveyors like twenty-two-year-old Wheeler, a Vermonter who had come to Lawrence because of the recent purchase of Delaware Indian lands by the government.[3]

93

Fresh-faced Hart, who walked into the bustling town from the countryside, was wise to distrust the dangers lurking along the side streets of Lawrence. Many reformers, including Sylvester Graham, cautioned impressionable youths against the temptations readily available in cities and towns like Lawrence. Henry Ward Beecher, a Connecticut Yankee and famed Congregationalist preacher who was also the brother of Harriet Beecher Stowe, wrote the most notable of the advice tracts addressed to young men alone in the urban landscape and surrounded by unknown faces.[4]

Hart was probably familiar with Beecher's *Seven Lectures to Young Men on Various Important Subjects*. In this 1844 publication, the preacher made an effort to warn youngsters against a man he called "the Enticer." As Beecher observed, "Every youth knows that there are dangerous men abroad who would injure him by lying, by slander, by overreaching and plundering him. . . . Few imagine that they have any thing to dread from those who have no designs against them." This nonchalance, though, was the guise of the Enticer. He did not come to a young innocent in the obvious form of a rowdy, thief, or solicitor of tawdry vice. Rather, the Enticer looked like a friend, someone who appeared to share a common background and similar sensibilities as his target. Once the Enticer created a bond with the unsuspecting young man, he then gently lured him to a friendly game of cards, escorted him into a theater filled with its fancy trappings and painted women, or perhaps coerced from him his vote. Beecher concluded, "[The Enticer] will use you, lead you on until you are useless; then, if the virtuous do not pity you, or God compassionate, you are without a friend in the universe." A fellow like Hart needed to be on guard lest his very soul be robbed by the Enticer, or, as Americans of the 1850s called this fiend in human form, the Confidence Man.[5]

How much Hart knew of the origins of this villain cannot be determined, but it is believed that the New York City press coined the term "confidence man" in 1849 to describe a man named William Thompson. This brash criminal looked the part of a gentleman casually strolling up the street when he engaged a well-to-do man in conversation. At some point, Thompson asked his new acquaintance whether he had his confidence and, if so, whether he would trust him with his watch. After the unsuspecting gentleman handed over his watch, Thompson took it, nonchalantly placed it in his pocket, and walked away. Thompson executed this confidence trick at least six times before he was hauled before a judge. The *New York Herald* coined the term for this particular kind of criminal who played on the trust of his victims. The paper soon assigned numerals to other men who were gulling their victims with confidence games—"Confidence Man No. 2," "Confidence Man No. 3," and so on.[6]

Even before the paper labeled this type of person a confidence man, American literature used his likeness as a stock character. The American character followed a British antecedent to the confidence man—Jeremy Diddler, a charming swindler in an 1803 play by James Kenney. "Diddling" soon became a synonym for "tricking" or "swindling." Edgar Allan Poe wrote a short essay, "Diddling: Considered as One of the Exact Sciences" (1835), in which he described mankind as the "animal that diddles" and wrote, "Diddling, rightly considered, is a compound, of which the ingredients are minuteness, interest, perseverance, ingenuity, audacity, nonchalance, originality, impertinence, and grin." The rest of Poe's essay describes myriad schemes characterized by dupes placing their confidence in respectable-looking strangers only to be taken for a ride.[7]

Herman Melville's *The Confidence-Man* further explores this figure. No doubt inspired by Kenney's Diddler, Poe's humorous and engrossing essay, the *New York Herald*'s confidence man, and perhaps even an incident in which a man took up the alias Herman Melville in 1850 to win the confidence of strangers who believed he was the famous author of *Typee*, the real Melville penned one of the strangest books in the nineteenth century and the incisive analysis of American culture at the middle point of that formative period.[8]

Set on April 1, 1857, April Fools' Day, the date the book was released, the story follows the titular confidence man as he boards a riverboat in St. Louis headed down the Mississippi River for New Orleans. Although the con man's many attempts to defraud the other passengers drive the story, it is difficult to know whether he is in fact one man or many people. Moreover, it is unclear whether this man is something more spiritual, like Jesus Christ returned to test the charity of his earthbound followers, or something sinister like the devil, or some cynical spirit come to possess the American soul at midcentury. Scarier yet, perhaps Melville's point is that there is nothing behind the masks—no God, no Satan, nothing but an empty shell. Melville used the interactions between the confidence man and the other characters aboard the boat—all archetypes of American culture, such as the planter, slave, businessman, and frontiersman—to explore the internal battle between cynicism and sincerity in the American psyche. Destabilized by industrial growth, capitalist pursuits, and westward migration, this society was full of unmoored people who struggled to trust others. Instead of making the confidence man's work more challenging, this fearful, vigilant climate served as the perfect environment for him to stalk his prey.[9]

As Melville's book demonstrates, it is impossible to detect a confidence man until after he plays his game. Because one's heart cannot be discerned, middle-class Americans in the mid-nineteenth century created a system through which one's sincerity might be displayed through dress, actions, and words. Young men and women learned what to wear and how to behave on the street, in the parlor, and at a dinner party or funeral so that they *appeared* to be sincere. This increased emphasis on the surface of reality, however, made it even easier for an outsider to infiltrate middle-class society by merely looking and acting a particular way. As middle-class Americans realized this, they became all the more vigilant, for the confidence man could be anywhere. He could be anyone, even the man least suspected. He could appear as a gentleman, a trusted local magistrate, a hale fellow, or perhaps even an unassuming kid fresh off the ferry.[10]

A wolf in sheep's clothing, Charley Hart was indeed a confidence man. The respectable citizenry of Lawrence remembered him as a ne'er-do-well, a part of the disreputable and even criminal group of men that lurked about at the edge of town and the dark fringes of their society. Whomever he associated with and whatever he and his comrades were up to, Hart was shifty. He did not stay around once his trick was discovered; he was gone by December 1860.[11]

Hart displayed many of the signs of a confidence man. He did not have a productive place in the community of Lawrence. He did not have employment, nor did he own any property or seem to possess any wealth. Wheeler, who sometimes shared a room at the Whitney House with Hart, "never heard of his having done a day's work at anything." Sydney Herd, who worked the ferry across the Kansas River from the Delaware reservation to Lawrence, befriended Hart. "If he had any money, to amount to anything, no one knew it," Herd recalled.

Moreover, Herd stated, "[Hart] did not appear to have any business or means of support so far as I know."[12]

Some suspected that Hart made his living outside the legitimate avenues of employment. "His associates were bad," Wheeler remembered, but he added, "Bad as they were, I believe he was worst of all." W. A. Johnson, who lived in Lawrence, said that Hart "and several young men about his age, all having assumed names, associated together for the purpose of stealing and robbery . . . They were detected in stealing horses and mules." Herd recalled how Hart proposed to rustle stock out of Missouri: "One thing certain, he was always willing to go into anything that turned up that had a dollar in it for Charley Hart." The attorney for Douglas County, Samuel A. Riggs, recalled that he attempted to prosecute Hart "during the summer and fall of 1860, for burglary and larceny, in breaking open and stealing from a powder-house of Ridenour & Baker; for arson, in setting fire to a barn in Kanwaka Township . . . and for kidnapping. These charges were all pending against him when he disappeared." Wheeler confirmed that Hart "was wanted by Sam Walker, sheriff at one time, in reference to breaking into a powder-house." Sheriff Samuel Walker attempted to serve a warrant on Hart for this crime, approaching him on Massachusetts Street one day. But Hart "started down the street upon the run, and bolted into the wagon shop of John Dean, closing and barring the door behind him." Walker then broke in, but he could not find Hart. "Years afterward Walker learned from John Dean that [Hart] spent the night following his attempted arrest at the house of a man named Reed," and that he "passed the night, with the Ex-Reverend John E. Stewart for a bed fellow." Stewart was infamous as a jayhawker, but why he shared a mattress with Hart is unknown. After he was given the slip, Walker gave up on hauling Hart into jail. Despite all this speculation and attempted prosecution, the courts never found Hart guilty of any crime.[13]

Years later, John Dean, a member of that sketchy group of compatriots in Lawrence to which Hart belonged, tried to deny his connection to Hart, claiming he always knew something was off about the man. "He was continually trying to complete some 'plot' that would 'work all right,'" Dean asserted. In addition, he said, "[Hart] was a very frequent visitor to my workshop, and was persistent in his efforts to gain my confidence and knowledge of my plans and doings." Dean believed that Hart was perhaps a spy. Contending that he himself was such an infamous abolitionist (at least in his own mind) that the slaveholders across the border wanted him dead, Dean claimed that Hart was working for the governor of Missouri. Missouri slaveholders no doubt wanted every jayhawker to swing, but it is doubtful that the governor knew Dean by name or targeted him, especially with many more infamous jayhawkers operating in the territory. In any case, Dean argued that "much of [Hart's] seeming character was 'put on.'"[14]

Wheeler also claimed that he sensed his roommate was hiding something unsettling. "He usually had the same room as myself," Wheeler remembered as he thought back to the summer of 1860, explaining, "During the very warm nights we frequently slept on the roof of the veranda." Wheeler further noted, "(Often I borrowed a pistol to put under my pillow. Why? Well, I don't know myself.)" Perhaps he was concerned that Hart might steal his blanket or poke him with a dagger in his sleep—these things being known to happen at night on the frontier—but he might have suspected something more nefarious. Although he was unable or unwilling to articulate the exact cause of his misgivings about Hart, Wheeler reiterated, "I was always suspicious of him; instinctively, I suppose."[15]

For his part Hart claimed he was engaged in a legitimate enterprise that required discretion. He told innkeeper Nathan Stone that he was "a detective for the Delaware Indians." Hart's designation as a "detective" probably indicates that he worked for the Delaware to help them retrieve their horses and other stock. On May 30, 1860, the U.S. government broke up the Delaware reservation so that the Union Pacific Railroad could build its transcontinental rail line through the area. In exchange, tribal households were allocated eighty-acre parcels of land and money intended to defray the losses incurred from white squatters' and settlers' theft of hundreds of ponies. The Delaware possibly used some of the funds in an effort to retrieve their stolen animals. Maybe tribal members, who were experienced in dealing with whites, believed that hiring a white man to deal with white horse thieves gave them a better chance at getting some of their ponies returned.[16]

Hart formed bonds with several Delaware men. Henry S. Clarke, a Canadian by birth who had lived in Lawrence since 1857, remembered that around the summer of 1860 Hart said "that he was living at the time with Henry Bascom, a Delaware Indian, out about three miles from Lawrence." When "later in the summer I saw him again," Clarke reported, "[Hart] said he was living with George Sarcoxie, another Delaware Indian, about five miles out from Lawrence, on the reserve." When Hart was not boarding at Stone's hotel, he lived among the Delaware.[17]

Hart had a complicated and sometimes antagonistic relationship with some members of the Delaware. Wheeler recalled one instance when "an Indian woman came into the hotel and told [Hart] she wanted seven dollars or her saddle." Exactly why Hart had her saddle is unclear. Maybe he stole it; maybe it was payment for a job he never performed. After Hart "got the saddle for her," she asked, "Where are my ponies?" According to Wheeler, Hart replied, "'I don't know anything about your ponies.'" Wheeler continued, "'Well,' she says, 'they will be back by to-morrow, or you will have trouble.'"[18]

As one might expect, Hart chose trouble.

In the next day or two, Hart joined a crowd of men and women in the sun-blasted streets of Lawrence, drawn there by the sound of snorting horses and hollering warriors. Clarke jostled through the same crowd as Hart to discover the source of the commotion, and he found "about half a dozen Delaware Indians" who were "very much excited." Before the dust settled, "White Turkey, a young Delaware, who talked pretty good English, and always sported an eagle's feather dangling from his hat, was telling the crowd about several of their ponies being stolen, and said they had traced them to the Kansas river near Lawrence, and that Charley Hart . . . was one of the men seen with the ponies." Clarke recalled the action that unfolded. Hart, "who was in the rear of the crowd, heard the remark, and stepped forward with a big bluff, warning White Turkey that that kind of talk did not go, and made a motion toward his revolver. White Turkey whipped out his gun and had him covered in less than a second." Hart was caught between death and dishonor. He "had his pistol out of the holster, but dared not attempt to elevate it, but backed out of the crowd." As Hart moved, "White Turkey slowly advanced toward him . . . until [Hart] . . . saw a chance to give his adversary the slip, which he was by no means too proud or reckless to do at the first opportunity." Pushing past the other onlookers, Hart fled the fight and saved his skin.[19]

The confrontation between White Turkey and Hart on Massachusetts Street might have resulted in the first duel of its kind. Dueling underwent several stages in America. A vestige of Old World tradition among the nobility, dueling was brought to North America by men of the upper ranks of British and European society. In this codified event replete with challenges, notes, and seconds, gentlemen used pistols to settle affairs of honor. Parallel to the violence of the upper classes, America's yeomen, laborers, slaves, and frontiersmen waged their own duels with bare hands, Bowie knifes, and rifles. In the U.S. West, these forms of dueling eventually intertwined and morphed into the quick-draw contest, a distinctly American form of individual combat in which men faced off against each other in some western town. If Hart raised his revolver, the first of these "Old West" shoot-outs would be attributed to an angry Delaware and a mysterious rogue.[20]

The outcome of the standoff between Hart and White Turkey depended on the eyes through which it was viewed. As a bystander, Clarke fairly assessed that Hart lost honor. However, in Lawrence few of the transplanted New Englanders and midwesterners had likely witnessed anything like the two men's confrontation. Without a frame of reference for the event, the town's residents leaned on their knowledge of the participants to understand the weird exchange. Perhaps they feared White Turkey and his band; maybe they thought the Delaware "who talked pretty good English" ambushed Hart; possibly neither an Indian nor a shifty fellow warranted more than a passing thought. The Delaware likely took note of Hart's cowardice and maybe saw this as a typical response for a white man. Possibly they expected more of a fight. For his part, Hart might have reacted instinctually, or perhaps his decision to retreat was informed by the transient nature of Lawrence and the West, a place where one's reputation and persona were fluid and situational.[21]

It is impossible to know Hart's mindset when he backed away from the confrontation with White Turkey, but at another point that summer he demonstrated an awareness of the transformative nature of the West. One can imagine Hart loafing about on the porch of the Whitney House on the afternoon of Saturday, June 23, when the census taker came through to record the residents. Putting down his pen and paper or perhaps a handful of playing cards, Hart told the government man he was twenty-three years old, born in Ohio, and a farmer. How he decided on farming as his profession of record remains a mystery. Perhaps he thought of settling down, breaking the land, and putting down roots. Maybe he made up something to tell the record keeper.[22]

Maybe Hart was pulling the census taker's chain. His story certainly sounded like a joke to his fellow boarders standing within earshot, eliciting guffaws all around. But this inside joke reverberated beyond the

This page from the 1860 Federal Manuscript Census records Quantrill as he lived under the alias Charles Hart. Entered on line twenty-five with the abbreviated version of his name, "Chas. Hart" is listed as a twenty-three-year-old farmer who was born in Ohio. The census taker did not enter any amount of value for either personal or real estate. In this document, we can see how successfully Quantrill covered his true identity with a false one, confounding future researchers seeking him in the most official of primary sources. (1860 Federal Manuscript Census, City of Lawrence, County of Douglas, Kansas Territory, p. 34, National Archives and Records Administration, Washington, D.C.)

Whitney House when it went with the census taker after he gathered up his forms, stuffed them under his arm, and left the premises. It was read; its contents were recorded. Eventually, Hart's explanation of his identity was filed away by government bureaucrats in the country's archives. It was just a blip, an oft-missed, statistically irrelevant hoax in the data, a prescient if unintended trick buried in what became the most fundamental source available to American historians, a mustard seed of doubt planted deep in that heaping, seemingly solid, unquestioned monolith of a primary source. Hart was quite an original.[23]

The ruse was deeper than a young wiseacre playing the census taker for a fool. One day while Wheeler lounged in a downstairs room at the Whitney House, Stone called him over to the front desk. As Wheeler recalled, "[The innkeeper] opened the day-book and showed me on the back page the name Wm. C. Quantrill, remarking, 'That is Hart's real name.'" Stone and Wheeler were likely the only two men who knew Hart was Quantrill's alias.[24]

This bizarre cover fit the odd methodology of Quantrill's con. Rather than put on airs or pull on a mask of legitimacy to cover an unworthy self, he did the opposite. Quantrill left his straightlaced, upright identity as the country schoolmaster to adopt a new identity as a sketchy idler. He covered his identity as a law-abiding citizen with the guise of a petty criminal, a member of the riffraff, a street tough of Lawrence's subterranean set. Quantrill's leaving the promise of the middle class for the uncertainty of a rogue's life seems to suggest that he was a shapeshifting agent of evil. As Charley Hart, he did not necessarily want to lighten the pocketbooks of Lawrence's upright men and women. He certainly did not seem to be conning strangers out of their gold watches or participating in some elaborate scheme to defraud them of large amounts of wealth. He might, however, have enjoyed deceiving the men he saw as the self-righteous, wealthy abolitionist merchants of Lawrence.[25]

Perhaps Quantrill became Charley Hart for the thrill of it. The persistent cynic in Melville's *The Confidence-Man* reminds two other passengers on the boat that deceit is not all about thieving: "Money, you think, is the sole motive to pains and hazard, deception and devilry, in this world. How much money did the devil make by gulling Eve?" If Quantrill was just a thrill seeker looking to separate the trustful from their faith, then he posed an existential threat to Lawrence's abolitionists and Free-Soilers. An avatar of the devil, an unassuming fellow like Charley Hart might join a cheerful debate in your shop, then saunter out and a short time later with a piece of your soul and a grin on his face.[26]

Whatever his motivations, there was something distinctly American about Quantrill's turn as Charley Hart. Some Americans seemed to appreciate a trick and placed value in one's ability to deceive another. The often-cited example of P. T. Barnum embodies this deep affection for the trickster. With circus acts featuring mermaids, ancient nursemaids, diminutive generals, and other curiosities, Barnum proved that Americans happily paid to get their legs pulled. The confidence man also represented the ability to change. Even before its founding in 1776, Europeans came to America to become something new—peasants aspired to be landowners, servants to be freemen, freemen to be gentlemen. Names changed, clothes changed, languages changed, and professions changed. Indeed, the people who immigrated to America believed that they changed. A man who failed in one city could move to the countryside and try his hand at farming, and so on. People celebrated metamorphosis as a central virtue of the New World. In that sense, all Americans were, in their own ways, confidence men and women, morphing and transforming into new people.[27]

Although Quantrill's alias indicated a new identity, it also revealed something about his essential self. When said aloud, "Charley Hart" brings to mind a fly-by-night gambler, vagabond troubadour, hapless gunhand, or cowpunching poet, but Quantrill likely imbued the name with meaning. Charley, or Charles, was derived long ago from the names of the greatest of kings, Charles Martel and his grandson Charlemagne. Quantrill also loved the name Charley, which was what he called his beloved warhorse during the Civil War. A legend arose that Quantrill and his horse were spiritually intertwined, with the horse becoming part guerrilla and the guerrilla becoming part horse. Hart played on "heart" and suggested love and affection. This iconography typically belonged to the fairer sex, but here Quantrill sported the softest of icons so that when he crossed the river and masqueraded into Lawrence, he did so as the king of hearts.[28]

Whatever the inspiration for his flamboyant persona, Quantrill's motivation for adopting the cover escaped his contemporaries. Even years after they discovered that Hart was an alias for Quantrill, men like Dean, Wheeler, and others speculated about his goals. Depending on the source, thievery, including theft of horses, as well as kidnapping, spying, or even assassination drove Quantrill. Uncertainty like this might suggest that he was a supervillain, an unlikely conclusion but still a popular theory among some of his biographers. A more reasonable assumption could be that his cover was so effective that the true nature of his pursuit remained a mystery long after he died. In either case, with Charley Hart unmasked, the stage is set to investigate the true nature of Quantrill's ruse.

CHAPTER 8: *Detective*

In the fall of 1860, a dozen prominent men met in secret in an up-stairs room of the Union Hotel in Paola, Kansas. Each man was there by special invitation. A couple of lawyers, a doctor, business owners, and the Indian agent for the territory—together these men represented the proslavery faction in this part of the territory. One man, younger than the rest and only known to a few, stood up in the middle of the smoke-filled room and interrupted the hushed banter. He introduced himself as Bill Quantrill and told the gathering that over the past few months he had lived under the alias Charley Hart and had been riding with jayhawkers, a revelation that likely shocked a few of the men. He explained that he was an undercover detective in the employ of Lieu-tenant Governor Hugh Walsh, who had tasked him with infiltrating a band of jayhawkers in an effort to bring them to justice. While among the jayhawkers, Quantrill had witnessed firsthand the murder of sev-eral proslavery citizens of Linn County, Kansas. He had also seen these same jayhawkers disrupt the U.S. district court in an effort to secure the release of three of their number indicted for stealing Indian ponies.[1]

Quantrill cut to the chase, warning these proslavery men that the jay-hawkers "contemplated a raid on Paola." He reported that the jayhawk-ers were "intending to rob the stores & the town, and also [that they] contemplated the robbing of the Kansas City, Paola & Ft. Scott Stage with the money that was expected to be sent to General Clover, the agent for the Miami Indians; some $30,000." Quantrill further disclosed that he had thwarted the attempt to steal the funds intended for the Indian agent. Apparently, he sent word to General Seth Clover, who ordered a company of U.S. infantrymen to protect the payment. The raid on Paola never materialized. Whether Quantrill had anything to do with prevent-ing the attack cannot be known.[2]

Quantrill's disclosure that he worked as an undercover detective goes a long way toward solving one of the most confusing mysteries of his life. His adoption of the alias Charley Hart, his relationships with members of the Delaware tribe, the accusations against him of horse thieving, and other rumors about his days in and around Lawrence in 1860—these seemingly disconnected bits of his story can now be linked together. His employment by Lieutenant Governor Walsh and General Clover—two southern-sympathizing officials—not only establishes a connection between Quantrill and the proslavery element in Kansas, but it also helps outline his transformation from a quiet free-state teacher into proslavery militant. Following him on his clandestine mission reveals much about Quantrill's days as Charley Hart, and it also exposes some of the deceptions at the heart of life on the border.[3]

Without any long-standing white inhabitants or American institutions and rituals, a man could easily reinvent himself in a town like Lawrence. Some families knew one another from the East. They came to the area as a part of the New England Emigrant Aid Company, helped found the town in 1854, and named it after their financier, Amos Lawrence. However, hundreds of people from every midwestern and northeastern state and quite a few European countries soon joined them in Lawrence. This was a town full of strange people speaking different languages and with different accents, all of them reading one another, assessing the character of their neighbors, and trying to decide whom to trust. This was a town full of strange faces, a town full of masks, a town full of new people, an American town.[4]

Lawrence was an opportunity for a man to change his identity. The settlement's mission to abolish slavery added new layers to the American masquerade. Historian Jason Phillips observes that the antislavery settlers of Lawrence and across the Kansas Territory wished to appear as quiet Christians and restrained men, but behind their veil of piety were gun-wielding warriors who knew that they needed violence to stop the spread of slavery. When Lawrence's first white settlers cut their old social networks in the East and moved to Kansas, they retained the dress of the clerk, minister, merchant, and farmer. However, they became new people, foot soldiers for an antislavery revolution. In essence, Lawrence's antislavery settlers were morally righteous confidence men. Their "Crate Politics," or the way in which Henry Ward

Beecher and members of his church "bought and shipped Sharps rifles to Kansas in crates labeled as Bibles," best illustrates their deception and explains why Sharps rifles became known as Beecher's Bibles. "Like restrained manhood, crate politics was self-contained," Phillips explains, and "northern filibustering cared about outward appearances, morality, and structural integrity."[5]

While crates and frock coats veiled the identities of many in Lawrence's white community, they also hid these citizens' involvement in the Underground Railroad. From the outset of settlement of the Kansas Territory, antislavery residents established the Underground Railroad as a part of their resistance to the spread of slavery, and they built the first "stations" in Kansas as early as 1854. Farmhouses, cabins, barns, and workshops containing secret cellars, attics, compartments, or lofts where a runaway slave could hide served as "stations." As stationmasters, antislavery settlers advanced the cause of freedom, even if they used illegal tactics. Under their coats or dresses conductors also concealed Colt revolvers, pistols supplied in the same manner as Beecher's Bibles.[6]

The metaphorical masks on the conductors of the Underground Railroad in the Kansas Territory covered white faces. Whiteness granted men and women more fluidity and freedom to create a new identity, while Blackness severely restricted African American men and women. African Americans might run away from slavery, but as long as they were in the United States, they still hid their faces away because they were in reach of the slave catcher. They might buy or win their freedom, but the law did not guarantee them equality. In white society, Blackness marked a man or woman as less, as a slave, a servant, a noncitizen, and the other. Blacks still used masks. They often played a part intended to please the whites around them while concealing their true feelings, and they often did so while working in secret to resist or escape their bonds.[7]

Some African Americans had access to a metaphorical white mask. Although legally considered Black, many children born into slavery had a family tree that was mostly white. Some of those who were light skinned enough to pass as white ran away from slavery to create a new identity as a white person. When these people made their way into white society, they left behind the community of Black people who made up their family. It was, as one scholar terms it, "a chosen exile," an exile often determined out of a desire for freedom, survival, social advancement, and the pursuit of a life with a broader range of opportunities. Even when African Americans were able to "acquire" a white mask, they still paid a price for their transformation. However, white people, and especially white men like Quantrill, had the privilege of changing whenever they pleased without much cost at all.[8]

In this community of masks—white, red, Black, mulatto—Quantrill masqueraded as Charley Hart, but the folks back east still knew him by his given name. As a result, he had to let Stone, the innkeeper, behind his mask if he wanted to receive correspondence from people at home. Perhaps Stone and Quantrill were friends, and maybe Quantrill trusted the innkeeper for some reason that precipitated his stay at the Whitney House. However, other than his real name, Quantrill hid much of his true self from Stone, and the hotelier probably did not trust his guest.[9]

Before he left Stanton, Quantrill told his mother and his sister and maybe others to send future correspondence to Lawrence. He received a missive from his sister in June. He wrote to his mother on June 23, 1860, the same date that the census taker came around. This was the last letter he sent home, or at least it was the last letter his mother kept. That date—just after the summer solstice—marked the turning of a page for Quantrill, the closing of a chapter and the beginning of a new one, the half-light that could be seen as the dawn or dusk of his life.[10]

This aforementioned letter contains a few bits of information that illuminate part of Quantrill's time as Charley Hart. Quantrill mentioned an unnamed man, the final anonymous friend to appear in his correspondence to his mother, who was suing the government. The man was going to give some of the money that he might win to Quantrill. His relationship to Quantrill, the cause for his suit, and the reason he planned to share his winnings remain a mystery. He might have been Bill's friend who was waylaid by Indians on the plains the previous year. Without more context, a number of scenarios are possible. Quantrill told his mother that should he receive money, he was going to send some to her to pay for a new roof for his familial home back in Canal Dover, Ohio.[11]

Quantrill confirmed his connection with the Delaware, stating, "I have been out with a surveying party on the Delaware Indian lands & was obliged to camp out under rather unfavorable circumstances." This is the only mention of him working "with a surveying party." Perhaps the surveyors asked Quantrill to guide the party because he knew the land and the people on it. He might even have worked to assist one or more of the surveyors living at the Whitney House. However, if Quantrill worked with any of the other boarders at the hotel, it is unlikely that they included his surveyor roommate, Wheeler, who never mentioned going out on the reservation with him.[12]

Quantrill's letter does not have much of a sense of finality. He explained his brevity by saying, "I stop at taverns & never can feel at home enough to collect my thoughts & write an interesting letter." Whether the result of writing in bursts when he found time or of the changes in his own mood, much of the characteristic sadness of Quantrill's letters from the previous winter and spring is absent. He told his mother, "Give my respects to my friends & my love to you all, hoping that soon I will see you all again." In the postscript—the very last words he wrote to his mother—Quantrill promised, "I will be home any how as soon as the 1st of September & probably sooner by that time I will be done with Kansas."[13]

A piece of overlooked evidence ties together the various threads of this part of Quantrill's life. This cold case, the mystery of his time as Charley Hart, has been trodden and retrodden by more than a few historical gumshoes who have generated a massive pile of documents. As with many cold cases, the crucial testimony was already in the existing record, hidden in plain sight. In a couple of letters to W. W. Scott, W. L. Potter, a proslavery settler in the Kansas Territory and the deputy sheriff of Lykins County, offered insight into Quantrill's actions over the rest of the summer and into the fall of 1860.[14]

Potter's testimony has been overlooked by historians. Connelley, who acquired Scott's collection of Quantrill-related materials after Scott's death, cast the Potter letters out of the canon of credible sources because they challenged his narrative, something he did with other pieces of evidence as well. "William C. Quantrill falsely represented himself to be Charley Hart, and he did so because of the criminal life he intended to lead and did lead," the author declared. Connelley claimed Quantrill joined a group of border ruffians that had some proslavery members and other members whose politics were simply piratical: "Quantrill took part in the expeditions and forays of the kidnappers and ruffians as soon as he was well enough known to have their confidence. . . . They transacted their business much as robbers and highwaymen . . . by making a raid and disposing of their plunder secured, then lounging and loafing about liquor-shops and skulking through thickets with fallen women for a time before again taking to the road." For Connelley, Quantrill "could not be true to any cause, for, of moral character, the foundation of devotion, he was devoid. Being false of heart and governed by self-interest solely, it was natural that he should be two-faced, untrue to everything and everybody, governed entirely by what he believed would make him the most money."[15]

Potter was credible, however. His testimony includes names, details, and events that make him a trustworthy witness. Potter's letters not only offer information that only someone who was there can know, but they are also full of mundane details and insignificant facts that suggest an authentic recollection. Moreover, it is difficult to see how Potter might have benefited from such a story.[16]

Adding Potter's recollection to Quantrill's biography helps bind together and confirm some otherwise disparate threads during this time. Quantrill told Stone he was a detective, which in those days commonly meant that he was a livestock detective. Apparently Quantrill told Potter "he had been among [the jayhawkers] as a detective." Potter also described Quantrill as follows: "We all understood [him] to say that he was in the employ of the Lieutenant Governor as a detective to find out the names of his Jayhawkers & to capture Jennison." This phrasing may suggest that Quantrill was trying to learn the names of these men *because* they were jayhawkers.[17]

However, Potter also mentioned that these jayhawkers were being hauled in for horse stealing. Although jayhawkers are so attached to the liberation of slaves in historical memory, they appeared to traffic in livestock as well, some of which came from slaveholders but a good deal of which came from their Native American neighbors. Potter claimed that Quantrill told the meeting that the jayhawkers "broke up the U.S. District Court and threatened to hang Judge Williams, who was presiding over the same . . . unless some two or three of their gang were turned loose & discharged from custody." Potter added, "Those three Jayhawkers were then under indictment for stealing Indian horses & were as I remember, confined in the U.S. jail at Fort Scott." Perhaps Quantrill was working to learn the names of these jayhawkers because they were pony thieves.[18]

As a livestock detective hired to return Indian ponies, Quantrill might have been employed by Indian agent General Seth Clover and Lieutenant Governor Hugh Walsh. Quantrill likely met Clover, a prominent resident of Paola, while teaching in Stanton in the fall of 1859 and the spring of 1860. Stanton was just a few miles from Paola. Colonel Torrey, who gave up farming and opened a hotel in Paola and was a neighbor to Clover, might have introduced Quantrill and the Indian agent. Perhaps Clover hired Quantrill to help recover ponies stolen by white men while focusing his inquiry on the horse-thieving jayhawkers. Although border ruffians also thinned the Indian herds, as a proslavery man, Clover likely turned a blind eye to their misdeeds and instead focused on northern men. Given Quantrill's changing political sympathies and his skill as an outdoorsman, as well as his familiarity with Native Americans, he was a good fit for the job.[19]

Quantrill's experience as an undercover livestock detective also illuminates a dimension of the border war that is in the shadows of historical study. Proslavery powers, whether local, territorial, or even national, had difficulty prosecuting jayhawkers for liberating slaves or terrorizing slaveholders. Perhaps this difficulty led proslavery authorities to focus their prosecutorial powers on a crime with which they could gain more traction. Horse stealing was a serious offense that garnered the government's attention in part because the Delaware made it central to their land negotiations in 1860. As a result, horse theft became a priority not only for the southern-sympathizing Clover and Walsh, but also for other government officials, even those with antislavery leanings. They sent Quantrill in to gather evidence or witness horse thieving firsthand and report back; his testimony possibly led to the indictment of those three jayhawkers in the U.S. district court.[20]

Potter's recollection also explains how Charley Hart found himself venturing into Missouri on a raid. "Jennison called on his men for volunteers," Potter wrote. "I think five in number to accompany him . . . to Missouri on a raid to steal some Negro slaves. . . . Quantrill was one of the volunteers." In this account, Jennison—the man whom Quantrill truly wanted to get—needed to attend to something else, so he handed the raid off to some other jayhawkers. Quantrill "could not refuse to go without exciting the suspicion of the Jayhawkers as he had at that time fully succeeded in gaining their confidence." Potter might have inserted the infamous Jennison into the narrative in place of a less well-known character like Dean with whom Quantrill was connected. However the

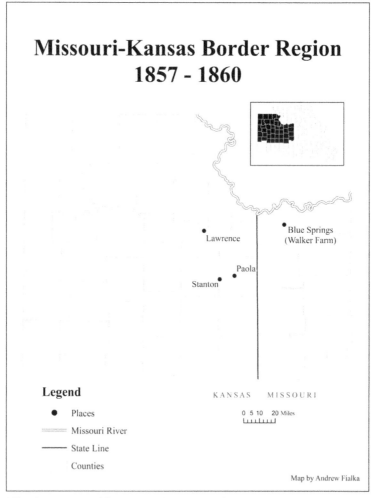

When he was not trekking across the western plains and mountains during the late 1850s, Quantrill lived along the Missouri-Kansas border. These points on the map demarcate the general boundaries of his stomping grounds. Quantrill lived and farmed not far from Paola in 1857–1858. He taught school in Stanton in 1859–1860. The guerrilla chieftain lived in Lawrence and then eventually befriended a family of slaveholders in Blue Springs, Missouri, in 1860.

plan came together or whomever it involved, Quantrill might have gotten in too deep to get out.[21]

It is unclear how long Charley Hart knew Charles Ball, C. T. Lipsey, and Ed Morrison before he joined the three jayhawkers on a raid into Missouri. Although the three other men trusted Hart enough to let him ride with them, they did not possess total faith in him. Ball, who spent time in Missouri scouting and preparing for this raid, led this expedition and kept the target of the attack from Hart, at least initially. As the four men rode into Missouri in the early winter of 1860–1861, while South Carolinians debated whether to secede from the Union, Ball, Lipsey, or Morrison might have told Hart parts of the plan. The group targeted a farm owned by wealthy enslaver Morgan Walker to liberate the people he held in bondage, take some horses, steal some money, and kill the man and his sons.[22]

The jayhawkers' mistrust of Hart was well founded. Whether Hart always planned to flip and saw his chance or became repulsed by the murderous actions proposed by his cohort, he decided to slip away from the others to warn the Walker men. The foursome reached the outskirts of the Walker property on December 10, 1860, and began observing the location and movement of the white men and enslaved people on the property. Hart was sent to reconnoiter a part of the Walker farm some distance from the others. After seeing a white man—presumably a member of the family—Hart stepped out of the dark tree line and into the open field.[23]

According to Andrew J. Walker, Quantrill told him a dramatic backstory that explained how he ended up at the farm. Quantrill said that he and his older brother had been attacked by a band of jayhawkers on the Kansas prairie, and that the outlaws had murdered his brother, liberated their Black servant, and stolen their wagon. After these events, Quantrill "made his way to Leavenworth. Here he joined the militia, and became an expert pistol shot, being known to his associates as Charley Hart." As Hart, Quantrill then sought revenge by killing all of his brother's murderers, except for three men. These same three men were now lurking in the Walkers' woods, planning to attack the family home that night. Walker's "natural mistrust of so extraordinary a story was disarmed by the frank manner of the stranger, no less than by the fact that [Walker] could think of no reason, in the range of ordinary possibilities, why he should seek to deceive [him]." According to Walker, after relating the story of his alias, Quantrill told him and his father, "Now take such action as you see fit."[24]

Quantrill's interaction with the Walkers and their neighbors showed him as a master of the confidence game. As the key to his ability to unlock the Walker's trust, Quantrill granted them power over the situation. He could not coerce them; he needed to let them make up their own minds. Consequently, Quantrill left them with a choice. They could seize and lynch him, or they could help him *and* themselves. Through their own free will, the Missourians chose to be agents of vengeance. Quantrill earned the men's confidence, and Morgan Walker, his sons, and his neighbors acted to win Quantrill's confidence.[25]

The fate of Ball, Lipsey, and Morrison offers the best and the bloodiest evidence of Quantrill's skills as a confidence man. All in their early twenties, about Quantrill's age, the three Quaker jayhawkers knew one another through a Christian church outside of Atchison, Kansas, led by the abolitionist preacher Pardee Butler. John Dean, the prominent jayhawker who once imagined that Charley Hart had been hired by the governor of Missouri to kill him, called Ball, Lipsey, and Morrison "Gods noblemen." Dean also remembered, "The party that left Osawatomie for Walkers numbered four men, the three Iowa men above given and Quantrill. I was there at the time on '*business*' and had the confidence and love of those Iowa men." According to Dean, he and Ball "freely talked about Quantrell, his 'fitness' for the work Ball thought he might *do*, and seemed to have more confidence than [Dean] in his frequent declarations that all he wanted was a chance to prove by '*work*' his honesty. [Dean's] counsil to Ball was *caution*." Dean instructed Ball to "give every man his place and duty and see that they kept their place and done their duty . . . with only a very limited measure of confidence in Quantrill, untill he had proved worthy."[26]

If any young men in the territory read and remembered the words of Henry Ward Beecher and the other reformers who instructed them to avoid the confidence man, Ball, Lipsey, and Morrison did. Although they believed in violence and intended to shoot down unarmed slaveholders in the dead of night, they remained Christian young men who likely learned about confidence men. They should have better heeded Beecher, who warned, "Enticers are mean, under the guise of magnanimity." Furthermore, confidence men like Charley Hart were "corrupt, under the appearance of virtue; with a great show of honor, they

[were] base; they cover[ed] a foul and pestilent heart with the show of modest[y]." In their willingness to trust that Hart was the person he said he was, and was a man who shared their righteous politics, they allowed him to join their group. Like an expert confidence man, Quantrill reflected the three jayhawkers' own views, enticed them, and earned their confidence. Under false pretenses, as the four men stood on Morgan Walker's porch on the night of December 10 and faced double-barreled shotguns blasting all around them, perhaps the men remembered one of Beecher's warnings: "If by any of these you are enticed to ruin, you will have to bear it ALONE!"[27]

In reality, Beecher would not have admonished these trusting jayhawkers. Directly or indirectly, he encouraged them to go to the Kansas Territory, helped send them there, and put guns in their hands. Along the way, Beecher and his ilk encouraged the type of subterfuge they had railed against a decade earlier. They sent settlers as warriors in disguise, shipped guns as Bibles, and had Underground Railroad stations in their houses. Nothing was what it seemed, but these subterfuges were acceptable because they served a good cause. Both the men and women funded by the New England Emigrant Aid Company and Quakers like Ball, Lipsey, and Morrison served as the Lord's own confidence men, their violence cloaked in piety and their piety cloaked in violence. Beecher did not account for Quantrill, though; no one saw him coming.[28]

For Missourians increasingly duped by mask-wearing slaves and deceptive abolitionists, a man like Quantrill was exactly what was needed to combat invisible enemies hidden behind white and Black masks. Although they never learned everything about Quantrill's past, Missourians embraced him, the lies he told, the masks he wore, and his previous acts of backstabbing; they saw value in his ability to trick and honor in his deception.[29]

After betraying the jayhawkers, Quantrill found a home with the Walkers. Andrew Walker described the events immediately after his family waylaid Quantrill's jayhawking companions: "We got to bed toward midnight, Quantrill with us, but I'm afraid we didn't sleep much. . . . Undressing there in the lamplight, all interest seemed to center in our mysterious new friend." Walker observed, "[Quantrill] was a very quiet man, but he answered our questions good-naturedly, and appeared to be well educated." In addition, the guerrilla "carried a sort of self-reliant, commanding look, and appeared to be strong physically."

Walker added, "He was twenty-four years old, he said, just a few weeks older than I."[30]

The next morning, Andy Walker took Quantrill for a ride around the property and showed him the family's lands, timber, creeks, and prairies while pointing out "the negro cabins, the stable, barn, shop, and smokehouse." Later the sheriff showed up and hauled Quantrill to Independence for questioning. After a hearing the next day, the sheriff discharged Quantrill, and Walker took him back to the lodging house. In the meantime, a crowd gathered with the intention of stringing up this stranger. Its members apparently only knew half of what happened and presumed that Quantrill was an enemy. However, before they could do anything, Andy Walker rode up on his big thoroughbred, "spurred among them and yelled out, 'I'll kill the first man that puts hands on him.'" "I succeeded in quieting a similar and even more determined mob around the corner near the hotel where I had left Quantrill," Walker recalled. The streets clear, Quantrill hopped up on Morgan Walker's buggy, and with Andy riding beside them, the men traveled back to the farm.[31]

The trust and friendship offered by the Walker men goes a long way toward explaining why Quantrill ended up with them when the Civil War broke out. The strength of this bond cannot be overemphasized. Up until this point in his life, Quantrill had roamed across the country and bounced between settlements and the wilderness. By late 1860, he felt adrift. His proslavery politics now differed from those of the folks he was raised alongside and many of the people he lived beside in Kansas. Quantrill was an alien, at least until he walked out of the trees and told the Walker men his tale. The Walkers appeared to touch Quantrill's heart when Morgan believed him and took him in, and when Andy befriended him and protected him from the angry mob in Independence. Something about these interactions made Quantrill feel that this place was like home.

After Quantrill returned with the Walker men to the farm, a slave from a neighboring farm located the surviving jayhawkers in the brush. Quantrill then accompanied the Walkers to the place in the woods where the Kansans were hiding out, and he watched as the Missourians surrounded and killed his old companions. After staying with the Walkers for "about two weeks after the shooting, Quantrill [then] went with Marcus Gill to Texas" to help Gill move some of his enslaved people deeper into the South. When Quantrill left, Walker lamented, "We had learned to like him, and rather hated to see him go. Father made him a present of his fine saddle horse, bridle and saddle, and $100 in money, and I gave him a suit of clothes."[32]

In the winter of 1860–1861, Quantrill trotted off to Texas as a new man. Assuming identities from the stranger taking the ferry into Lawrence to a turncoat walking into the lives of the Missourians to the rider of a fine saddle horse headed South, he was an ever-shifting, freshly dandified rogue. Like Stone's register, Quantrill's identity changed with the turn of a page, or, to use the metaphor the young Quantrill preferred, the turning over of a new leaf. This stage of his life, more than any other, demonstrated that he felt the invisible boundaries of mainstream culture and learned to wriggle through the cracks that were unseen by most nineteenth-century men. He donned several costumes that each served a purpose and changed them when they no longer suited him. As he left Missouri and rode southward, it seemed that Quantrill's career as an undercover detective had run its course and the most mysterious chapter of his life had ended.[33]

CHAPTER 9: *Overseer*

With the reins of his fine new saddle horse in one hand and a whip in the other, Quantrill helped Marcus Gill move his enslaved property from Missouri to Texas. Although the whip is not mentioned in any documents, it or another tool of discipline must have been a part of Quantrill's gear. Whether it was a cat-o'-nine-tails, a flail, a long bull-whip, a rod, a cane, a staff, a club, a truncheon, or a cudgel, Gill gave Quantrill something to keep his slaves in line and on the move. Any white man who found himself disciplining or driving slaves carried a weapon. With clotted blood specks at its end, it was not simply a tool for maintaining supremacy over enslaved Black people; it was a symbol of racial hierarchy in nineteenth-century America. When Quantrill took the whip, he confirmed his allegiance to slaveholding Missourians and proclaimed his beliefs in favor of slavery and the superiority of the white race without saying a word.[1]

Although Quantrill's status as an overseer was temporary, limited to moving Gill's slaves to Texas, he joined a segment of white labor that managed the plantations of the South. How many overseers there were from year to year is unknown. Some very large plantations probably had multiple managers, overseers, suboverseers, or agents, but smaller plantations did not necessarily hire a full-time overseer. One scholar calculates that 37,883 men were hired to oversee slaves on the 46,000 plantations across the slave states in 1860. These white men were paid employees and were vulnerable to the same exploitation as other wage laborers in the nineteenth century. As dependent workers, they were men of a second class, and the economics of slaveholding gave planters little incentive to pay these men a penny more than they had to. Overseers rarely advanced beyond their class or became able to own land or slaves.[2]

However many there were or how much they were paid, overseers were the middle managers of the slave system. In the eighteenth and nineteenth centuries these figures were known not just as overseers but also as agents and managers. As these titles suggest, they were a part of a business operation, their place being between the enslaved laborers and the planters. Overseers organized the day-to-day operations of the plantation, enforced discipline, and acted as the planters' men on the ground. Overseers also held different levels of authority. Some planters entrusted them with huge operations requiring them to manage hundreds of people and huge swaths of land, and to cultivate thousands of dollars' worth of cash crops. Other planters used their overseers more as brutes, figures who intimidated, beat, and otherwise pushed gangs of slaves through their daily labor to achieve the highest possible output. For many slaves, the overseer was the very embodiment of slavery's brutality.[3]

The whip in Quantrill's hand pulled him deep into the world of slaveholding. In early 1861, Gill owned eighteen slaves, but ten had run away, likely across the border into the Kansas Territory. Those who remained to travel to Texas included a twenty-five-year-old woman, a twenty-one-year-old man, a sixteen-year-old girl, a thirteen-year-old boy, a twelve-year-old girl, an eight-year-old boy, a two-year-old girl, and a one-year-old boy—all nameless, partially masked by the 1860 Slave Schedule. Some of Gill's younger slaves were listed in the census with the letter *M* in the box denoting skin color, thus indicating they were mulatto. Their father was probably a white man, maybe even Gill himself. When the war broke out a few months later, Quantrill was well acquainted with the brutality and barbarism of slavery that he chose to protect.[4]

After Quantrill helped move Gill's property to Texas, he disappeared from the historical record again for much of the year. During this moment of silence in Quantrill's record the nation experienced the uproar of the secession crisis. South Carolina left the Union on December 20, and the rest of the Deep South followed shortly afterward. Quantrill was likely in Texas when that state left the Union on February 1, 1861, but he did not stay there long. He made his way back north toward the borderland and directly into the winds of the approaching war. Quantrill returned to his old haunt around Paola perhaps to collect unattended belongings or perform a mysterious task.[5]

120   CHAPTER NINE

Quantrill made his way to the safe harbor of the Benning family homestead in March 1861. After discovering Quantrill's location, a few jayhawkers decided to avenge the death of their comrades at the Walker place and contrived a horse-thieving complaint. A sympathetic judge swore the jayhawkers in as a posse comitatus, and with a warrant in hand they rode to the Benning place, besieged it, captured Quantrill without a fight, and took him to Paola by way of Stanton. A group of friends and sympathizers, including W. L. Potter, came to Quantrill's aid. Potter rounded up attorneys who pleaded Quantrill's case before Judge Thomas Roberts. In the Kansas Territory, the law and sectional tensions were tied together, with many suits revealing the tension between the institution of the law and the extremist politics pulling at its foundations.[6]

In this instance, however, the law prevailed over political influence. "I saw him [Quantrill] in the early summer of 1861[,] he was confined in the county jail of Miami County (then Lykins Co.) Kansas," remembered Roberts, who "was then acting as Probate Judge of said county." The judge was familiar with Quantrill, who as a young schoolmaster had boarded with Roberts's family during the previous year's school term. The jayhawkers could not establish that Quantrill had committed a crime. As Roberts recalled, "He was taken out and brought before me on a Writ of Habeas Corpus and . . . was released from custody their [sic] being no legal cause for his confinement."[7]

At that point, news of the war was in the air. Quantrill heard that thousands of South Carolina militiamen had fired their cannon at a U.S. fortress in the middle of Charleston Harbor as he rode down the Santa Fe Trail. He further learned that Lincoln had called for seventy-five thousand militiamen to come to the defense of their nation and put down this rebellion. Before reckoning with that news, though, he was informed that Virginia, North Carolina, Tennessee, and Arkansas were following their fellow slaveholding states out of the nation.[8]

Reaching the Indian nations, Quantrill looked to see which way the wind was blowing. Legend says that during the spring and summer of 1861, he stayed with Joel B. Mayes, a young, well-educated man from a prominent family. The Cherokee was a few years older than Quantrill, and when he enlisted in the Confederate military, Quantrill likely entered service with him. "Quantrill joined the company of Joel Mayes, the Cherokee chief," recalled Andrew Walker, who likely based his information on the story he heard from Quantrill.[9]

Quantrill and Mayes fought at Wilson's Creek on August 10, 1861. Union general Nathaniel Lyon, a terror to secessionist Missourians, was killed in this first major battle west of the Mississippi. The fighting occurred a few miles outside the town of Springfield, Missouri, and it featured back-and-forth charges and countercharges, miscommunications, and misidentifications. In an effort to stem the tide, Lyon led a charge against southern lines; Confederates shot him during the action, and he became the first martyred hero for the Union. After Lyon's death, Union forces retreated, leaving the field to the Confederates and giving them a significant victory. During the engagement, "Quantrill's horse was shot under him." After the battle ended, Quantrill fell ill and "was left at a farm house to recover."[10]

Like Quantrill, other men who became prominent guerrillas began the war in the Confederate army or the Missouri State Guard (MSG). Frank James joined the MSG and fought at Wilson's Creek. Andrew Walker also enlisted in the MSG, but not in time to participate in that battle. Rather, he was a part of the thousands of men who reinforced the guardsmen in their siege at Lexington in September 1861. George Todd, who became an important guerrilla leader, was with the MSG early in the war. It is likely that quite a few lesser-known guerrillas answered the call of Missouri governor Claiborne Fox Jackson and volunteered to serve the Confederate cause.

Participation in the formal Confederate armies suggests that these men originally wanted to fight as uniformed soldiers. When they heard about Fort Sumter and Lincoln's call for troops, Quantrill, Walker, Todd, James, and many others did not immediately throw on guerrilla shirts, grab pistols, hop on horses, and ride into the bush. Rather, like boys and other young men across the South, they envisioned a romanticized version of linear warfare. They pictured themselves campaigning as a part of a large army, marching in columns, standing shoulder to shoulder with their comrades in the face of the enemy musket fire, and charging headlong with bayonets fixed.[11]

Historians of the guerrilla war tend to present partisan warfare as the first and only option for the men who became bushwhackers in Missouri. Michael Fellman suggests that young men in Missouri were champing at the bit to go bushwhacking. When the North and South took up arms against each other, these Missourians went straight into the brush and used the war as an excuse to plunder and kill their neighbors. In *A Savage Conflict*, Daniel Sutherland demonstrates that the desire to fight as guerrillas from the war's outset reached well beyond Missouri. He contends that in 1860 and 1861, a great many southerners preferred guerrilla warfare to a more linear form of fighting. It was, according to Sutherland, the most appealing form of action for men who grew up with stories of "Light Horse Harry" Lee and Francis Marion defeating the British in the American Revolution.[12]

However, in western Missouri, it took vast strategic shifts for the local population to turn to guerrilla warfare. The Confederate army that emerged victorious at Wilson's Creek broke up because of a dispute between the commanding officers, Missourian Sterling Price and Arkansan Ben McCulloch, about strategy and supplies. The Missourians marched north to Lexington, besieged the prominent river town, and won a victory there. The Texans, Native Americans, and Arkansans led by McCulloch retreated into Arkansas to regroup. However, Price and his men soon marched back down to southwest Missouri. Price seemed to lack the gumption to either travel down the valley to St. Louis, or to stay and take crops and livestock from his fellow Missourians in order to feed his army and keep its soldiers in the area.[13]

There was a lull in the operations of the formal Federal and Confederate armies until Henry Halleck and Samuel Curtis initiated a winter campaign against Sterling Price in February 1862. They drove the MSG into northwestern Arkansas, where they were united with McCulloch's Arkansans and Texans under the command of General Earl Van Dorn. On March 7 and 8, Curtis's U.S. Army of the Southwest defeated the Confederates. The battle effectively drove formal rebel forces from the state for the rest of the war.[14]

Abandoned by the Confederacy in the fall of 1861, the southern sympathizers of Jackson County and the rest of Little Dixie, Missouri, were left to their own defense. After the "army marched away," Walker remembered, "Quantrill got well he returned to us." Quantrill was pulled back to Blue Springs by his bond with the Walker men. Upon his return, he likely returned to his role as a hired hand, helping out on the farm where he could. Many of the efforts on the farm concerned dealing with the evolving wartime situation. Andy Walker, Quantrill, and the other white men likely moved livestock and slaves here and there, hiding them from U.S. troops and jayhawkers. In addition, the men at the Walker farm were constantly on the lookout for patrols and raiding parties. At some point, Andy Walker formed a neighborhood patrol that included Quantrill and other hired men from Blue Springs, and this patrol became the basis for Quantrill's guerrilla band. Much of Quantrill's experience in the war—where he fought, whom he fought with, and how he fought—can be explained by the simple concept of friendship. Just as homosocial bonds buoyed him in the 1850s, they propelled him during the Civil War. Quantrill went to war for his friends.[15]

Through these men, Quantrill developed bonds with slaveholding and proslavery households across western Missouri. Later, when insurgent warfare became the dominant mode of fighting along the border, women on these farms provided Quantrill and his men with nearly all of their supplies. The mothers, sisters, cousins, and sweethearts of the men in the brush produced food, both hot meals eaten at their own tables and cold baskets of food carried away into the guerrilla camps in the timber bottoms. They made much of the clothing the guerrillas wore, from socks and pants to the iconic guerrilla shirts. The women who manned the insurgent supply line also cared for horses, gathered and passed along information, stored gunpowder and percussion caps, nursed wounded bushwhackers, and helped to bury the dead. They were the logistical branch of the guerrilla war effort, and in that capacity they were as much guerrillas as Quantrill and his men.[16]

Warfare grounded so firmly on the household was an outgrowth of southerners' worldview. The household was the central social, cultural, and economic institution in the antebellum South. It was the site of production and reproduction, and all people and things emanated from it. When men across the South marched to war, they did so with clothes on their backs and food in their bellies and their packs, all of which was made by their kinswomen. In areas far removed from the battlefront, households continued to generate wartime supplies indirectly and supplies often followed convoluted and circuitous paths to the front. However, in western Missouri, the war was fought around and inside these households, allowing them to provide direct support for their men.[17]

Quantrill's reliance on the household was an efficient alternative to the wasteful logistics of large Confederate armies. At his peak strength, Quantrill led somewhere between 250 and 400 guerrillas—a much smaller outfit than a single regiment at full strength. The southern community of western Missouri was better prepared to sustain a fighting force of this size over the course of the war. Whereas Price's army, with more than twenty thousand men camped outside Lexington, put undue stress on local farmers, the guerrilla war effort did not overextend the resources of sympathizers. Rather, farms supporting the guerrillas were providing for roughly the same number of people as they had before the war. Anywhere Price's MSG or another Confederate army campaigned in Missouri, soldiers emptied corncribs and smokehouses, drank up all the clean water, and even took shoes, socks, pants, shirts, and coats from the local populace.

Fighting close to their homes allowed the guerrillas to protect their households. Certainly this meant defending their womenfolk, whom they imagined perched on a pedestal, but it also meant defending their slaves. A slaveholding community absent of young men was vulnerable. Slaves in western Missouri started to run away at higher rates when the troubles in the Kansas Territory began, and when the war broke out, the impulse to flee grew stronger among Black men and women. Furthermore, fear of a slave revolt grew, with Black men rising up with the help of jayhawkers and the U.S. Army to kill their owners and free themselves. The presence of mounted and armed young men might deter some enslaved people from taking flight and would almost certainly eliminate the possibility of an armed rebellion. After serving as an overseer for Gill and helping to move his property to Texas, Quantrill understood these priorities and kept them in mind as the war in western Missouri evolved.[18]

Warrior

1861–1862

CHAPTER 10: *Killer*

"Kill 'em all, Andy!" Mary Stone's cry cut through the pounding of horse hooves and the whooshing of air and came to the riders like an order from a general shouted over the din of battle. Andrew Walker, the leader of the neighborhood patrol for Blue Springs, Missouri, in the fall of 1861, glanced back to see Stone shaken, enraged, and pointing a finger toward the Thompson farm. It was there that a band of Union troopers headed after they had pillaged her house and beaten her with a pistol. Walker had formed a group of eleven men, including William Clarke Quantrill, to deal with unruly abolitionists and their allies in the U.S. Army who were raiding the farms of slaveholders. In less than a minute the patrollers fell on their prey. The ensuing pistol fire, sporadic and inaccurate, threw shot around the farm, adding a new dimension of chaos to the bedlam already underway. The Union soldiers ran this way and that, most getting to their horses and riding into the woods. When the gunfire gave way to relative silence, the patrol took measure of the day's deeds and found one Union trooper lying dead—apparently the man who had abused Mary Stone.[1]

Quantrill signed his name to the death of this man, branding himself a killer. In the wake of the shoot-out at the Thompson farm, the U.S. authorities occupying Jackson County arrested Strawder Stone and William Thompson with the intention of executing them for the murder of the fallen trooper. To protect these men, Quantrill went to the justice of the peace and swore to killing the soldier, then endorsed his admission and had a boy deliver it to the U.S. commander. Walker, Quantrill's closest friend at the time, warned against this act of sacrifice, predicting that the U.S. Army would come after him. Walker could not foresee, though, that his friend would slip and duck Union patrols over the coming days and weeks. In so doing, Quantrill became something of a living martyr and a beacon for the southern resistance in western Missouri. Young white men, sons of slaveholders and southern sympathizers, went into the brush to fight and to join this apparently selfless, avenging killer, beginning the most widespread guerrilla movement of the war.[2]

Quantrill's status as a killer propelled his rise to infamy. By taking a life in this skirmish, he demonstrated to his friends—all mostly untested men—that he was up to the challenge. There were very few times during the Civil War when the killing of an individual so marked a man. It was no coincidence that the first guerrilla to kill the enemy became the leader of the bushwhacker community in western Missouri.

Quantrill's biographers agree so rarely, but on this point—that he was a prolific assassin—they are in general accord. Perhaps such a consensus should be a relief, but such an unnatural alliance triggers a deep, gut-level suspicion. The long tally of kills that Edwards and Connelley attributed to Quantrill serves both biographers' arguments. They used the stack of bodies as a malleable heap of evidence. For Edwards, the kills proved Quantrill's virtue and honor; for Connelley they confirmed the guerrilla's innate depravity. In other words, Edwards and Connelley did not care so much about killing. They just used it as another avenue for pushing their assertions about Quantrill and the war.[3]

Although they tend to agree that Quantrill walked through life ankle-deep in gore, biographers argue about the moment when he first killed. Assertions, insinuations, and rumors depict Quantrill killing long before he took the life of the Union soldier at the Thompson place. Connelley contended that his subject demonstrated the character of a psychotic murderer at a young age. According to Connelley, "He [Quantrill] had few friends, for there was little in common between him and other boys his age. . . . [He] maimed domestic animals for amusement." The biographer further claimed that Quantrill "would often nail a snake to a tree and let it remain in torture until it died. . . . He would stick a knife into a cow by the roadside, or stab a horse. He often tortured dogs and cats to enjoy their cries of distress." Connelley's evidence for *all* of these claims comes from an interview that Quantrill's boyhood friend W. W. Scott gave the *Morning Herald* of Joplin, Missouri. Scott was quoted as saying that he saw Quantrill shoot a pig through its ear "and then he would laugh immoderately at its antics."[4]

Well before the early twentieth century, when Connelley made these allegations, society believed that a child who abused animals became a depraved adult. Among the more vivid pieces of evidence for this observation are William Hogarth's 1751 woodcuts *The Four Stages of Cruelty*. The first stage offers a scene of animal abuse by boys: a rooster being shot, cats being tied and tortured, and a dog being assaulted with a hot poker stabbed in its rectum by a boy named Tom Nero. The next stage shows Nero beating a horse. The third stage bears witness to Nero turning his violence on a person—his pregnant lover. Finally, in the fourth scene, the state turns violent toward Nero, as he is executed for the crime of murder, after which his body is dissected in public. Knowing that this trajectory of violence—from the abuse of small animals, to that of larger animals, and eventually of people—was a commonly held belief, Connelley sought to brand Quantrill as twisted, someone who as a child shot a farm animal for a chuckle.[5]

Quantrill did shoot a pig's ear—two, in fact. Although Connelley probably did not realize it, Scott gave several interviews similar to the aforementioned one in the *Morning Herald*. Scott told the *Louisville Courier-Journal* that, "at fourteen years [of age] while hunting along the Tuscarawas river lowlands, west of the town, [Quantrill] demonstrated his marksmanship by boring a hole through each of the ears of a pig with a rifle bullet at a distance of over 250 yards." He did not retell the story to highlight Quantrill's malice, but to show his skill with a rifle. In antebellum America, men demonstrated shooting prowess by hitting the body part of an animal placed at some assigned distance. In a shooting contest, a commonly known part of an animal's anatomy, like a pig's ear, served as a mark in the absence of a standardized paper target—shootists aimed at a bull's eye rather than a bullseye. It was likely that the pig in Scott's story about Quantrill had already met the butcher, and that its removed ears served as targets. The winner of the shooting contest probably received the ears as proof of the deed and a part of the pig as a prize. With all this in mind, it is likely that the Joplin *Morning Herald* misquoted Scott or Connelley embellished the tale.[6]

A few pages after his claims about Quantrill's childhood animal abuse, Connelley asserted that Quantrill fulfilled his destiny as a murderer in Mendota, Illinois, during his brief stay in 1855. The guerrilla's actions there explained his departure. To support his argument, Connelley cites a note written on a slip of paper bearing the letterhead of one S. S. Scott, the owner of Scott Fountain Pen Company in

Chicago, Illinois. This message, which is otherwise anonymous, asks whether Quantrill "shot & killed a man whom he said knocked him down with the intention of robbing him" in Mendota or in Ottawa, Illinois. This question, lacking context and an answer, is far from conclusive evidence. It leaves room for a panorama of conjecture, especially when considering that the slip of paper is not addressed to anyone or signed.[7]

Presuming he did not gun down a robber in self-defense in northwest Illinois, Quantrill's first kill possibly came on the Kansas plains. Edwards, who added his typical Lost Cause flourish to the story, took Quantrill's own assertion that he was avenging a murdered brother to the extreme. According to Edwards, after Quantrill made his way into the good graces of the jayhawkers, he made an unnamed comrade his first victim. As Edwards told it, Quantrill went to meet a "wagon load of negroes" with three other men, but "one of the three men failed to return. . . . Nor could any account be given of his absence until a body was found near a creek several days afterward. In the centre of the forehead was the round, smooth hole of a navy revolver bullet." Then Jack Winn got it. Edwards said that Winn "had been shot just inside the fence of a cornfield . . . There was the same round hole in the forehead." The biographer also claimed that the killings happened in the same way, one after another, a single bullet in each head, until Quantrill left his gruesome mark on two dozen men. In this telling, the pattern became evident because of the identical bullet holes—the killer's signature—leading Edwards to exclaim, "Somebody's hand-writing was becoming to be legible!"[8]

Edwards could spin a yarn. It is fanciful to imagine any man infiltrating a group of vigilant killers like a band of jayhawkers and taking them out one at a time without raising an eyebrow, but Edwards thought he could convince his readers. If someone read this passage of *Noted Guerrillas* and nodded along affirmatively, either they already believed that Quantrill was a mythical killer, or they wanted to be taken for a ride.

Quantrill could dangle a story as well, and in his tale he was heroic, a man wrapped in vengeance. After he sold out his comrades at the Walker place, he told the Missourians that he had been traveling to Pikes Peak from his home state of Maryland with his brother and a Black "servant boy." Quantrill said that jayhawkers had ambushed them, killed his brother, and taken the "servant," wagon, and horses.

They had left Quantrill wounded and stranded in an unfamiliar land until Golightly Spybuck found him next to a creek and took him back to his shelter, where he and his wife nursed him back to health. After recovering, Quantrill had infiltrated the band of jayhawkers responsible for his brother's death and killed them one at a time until only a few were left.[9]

While it seems likely that Spybuck did exist and came to Quantrill's aid in some way or another, the guerrilla constructed other parts of the tale to ingratiate himself with the Missourians. Jayhawkers did not attack him, but Indians did. He was not from the slave state of Maryland, but rather the free state of Ohio. He did not own any "servants," but he knew the feelings of the Missourians on the matter of slavery. The raiders gravely, and perhaps mortally, wounded his companion, but Quantrill did not have an older brother, let alone one who had traveled with him in Kansas.[10]

Despite the discrepancies, Quantrill's story cannot be tossed out completely. It is bursting with the themes that he found important, and it offers a window through which to view his motivations. First, the attack created a lingering trauma, compounding what occurred had in the mountains. Maybe he subconsciously conflated his disdain for the people of Lawrence with the attack, or through some twisted logic blamed the abolitionists for his friend's fate. Quantrill continually pointed to this event as the origin of his angst with the Kansans. Second, the attackers did injure or kill the unnamed man with whom he was close. If Quantrill thought of the man as kin, he was not the first man to elevate kith to kinsman after sharing an intense experience.

In addition, Quantrill told a tale of revenge. His story echoes a theme alive in the popular imagination of nineteenth-century men, especially in the South. Revenge appears in some of the most popular stories published in the decades preceding the Civil War. Quantrill was almost certainly familiar with the writing of Edgar Allan Poe, Alexandre Dumas, and Sir Walter Scott. *The Cask of Amontillado* and *The Count of Monte Cristo* offer tales of revenge, while *Ivanhoe* is rife with the language of honor-bound vengeance. Each author tapped into compelling and ancient desires for power and righteousness that remained bound up inside men of this era. Although there is some debate in these works over the legitimacy of revenge, all are sympathetic to the vengeful man. Folktales, too, provide a distinctly American face for revenge. One such tale that swirled around campfires and hearths from the Pacific to the banks of the Missouri as it cut through Little Dixie was the story of Hugh Glass, a hunter and mountain man living in the West. Glass was left for dead by his companions after he suffered life-threatening wounds in a grizzly attack, but he survived and tracked his betrayers over hundreds of miles of wilderness. His true story quickly took on mythic proportions. Quantrill and his fellow travelers across the snowy Rockies knew of Glass and dozens of other men who lived and died in mythical ways.[11]

After Quantrill told Morgan Walker and his boys his story of vengeance, they used powder, ball, and fulminate to help write the conclusion. Morgan and Andrew Walker inserted themselves into the script at this critical moment and helped provide an end to Quantrill's tale. By extension, the Walkers' participation in the shoot-out at the very end of this story loaned credibility to the entirety of the narrative Quantrill created.[12]

After the incident at the Walker farm, the Missourians accepted the embodiment of a revenge tale in their ranks. They needed such men by the end of 1860. For years, the border war between the abolitionists who settled in the Kansas Territory and the proslavery Missourians heated up, and it finally reached a nearly combustible temperature. At any point, the periodic raids from jayhawkers and the retributive violence from southerners could explode and engulf the region in open warfare. Walker observed, "[During this period] it was hard to resist joining one's angry neighbors in visiting retribution on these meddlesome and blood-thirsty Yankees . . . whose zeal promptly manifested itself in stealing and driving off our slaves." Indeed, "each succeeding act of outlawry was as coals added to consuming fires of hatred" that "burned on both sides of the line." When Quantrill entered this cauldron of hate, the Missourians needed men already tempered and hardened by fire, men capable of enduring the flames of war that were certain to come.[13]

Quantrill's earliest documented killing took place at the Thompson farm in 1861. None of the other claims about killing, whether his own or his biographers', can be corroborated. There is not a single piece of evidence of Quantrill taking a life before the Civil War. He was a killer, and he wanted to be seen as a killer, but he only made his bones in the context of the war.

Quantrill knew something about killing in wartime: the act was imprinted on both the killed and the killer, the dead and the deadly. Beginning with his kill at the Thompson place, Quantrill complemented his bloody deeds with words to assign some meaning to the moment. With these few words scrawled on slips of paper or uttered to his compatriots as a starting point—a Rosetta Stone of sorts—it is possible to translate these actions and read them as a sort of text. In a type of warfare that was almost wholly unwritten on one side and mostly absent of traditional battlefield symbols like flags, acts of killing become a form of language. Each instance in which a man was gunned down or strung up offers an opportunity to decipher the strange linguistics of blood and suffering. In studying these violent acts performed with intention, a metanarrative materializes, and a story unfolds like a note with a few grim lines undersigned W. C. Q.[14]

Word of the mysterious, avenging stranger who killed a Union trooper and then swore to it in writing spread from neighborhood to neighborhood. It was not long before "young men of the neighborhood began joining [Quantrill]." Whether they came early or later—whether like William H. Gregg, who joined Quantrill on Christmas Day 1861, or like Cole Younger and John McCorkle, who came out to the brush at different times in 1862—the men who flocked to Quantrill stated their motivation as vengeance. A desire to redress grievances pulled these men away from the formal southern armies and pushed them to wage their own private wars in the brush, where they sought "the comradeship of the bushwhackers." "Quantrill's career as a great guerrilla chief began" once he had enough recruits and started "bushwhacking the Federals," providing "the only effective resistance possible, to the domineering of the troops and villainies of the Red-legs."[15]

Quantrill's followers wanted to kill Union troopers and make names for themselves, but becoming a killer was not an easy task. One of the first Union reports to mention the activities of Quantrill and his guerrillas describes some successes against them. Union captain William S. Oliver of the Seventh Missouri Volunteers claimed that his men were able to kill six members of Quantrill's band over two days of ambushes and skirmishing. However, without giving details of the events, Oliver reported "1 man killed and 2 wounded during the expedition referred to." As U.S. troops attacked them, the guerrillas killed their enemies and *became* killers, becoming new men. One at a time, they left their mark on the war and were marked by it. Eventually, they would all become killers, be killed themselves, or both.[16]

CHAPTER TEN

Under Quantrill's command, killing was not limited to vengeance against U.S. troopers; it was also used to enforce wartime law within the southern community. Quantrill invoked draconian punishments early in the war for anyone who attacked southern sympathizers. In response to reports that one or more horse thieves were operating in the area, he tasked his men with tracking down the culprits. After a brief investigation, Quantrill learned that Searcy, a Confederate deserter, was the rustler in question. In January 1862, the guerrillas found Searcy's corral hidden beside the Missouri River and placed him under arrest. After discussing it with his men, Quantrill decided to hang Searcy and return the horses to their owners. Like a Colt Navy, a hemp rope could be used to give Quantrill's leadership legitimate authority within the southern community of western Missouri.[17]

Furthermore, being a killer helped Quantrill establish a code of discipline among the guerrillas. The Searcy hanging made evident his willingness to use capital punishment against anyone, even southerners, who hurt the cause. As a case in point, Quantrill threatened Bill Anderson with death in an attempt to keep him in line. Anderson and a few others "had been stealing horses from Missourians . . . and operating along the Kansas line and near Little Santa Fe." As their horse thieving, maybe directed at Unionists, made the guerrillas look bad, "Quantrill warned them to not steal anything more where he could get hold of them if they valued their lives." The initial warning did not take, for in the fall of 1862 Anderson faced similar accusations. Quantrill then ordered William H. Gregg to bring Anderson and his men into his camp. There, after disarming the thieves and taking their mounts, "Quantrill told Anderson in short and sharp words that if he ever stole again and he could get hands on him he would hang him and his men to the first tree he came to that would bear their weight. And he sent them afoot and unarmed from camp." Until their falling-out in 1864, Anderson heeded Quantrill's words.[18]

This code extended to the act of killing itself. Although the scope of violence broadened over the course of the guerrilla war, as it did across the Civil War landscape at large, little evidence indicates that Quantrill or his men murdered indiscriminately in the fall of 1861. To the contrary, restraint reigned. In the first months of the war, Gregg recalled that "Quantrill and his men did little more than stand the enemy off after [he] joined the command until spring, during which time [they] captured many of the enemy whom [they] universally paroled. Quantrill and his men were vying with each other who should be most magnanimous toward prisoners." In the beginning, killing was guided by the tenets of chivalry: only armed enemy men were shot down, unarmed combatants were shown mercy unless they perpetrated some crime, and noncombatants were left alone, especially women and children.[19]

Early in the war, this growing band of guerrillas wanted to leave its mark on Kansas. On March 7, 1862, the men dashed into the small settlement of Aubry, south of Kansas City and just over the border. Although the raiders seemed prepared to spare all of the residents and focus on plunder, they faced a bit of resistance at a tavern. Union lieutenant Reuben A. Randlett, who was on leave and sleeping upstairs in the tavern, claimed that he and his fellow boarders awoke and realized they were surrounded. The guerrillas killed three men on the first floor who possibly defended themselves with arms or ignored the outlaws' demands and made a run for it. During the ruckus, Quantrill caught sight of a figure peering furtively out of one of the tavern's second-story windows. Perhaps suspecting that the man was involved in the shooting in the building and looking to take a shot at the guerrillas outside, Quantrill unholstered a Colt revolver and shot the man through the windowpane. As a result, the guerrillas gunned down four men in the raid.[20]

Realizing he could not resist the guerrillas, Randlett dressed, walked downstairs, and formally surrendered. The guerrillas then took him captive and interviewed him. While speaking to Randlett, Quantrill looked across the room, saw a man with his face covered in blood, and recognized him as his old acquaintance Abraham Ellis. Ellis, a school inspector from Ohio before the war, knew Quantrill's father and had met Bill after both men moved to the Kansas Territory. As the superintendent of schools for Miami County, Kansas Territory, Ellis had visited Quantrill's schoolhouse in Stanton to observe his teaching and certify him. After Ellis had watched Quantrill teach, he shared the young man's bed. Now one man had a bullet lodged in his head, and that bullet had been fired by the other man. It made little difference to Quantrill that Ellis was serving in the U.S. Army as a quartermaster. He was a friend.[21]

Abraham "Bullet Hole" Ellis lived for another twenty-seven years after Quantrill's bullet crashed into his forehead, longer than many of the men who participated in the war on either side. But the hole in Ellis's forehead marked him as an exception. Despite their friendly interaction, Quantrill pulled his gun with the intent of killing the man he saw in the window. His prowess within the guerrilla band depended on his ability to hit the target. Quantrill knew better than anyone that killing was a test of manhood. Perhaps his years in the West taught him that a warped kind of power came with *being* a killer, especially in wartime when society needed killers; in war, *real men* killed. Only as a killer could Quantrill hope to lead the loose band of men—fellow killers and wannabes alike—who gathered around him in those first months and followed him through the early years of the war.[22]

CHAPTER 11: *Captain*

In his capacity as a guerrilla captain, Quantrill did not fly a black flag—not a *real* one. After the war, a few partisans insisted that both sides carried actual black flags. In their memoirs, former guerrillas depicted the sable banners as a physical symbol of a no-quarter policy. Any warriors—bushwhackers or U.S. troopers—who rode into battle under such a flag would not take enemy combatants as prisoners. There is no material evidence or reliable postwar testimony to suggest that either side in fact charged into battle waving a black flag. Yet these fictive artifacts pop up often enough, and guerrillas' insistence on their reality reveals the mindset of these veterans. Not just fibbing or embellishing their memories, these old men wanted their readers to know that these no-quarter policies were real, that their experience as fighters differed from that of other Civil War veterans, and that death constantly loomed over them.[1]

Historians, even those most skeptical of veterans' romantic embellishments, describe the guerrilla conflict in terms that echo sanguineous language of former bushwhackers. In *Inside War*, Michael Fellman asserts that Civil War combat was a cyclone of chaos in which violence was boundless. Almost as soon as the fighting began, neighbor attacked neighbor, and communities collapsed in on themselves. Men killed, overkilled, and mutilated their enemies, but they often targeted noncombatants and even their own people. Other scholars have built on Fellman's compellingly dark vision of the Civil War, using it to explain other guerrilla theaters across the South, and even projecting it onto the partisan war writ large.[2]

Both postwar talk of the black flag by veterans and historical depictions of unfettered violence have cast a shadow over the nuanced and surprising ways in which killing evolved through the early years of the guerrilla war. By examining the written documents and reading the performances of Quantrill and his men as texts, it is evident that his and the guerrillas' collective ideas about killing evolved incrementally. Guerrillas did not spring from the womb fully formed as brutal monsters. Rather, they learned how to kill. Not only was there a process to men becoming killers, but the way in which men killed also changed over time from the beginning of the war to the end. Thus the act of killing should be read historically. Whether a shocking assassination, a word whispered into a dying man's ear, blood streaming from a hole in a man's head, or "QUANTRELL" sewn in white letters across a black flag, every recorded act, word, and memory can be translated and pieced together into something that we can comprehend, if not condone.[3]

Although many of the guerrillas and their enemies were already experienced killers, the act of killing in Civil War Missouri began a dramatic transformation after Union general Henry Halleck wrote and published his no-quarter directive on March 13, 1862. General Order No. 2 declared that guerrilla warfare was "contrary to the rules of civilized warfare, and . . . every man who enlists in such an organization forfeits his life and becomes and outlaw. All persons are hereby warned that if they join any guerrilla band they will not, if captured, be treated as ordinary prisoners of war, but will be hung as robbers and murderers." The order granted Union officers and soldiers serving in the Department of the Missouri unprecedented license to identify irregulars and execute them. Halleck even established a legal precedent for this draconian measure, albeit after the fact. His friend Francis Lieber, a renowned scholar of international and military law, consulted on these policies. Lieber's August 1862 response to the questions about guerrilla warfare not only justified Halleck's Order No. 2, but it also served as the cornerstone and inspiration for General Order No. 100—the Lieber Code—and the Union army's turn toward hard war policies more generally.[4]

Although the Lieber Code focused on a range of acts, the justification for redefining killing in Missouri in early 1862 was not grounded in a reality that Quantrill or his men or any guerrillas were murdering indiscriminately. Although some historians view Halleck and Lieber as a cohesive intellectual unit because of their work on General Order No. 100, some of their cornerstone ideas did not actually harmonize. Halleck's central, and at one time *only*, reason for outlawing guerrillas was their destruction of the logistical infrastructure of the Union war effort. In December 1861, he issued General Order No. 32, which highlighted this devastation: "Insurgent rebels scattered through the northern counties of this State, which are occupied by our troops, under the guise of peaceful citizens, have resumed their occupation of burning bridges and destroying railroads and telegraph wires. These men are guilty of the highest crime known to the code of war and the punishment is death." Similarly, General Order No. 2 said nothing of indiscriminate killing, instead beginning with a discussion of the railroads and telegraph lines, again implying that the safety of the logistical infrastructure was Halleck's number one concern.[5]

Halleck first mentioned the guerrillas' violence against people to Lieber in August 1862, nearly six months *after* General Order No. 2 declared that guerrillas would receive no quarter. The general reported, "Rebel authorities claim the right to send men, in the garb of peaceful citizens, to waylay and attack our troops, to burn bridges and houses, and to destroy property and persons within our lines." At the risk of parsing words and splitting hairs, it might be observed that Halleck did not, however, say that the guerrillas were killing *indiscriminately* or killing *prisoners*. While he did suggest that these combatants were targeting "persons" in addition to "troops," his statement read more like an afterthought. Moreover, the general failed to acknowledge that the guerrillas adjusted their methods *in response* to General Order No. 2. Even if the guerrillas responded to the directive by destroying persons without discretion, evidence of which is sparse, Halleck seemed to consider safeguarding these human lives less important than his conventional job of protecting bridges, railroads, telegraphs, and soldiers.[6]

Regardless, Lieber's response revealed that he assumed the guerrillas in Missouri were killing wholesale. In his letter he imagined a much bloodier picture of the conflict in Missouri than even the one painted in Halleck's missive, or the one portrayed in the guerrilla-produced sources. In a long response, Lieber offered his most poignant characterization of the guerrillas, telling Halleck, "[Some people] connect with the guerrillero the idea of necessitated murder, because guerrilla bands cannot encumber themselves with prisoners of war; they have, therefore, frequently, perhaps generally, killed, their prisoners, and of course have been killed in turn when made prisoners, thus introducing a system of barbarity which becomes intenser [*sic*] in its demoralization as it spreads and is prolonged." Rather than correct Lieber, Halleck took the scholar's historical generalization and used it as a retroactive explanation for his own no-quarter policy in Missouri.[7]

Whatever the justification for General Order No. 2, it illustrates that Halleck viewed the guerrillas as illegitimate combatants. The Confederate army commissioned Quantrill as an officer in the summer of 1862. Documentation of this commission has not been found, but it seems likely that he was considered a partisan officer in the Trans-Mississippi Theater, where the Confederate army was often left to create and maintain its own edifice of legitimacy. None of this mattered one way or another in the eyes of the U.S. government. Halleck and other officers in the Department of the Missouri did not grant Quantrill or any of his lieutenants any standing as legitimate officers.[8]

The guerrillas initially reacted ambivalently to the news that Halleck had raised the metaphorical black flag against them. William H. Gregg recalled that Quantrill and his men learned of Halleck's new no-quarter policy on March 20 from a copy of the *St. Louis Republican* that caused many of the guerrillas to quit the war. Gregg wrote, "When we received Maj Gen Hallecks order, telling his officers, and men to shoot or hang Quantrill or his men wherever caught or found, at this date we had sixty men, twenty of whom had come to us only the day before, and when the order was read and explained to them, these recent recruits left us. . . . They were disgusted at the idea of being outlawed and the hoisting of the black flag by the enemy." However, the recent deserters eventually came back when they realized that, with General Order No. 2 as legal validation, "federal troops began murdering by wholesale, old men and boys, and, were so insulting to the women that they too often hid out on their approach."[9]

A few guerrillas remembered this event differently, suggesting that at this moment Quantrill raised the black flag. Partisan, outlaw, and postwar storyteller George Shepherd insisted that this banner was not a metaphor but a very real standard. He recounted that a girl named Annie Fickle showed up at the guerrillas' camp in the spring of 1862 with a copy of a local newspaper that printed the Union army's declaration of no quarter toward the guerrillas. Shepherd claimed that after Fickle had read the order aloud, she gave a rousing speech in which she evoked true manhood, "the love of God," and the "principles of the Confederacy." Upon finishing her remarks, she unfurled the black flag. Writer J. W. Buel described the standard thus: "The banner was made,

A depiction of the mythical presentation of the black flag as George Shepherd told it. Here is the fictional moment when Ann E. Fickle unveiled the sable "Quantrell" banner to the guerrilla chief and his men. This image appears in J. W. Buel's 1881 *The Border Outlaws* alongside George Shepherd's version of events. Buel used stories and illustrations like this one to amplify many of the romantic, pro-guerrilla Lost Cause myths first outlined by John N. Edwards. (James W. Buel, *The Border Outlaws* [St. Louis, Mo.: Historical Publishing, 1881], illustration between pp. 38–39)

by Annie's own hands, of quilted alpaca, four thicknesses, and its dimensions were three by five feet. In the center was deftly worked, in sombre colored letters, the name 'Quantrell,' running endwise through the middle of the flag." Shepherd intertwined in his fantastic tale many of the same threads of memory as other postwar reminiscences: He whitewashed any discussion of slavery or race from the motivations of the guerrillas, and he elevated and purified the white woman and connected her directly to the cause and the conduct of his war. In addition, he romanticized what was in reality a dark and depressing moment for the men in the bush. This is a much better tale than Gregg's version of events.[10]

However, Gregg's story stays much closer to the truth. Halleck's order affected the guerrillas as intended, at least initially. The men in the brush, without any women to lift their spirits, felt as if the war were over. Above all else, Quantrill and his men did not want to raise the black flag, and they did not want it raised against them. They wanted to fight like their idealized version of a soldier and be recognized as such.[11]

142   CHAPTER ELEVEN

Quantrill could have scribbled down a response to Order No. 2 and nailed it to the door of some prominent Unionist. However, he believed in the primacy of actions over the written word. Like many other men of the Civil War generation, he thought that to do something was to leave an impression on society in the present, and that a truly impactful deed might be recorded for future generations. In one of his last letters to his mother, Quantrill lamented his life up to that moment, saying, "[It reads] like a sheet of paper, on the first page of which there are a few signs, showing that something has been commenced, and then all the rest left blank; telling you not what was the purpose of the writer, and leaving you to surmise. . . . And my conscience tells me that if something noble is not done in the future to fill up this blank [then my life will be for naught]."[12]

Whatever we think of their nobility or ignobility, Quantrill's actions authored a bold response to General Order No. 2. On March 22, two days after Quantrill and his guerrillas learned their lives were forfeited by going into the brush to wage war, "the men killed a Dutch sergeant guarding a bridge just outside of Independence." They also set fire to the bridge, punctuating the killing in a way that would get Halleck's attention. Walker recalled that at some point after they shot down the German soldier or militiaman, "Quantrill remarked that 'they issued the order, but we draw first blood.'" Other versions of the bridge burning exist. One claims that the guerrillas actually killed two men, a soldier as well as Unionist George Allison, while a nine-year-old boy watched in horror. A newspaper quoted someone who claimed to have witnessed the killing from a distance, and who said that the two men and the boy "met Quantrill and his men. The three dismounted. Saw Allison and the soldier shot. Quantrill then turned to the boy and said, 'Boy, go back to Kansas City and tell the sons of b——s you saw Quantrill's band kill your father.'" With reins in one hand and a smoking pistol in the other, Quantrill embodied well the devil-may-care warrior on a dancing, wheeling mount.[13]

Hours after the violence at the bridge, Quantrill performed an encore at the Tate house. Having followed the guerrillas' trail to the home that cold, rainy night, U.S. soldiers surrounded the residence, and a firefight began. A brief truce was called, and after the Tate family was allowed to leave, a Union officer made his way onto the porch. The record of what happened next varies. John McCorkle, who was not present, claimed that the officer was trying to force the door open when

Quantrill said, "Boys, get away from that door a minute." The guerrilla "then he fired his pistol through the door and the Federal officer fell, mortally wounded." McCorkle also stated that Quantrill killed another man through the door, next ran upstairs and shot men down with a shotgun, and then shot the first Union soldier he saw upon running from the house, leading the breakout through the enemy lines.[14]

Andrew Walker told a slightly different story, but he still depicted the guerrilla chief in a glowing light. He remembered that when the officer approached the house, "Quantrill took up the parley with the commander at the door." "And at last, when he could temporize no longer," Walker added, "I could see that some audacious deed was about to be perpetrated." Walker "kept [his] eyes on Quantrill" and saw "a bright flash—and a pistol shot rang out. He had shot the commander through the door panel." The firefight continued, and Quantrill gave a brief speech with "a note of defiance, of joy-in-conflict, of never-give-up" in his voice, after which he led the men sprinting into the darkness and the safety of the woods.[15]

Union reports and newspaper stories of the Tate house fight challenged some parts of the guerrillas' versions of events. Union colonel Robert B. Mitchell, commander of the troops engaged in the skirmish, offered a narrative of the event that only confirmed that an officer was shot through the door of the house. Rather than saying his soldiers tracked the guerrillas, Mitchell claimed he "sent Major Pomeroy about 3 miles from the town, with instructions to arrest one David Tate." If we believe Mitchell, it was by sheer luck that the soldiers arrived after the guerrillas. Mitchell, who was not present, said that Pomeroy was shot through the door when he went to the door alone to arrest Tate. The ball entered his leg, nicking an artery. With a gruesome wound in his thigh, Pomeroy limped from the building as a firefight ensued. Later in the fight, a private was shot and killed.[16]

Despite discrepancies in the guerrillas' accounts of the incidents on March 22, 1862, Quantrill authored a narrative reaffirming his base of power within the band. He recognized he needed an act of violence to show his most immediate and important audience—the men in his company of guerrillas—that they would not be threatened or scolded. Quantrill also wanted to offer a response to the Union army for Order No. 2, a rebuttal that was performed and recorded by witnesses and echoed through newspaper accounts and officers' reports. However, as the story took off, it was changed and interpreted in ways he could not control. Union officers and Unionists received some of Quantrill's intended messages, but others came to them without context and were misinterpreted or missed altogether. As he was writing his narrative of the war it was being co-opted, plagiarized, and misrepresented.[17]

Even after the outburst of killing at the bridge and Quantrill's quick trigger at the Tate's front door, the guerrillas' antebellum conception of killing did not wholly change. Throughout the spring and summer of 1862, the partisans reverted to their old rules of engagement. They still took enemy soldiers as captives and tried to exchange them. In late March or early April 1862, the guerrillas "captured a first lieutenant of a Kansas cavalry regiment whom [they] held to exchange for [Perry] Hoy. Quantrill wrote the commanding officer at Fort Leavenworth asking that the exchange be made but got no answer. He then sent the lieutenant to Leavenworth to effect an exchange." The U.S. lieutenant returned and told Quantrill that the commander of Leavenworth would not make the exchange. In response, "Quantrill told him to go home. The lieutenant remarked that he would go home and stay there, that he would not fight for a government that would not exchange a private for him."[18]

Whereas the Union authorities did not recognize the legitimacy of the guerrillas, Confederate officials did. On August 11, 1862, these soldiers assisted Confederate forces in their victory at Independence, Missouri, and a few days later, they defeated U.S. troops at the Battle of Lone Jack. In between the two engagements, Quantrill received a military commission. Gregg remembered, "Two or three days after the taking of Independence, Quantrill and his men were sworn into the Confederate service and reorganized by electing Quantrill captain, William Haller first lieutenant, George Todd second lieutenant, and William H. Gregg third lieutenant, with 150 men." Colonel Upton Hays or Colonel John T. Hughes, who were both active in the area during the Battle of Independence and afterward, probably officiated at Quantrill's swearing in and his independent command. However, the commission most likely came down through the Confederate command in the Trans-Mississippi Theater. Within that section of the war, the Confederate army cosigned Quantrill's actions.[19]

After the Battle of Lone Jack, Captain Quantrill transformed the way the guerrillas killed. Quantrill was sitting beside a table at the partisans' camp in the woods reading a copy of the *Missouri Republican* when Gregg joined him. In addition to being one of Quantrill's lieutenants, Gregg also functioned as his adjutant. He waited for his commander to finish reading the newspaper so that he might read it or hear the news, when he "suddenly . . . saw a change in Quantrill's countenance, and the paper fell from his hand." "Without saying a word," Gregg remembered, "he [Quantrill] drew a blank book from his pocket, penned a note on a leaf, and folded and handed it to me." Quantrill told Gregg that Hoy had been killed, and that he wanted him to take the note to Andrew Blunt, a guerrilla who was in charge of the U.S. prisoners captured during the Battle of Independence. As Gregg left, he opened the note and read the following: "Take Lieut. Copland out and shoot him, go to Woodsmall's camp, get two prisoners and shoot them." After the executions, "the men were ordered to saddle up," and Quantrill told them that they "were going to Kansas to kill ten men in revenge for poor Hoy."[20]

Even as Quantrill ordered a brutal response to Hoy's execution, he did not initiate uncontrolled violence. When the guerrillas entered Kansas in early September 1862, they " had killed ten men before [they] reached Olathe, but [they] had started to take Olathe." Quantrill dispatched Gregg with approximately sixty men to surround the little town to make sure no one could escape to sound the alarm. The main body of guerrillas rode ahead. "On the arrival of Quantrill at the court square," he and his men "found 125 soldiers drawn up on the sidewalk south of the square, so a plan was adopted to capture these men without bloodshed." Hitching their horses and hiding behind them so that the U.S. soldiers did not see them, the partisans emerged on the streets with pistols drawn, got the drop on the soldiers, and captured them. Gregg wrote, "One man refused to give up his gun and was shot and killed. So we had killed fourteen men for Hoy." The guerrillas then paroled their prisoners "and turned them loose—notwithstanding Major General Halleck's order to shoot or hang Quantrill and his men wherever caught or found." Testimony from Kansans and from U.S. Army officers confirms both the brutality of the guerrillas in killing ten men on their route to Olathe and their restraint in sparing the lives of all the people in the town itself, including nearly all of Company H of the Twelfth Regiment, Kansas Infantry.[21]

Still, Quantrill's response to Hoy's execution escalated violence in Missouri. Historian Lorien Foote, author of *Rites of Retaliation*, explains

146   CHAPTER ELEVEN

that during the Civil War retaliation was framed by limits. One of the most important limitations was that "retaliation had to be proportional to the offense." Put simply, if an enemy violation of the laws of war resulted in the murder of *one* of your men, a proportional response would be to kill *one* enemy prisoner of the same rank. Quantrill's decision to kill (more than) ten men for the one man was disproportionate. It fell outside the bounds of a legitimate act of retaliation. Instead of deterring or preventing future violations of the laws of war as he understood them, Quantrill pushed his enemies to act even more violently toward his men after they were captured. Foote makes this point well by citing Lieber's warning: "If one belligerent hangs ten men for one; the other will hang ten times ten over the ten, and what a geometrical progression of skulls and crossbones we would have!"[22]

Lieber's imagery suggests another cause of the escalation of violence in Missouri. By invoking the Jolly Roger, Lieber suggested that the exponential increase of death would lead both sides in the conflict to become like the criminal, dishonorable, barbarous pirates of lore. Here, this black flag symbolized savagery and illegitimacy. Yet Quantrill and his men believed that Halleck and the U.S. government were the first to fly a black flag, making the Union commander and his men the unlawful scalawags. Unsurprisingly, because each side deemed the other piratical, it was difficult for guerrilla officers like Quantrill or his U.S. counterparts to enter into a ritual of retaliation. Neither side listened to the other. U.S. officers dismissed Quantrill's letters, and the partisans refused to heed Halleck's or other U.S. officers' warnings to leave the brush and join the formal Confederate army. Quantrill's guerrillas and the U.S. Army in Missouri were like two ships passing in the night, each one flying its own version of the skull and crossbones.[23]

As the guerrillas gradually pivoted from their idealized version of warfare to something more brutal, they did so in Quantrill's name. He signed the orders to execute the prisoners held by Blunt and then ordered his men to Olathe, but Quantrill's name also appeared on a flag that the guerrillas brought with them into Kansas. In the wake of the raid, Jonathan Millikan discovered an odd little pennant that resembled the first flag of the Confederate government, the so-called stars and bars. In the formal armies, a flag this small would complement a unit's battle flag, flying above or just below a much larger standard on the same staff, and perhaps denoting a specific regiment within a brigade. This particular flag had a unique design within the sea of blue.

It had no stars but instead featured a crudely fashioned palmetto tree of white cloth on the blue backing, as well as an abbreviated name of Quantrill—"Quant."—stitched within the tree.[24]

Besides the obvious homage to the guerrilla leader, the flag established a connection to South Carolina and the larger Confederate movement. The palmetto was added to the South Carolina state flag in the weeks following that state's secession from the Union. Because the Palmetto State originally stood alone against the Union, this was the first flag of the rebellion. Speeches given by South Carolina secessionists to rally other southern states to their cause make it evident that this banner stood for white southerners' desire to maintain slavery and supremacy over the Black race. Adding the red-white-red bars of the first national flag of the Confederacy to the palmetto effectively married the original vision of South Carolina to the goals of the Confederacy. Stitching Quantrill's name on these symbols spelled out the political ideology of the guerrillas: they were proslavery white supremacists led by a man believed to embody those values.[25]

Makeshift and infused with political ideology, *this* flag represented the guerrillas and their warfare in the early stages of the conflict. Instead of heaving some outsize, garish, and overly theatrical black banner mounted on a heavy staff, one of Quantrill's men more likely carried this little flag, tucked in a saddlebag or a shirt pocket, into Olathe. Not unlike Shepherd's fictional black flag, this flag was likely made with love by a guerrilla's kinswoman. In fact, most Civil War battle flags were made by women with love and high hopes for their kinsmen and other young men from their region who were marching off to war. The Olathe flag was based on a popular design already imbued with political and cultural meanings. This petite standard was not intended to be flown, but to be tucked away as a keepsake and kept close to a guerrilla's heart. It was probably given to a guerrilla by his mother, or perhaps his sweetheart, when he left home for the brush—a moment not altogether unlike so many others across the country when women presented the locally raised regiment with hand-sewn regimental colors. Personal in its origins, decidedly Confederate and identifying with Quantrill, this flag was a guerrilla flag.[26]

Like the Olathe flag, Quantrill put his name on a policy of no quarter that was congruent with the guerrillas' preexisting principles. By personally ordering the execution of prisoners, a cosmic echo reverberating back from the first time he signed his name to the death of a man at the Thompson place, Quantrill took responsibility for the bloodshed. When he determined that the guerrillas would ride into Kansas and kill ten men, Quantrill absorbed much of the guilt for what was to be done. Furthermore, in proclaiming that the killings were being done "in revenge of poor Hoy," he reaffirmed that his men rode into the future under a figurative black flag woven from those dark threads of memory stretching back into their past. These threads recalled every slight and personal injury suffered at the hands of the Union.[27]

Following Quantrill's example, some of the guerrillas wrote their own bloody deeds. When not under the direct command of Quantrill, groups of men numbering from three or four up to ten or twenty rode off to operate in their own neighborhoods, acting and writing policy in much the same way as their leader. In the winter of 1862–1863 the guerrillas punctuated with ink a statement already made with blood. Andrew Walker spent the first weeks of winter in a dugout in the brush with three other guerrillas—Cox, John Keagan, and Al Ketchum. Union troopers eventually saw the smoke from their fire and trapped them. The partisans made a desperate breakout. Walker escaped safely, albeit almost naked, as did Cox. The Union troopers wounded Keagan and left him for dead, and they killed Ketchum and riddled his body with bullet holes. Ketchum's fate was emblematic of the type of overkill intended to dehumanize and humiliate that became increasingly common in this war. Walker rejoined George Todd's band, which remained active even during the winter. In one of the first skirmishes after Walker's return, the bushwhackers gunned down six Union troopers and mortally wounded their captain. After making a count of the bodies, "Fletch Taylor dismounted." He then "rolled one of the dead men over, and taking a scrap of paper, scrawled thereon: SEVEN FOR KETCHUM."[28]

Some of the guerrillas' notes directly referenced vengeance as a cause. In May 1863, Jim Vaughn inexplicably rode into Kansas City, hopped off his horse and tied it up, and then sauntered down the street and into a barbershop. The fearless, if foolish, Vaughan made an immediate impression on the citizens of the Union-held town, especially the red legs and jayhawkers who lounged about the streets. A jayhawker might have known Vaughn personally or recognized the swagger and dress of a bushwhacker. However he recognized Quantrill's comrade, a jayhawker quietly sounded the alarm. Vaughn had removed his gun belt to sit comfortably in the barber's recliner, and he was captured without bloodshed before being tried and sentenced to hang.[29]

On May 29, Vaughn stood on the gallows and uttered a searing declaration of righteous contempt: "You may kill me, but you'll never conquer me, and taking my life today will cost you a hundred lives and this debt my friends will pay in a short time." Less than a month later, a group of guerrillas that included many of his close friends skirmished with and killed quite a few Union troopers. According to John McCorkle, in the aftermath of the fighting "Will McGuire rode up to a dead Federal officer who had assisted in the hanging of Jim Vaughan." Like Fletch Taylor before him, McGuire dismounted, " wrote upon a slip of paper, 'Remember the dying words of Jim Vaughan,' and placed it in the teeth of the dead Federal."[30]

Like Quantrill, these killers wrote policies that impressed the past on the future. The slips of paper with hand-scrawled messages offered the guerrillas' responses to Halleck's Order No. 2, representing their particular application of no quarter. The man who pulled the trigger knelt over the dead body and articulated the reason why with a pencil and paper.[31]

On at least one occasion, Quantrill went beyond the handwritten missive and printed a set of general orders for the public. The *Emporia News* published the directives on August 23, 1862. According to the Kansas newspaper, the paper on which the three orders were printed was "found near Lexington, Mo.," perhaps pinned to a tree or nailed to a courthouse door at some prominent crossroads. The first order and the third order tracked with other Confederate policies at that moment. General Order No. 1 focused on recruiting. Looking to capitalize on Confederate victories at Independence and Lone Jack, this edict stated, "All persons wishing to escape this draft into the Federal army . . . [may] come to any of the camps now in the brush, where they will find arms and ammunition with which to operate against Federal troops at every possible point."[32]

When Quantrill undersigned Order No. 3, he was aligning himself with the broader efforts of the Confederacy to maintain white supremacy over the enslaved African American community. The command said, "Any one known to have paid money to the Federal Government, to exempt him from military duty, is liable to have his chattel property taken for the use of the Southern army." Seeing slaves as a sort of hostage or bargaining chip, this third order was a Confederate response to the Union's Confiscation Act issued earlier that summer. Quantrill aligned himself most explicitly with the racial views of these southern reactionaries. The guerrillas conflated the defense of slavery and their rights as slaveholders—or potential slaveholders—with a direct defense of home and family, but slavery was as much the cause of the war on the border as it was across the South, if not more so.[33]

Although Order No. 3 tracked with other Confederate policies, Order No. 2 differed from the formal policies scripted by the Confederate government and instead spoke directly to the guerrilla war and its participants. Order No. 2 expanded the limits of Quantrill's no-quarter policy, declaring, "All persons who shall be found going to any Federal military post, who is [*sic*] liable to be drafted into the Federal army, shall be shot where taken. Any one who is known to have reported to any military post the whereabouts of Southern men shall be shot." The *Emporia Times* opined, "It sufficiently explains why so many Union men have lately been assassinated in the vicinity of Lexington, Independence, and Westport." This order was signed by Upton Hays and W. C. Quantrile—the spelling presumably misprinted, misread, or both. By mirroring the enumeration in Halleck's no-quarter policy, Quantrill sent a clear message to U.S. authorities.[34]

Quantrill might have made his orders public because he feared the public had not noticed previous messages. Quantrill's suspicions that the guerrillas' missives—slips of paper found on moldering bodies deep in the brush—did not reach the men and women outside the guerrilla community and the Federal military proved correct. The brief editorial preceding the publication of Quantrill's general orders showed the degree to which onlookers misunderstood the violence in Missouri in 1862. The *Emporia Times* chirped, "The rebel Secretary of War recognizes guerillas as regular soldiers. Let him compare the order of his soldier, Up Hays, with those of Gen. Pope, which so recently excited his ire, and he will find that retaliation is a game that we too can play at." This baiting editorial suggested that Quantrill's orders instigated a no-quarter policy requiring a violent rejoinder from the United States instead of recognition that the guerrilla chief was responding to Halleck's Order No. 2.[35]

As a result, the public did not understand Quantrill's references and mistook his winks as the twitches of a nervous psychopath. Blustery proclamations like his Order No. 2, when read from a hundred miles away or a hundred years away, seemed to suggest that his willingness to kill was deeply rooted in a frailty of the mind. The public and some historians misread Quantrill's performance as a cheap shtick, some antecedent to a vaudeville horror show, an action so over-the-top that it was more humorous than serious. Quantrill and the guerrillas performed uncounted violent deeds with few wartime records to explain them. They did not make it easy to interpret their warfare, let alone make it possible to offer a sincere read of their bloody messages. But the messages were there, for better or worse, scripted in blood and imprinted with meaning. Each death inscribed a permanent mark on the great cosmic tablet.[36]

In their recollections of the early years of the war, guerrillas communicated that the killing was not an orgy of bloodshed from start to finish. Instead, it evolved. Although a few veterans of the war swore that the black flag was real, most bushwhackers wrote and spoke of the black flag in a metaphorical sense. In their postwar narratives, guerrillas used the literary concept of "raising the black flag" to signal the transition from what they thought of as gentlemen's warfare to a war without mercy.[37]

Even though there were no real black flags with the name "QUANTRELL" embroidered on them, Quantrill will forever be associated with the merciless brand of warfare that took hold in Missouri after 1862. By putting his name on their fictitious standard, guerrillas like Shepherd credited Quantrill with their way of war. The unknown woman who stitched the small "Quant." flag did the same. Shepherd's Annie Fickle and the real but anonymous seamstress both asserted that the guerrillas killed in Quantrill's name, and there is truth to this accreditation. Quantrill wrote vengeance into his bushwhackers' no-quarter policy and gave these revenge killers an identity beyond that of a soldier. In sanctioning the deaths of so many men, Quantrill marked himself and those who rode with him. He signed his name to these men's pasts and their futures, and he authored the first ghastly draft of the history of the guerrilla war in Missouri.[38]

CHAPTER 12: *Partisan Ranger*

Quantrill took leave of his command in the fall of 1862. The rest of the guerrillas attached themselves to J. O. Shelby's Missouri Cavalry in Arkansas and reported that Quantrill headed to Richmond, Virginia. To travel from one end of the Confederacy to the other required knowledge of the fragile southern infrastructure, a feel for the ever-shifting lines of battle, and papers to facilitate his passage, as well as a letter of introduction upon arrival at the Confederate capital.[1]

Around the time of Quantrill's journey, the military situation in the Western and Eastern Theaters was fluid. Depending on the direction Quantrill took across the country, he might have edged close to the Union and Confederate armies dueling near the Kentucky-Tennessee border. On October 7, lead elements of U.S. general Don Carlos Buell's Army of the Ohio skirmished with Confederate general Braxton Bragg's Army of Mississippi outside Perryville, Kentucky. The next day a general engagement ensued. The Confederates fought well and outperformed their northern counterparts, but Bragg ultimately gave up the field to the U.S. Army. The Battle of Perryville, though not as large as other better-known Civil War battles, was one of the bloodiest, and its outcome reverberated throughout the theater. Barring cavalry raids and significant guerrilla action later in the war, the strategic victory at Perrysville would allow the United States to retain Kentucky until the fighting ended.[2]

Quantrill would find the situation in Virginia just as precarious as the one in the Western Theater. In early September, Lee's Army of Northern Virginia invaded Maryland. A couple of weeks later, the Confederates suffered a significant defeat at Antietam and retreated into Virginia without much to show for their first attempt at taking the war to northern soil. Within a couple of months, the Federal Army of the Potomac and the rebel Army of Northern Virginia were squaring off again at Fredericksburg, about sixty miles north of Richmond. Between the two forces, there were close to two hundred thousand men amassed on either side of the Rappahannock River. The Battle of Fredericksburg began on December 11, resulting in massive casualties over the next few days. Losses were especially bad on the northern side, as U.S. commander Ambrose Burnside launched frontal assaults at well-positioned Confederate lines on Marye's Heights above the town. At the end of the battle the Confederates held the field, and there was a lull in fighting until the spring of 1863.[3]

As Quantrill weaved his way around the fighting, he probably heard about the Emancipation Proclamation. The proclamation, which Lincoln issued on September 22, said that the following measure would take effect on January 1, 1863: "All persons held as slaves within any State or designated part of a State, the people whereof shall then be in rebellion against the United States, shall be then, thenceforward, and forever free." Preceding the Emancipation Proclamation, Congress had passed pieces of legislation that chipped away at the institution of slavery. These included the Confiscation Act of 1862, which justified the armed liberation of the slaves of individual rebels, and the Militia Act of 1862, which empowered the president to use Black men as soldiers. Lincoln now proposed something more sweeping. Except in the states of Missouri, Kentucky, Maryland, and Delaware, and in certain occupied or loyal regions, the U.S. government was freeing all of the slaves across the South. Most in the North and South saw this action for what it was, the first step toward the total abolishment of slavery. We cannot know Quantrill's reaction to the Emancipation Proclamation, but his feelings were probably similar to those of the slaveholders he fought alongside.[4]

In this volatile climate Quantrill approached the Confederate capital in search of a commission under the Partisan Ranger Act. Legitimacy and ambition seem to have been the twin motivations for the journey. Some said that Quantrill sought a captaincy, but given his standing as a captain in the Trans-Mississippi Theater, he more likely wanted a colonelcy. The most men he ever directly commanded at once in the first year of the war was between one hundred and two hundred. However, if one counted all the people who were a part of the guerrilla community he headed—such as the women and men who supported his

154 CHAPTER TWELVE

fighters, and not just the fighters themselves—then six to seven times the number of soldiers followed his lead. Quantrill's influence over the war in western Missouri was still perhaps greater than a mere tally of the fighters and supporters he led.[5]

The Confederate Congress passed "An Act to Organize Bands of Partisan Rangers," on April 21, 1862, to give President Jefferson Davis the power to commission officers to form bands of partisans. This piece of legislation empowered men to defend their own communities against enemy invasion in the absence of a formal Confederate army. The law gave the executive branch broad powers to commission men to fight on their own hook in the hope that the president might appoint a new Swamp Fox, Wizard Owl, or Lighthorse Harry—those distinctly southern heroes of the American War of Independence.[6]

However, Section 2 of the act demonstrated the law's ignorance of partisan warfare. The law stated, "Such Partisan Rangers, after being regularly received into the service, shall be entitled to the same pay, rations and quarters during their term of service," and "be subject to the same regulations as other soldiers." It was a difficult proposition for these men who fought on their own hook beyond Confederate lines to be "regularly received into the service." Equally problematic was the idea of enforcing the same regulations to which the Confederate government subjected other soldiers. These issues were not addressed in any satisfactory way, as the Confederate legislature was writing laws faster than it could debate them.[7]

The exact number of men officially enlisted as Partisan Rangers is difficult to know. What is left of Confederate records is incomplete; however, based on extant available documents, historian Barton A. Myers says that around one hundred partisan companies were formed and either commissioned or applying for commissions from every Confederate state except Texas, Arkansas, and Tennessee by September 1862. Based on this information and other evidence, Myers estimates that at least six thousand men served as partisans, and probably more. Likely there were thousands more who joined the Partisan Ranger ranks during the following year. For instance, Lieutenant Colonel John S. Mosby did not begin his famous career as a Partisan Ranger until January 1863.[8]

However many men became partisans, the Confederate high command debated their usefulness to the war effort. Mosby and a few others who worked closely with Generals J. E. B. Stuart and Robert E. Lee achieved success on the battlefield, while raiding, and in other capacities. They were lauded by the upper echelon of the military and government, as well as the newspapers. Generals like Lee, though, doubted the viability of the partisan system as a whole. Lee wanted to wage a conventional war with formal armies, and the Partisan Ranger Act weakened his ability to do so. He and his allies seemed to believe that the act gave too much power to untrained and undisciplined men, kept them out of the formal Confederate forces, and sparked brutal, anarchic local wars across the South that ultimately distracted from and weakened the southern war effort. Lee himself lobbied to have the law rescinded, and he and his allies got their way on February 17, 1864.[9]

Quantrill held a different perspective than Lee and other members of the Confederate high command on the best way to conduct the war. After fighting in the Confederate army and as a bushwhacker, Quantrill believed that guerrilla warfare was superior. Guerrilla warfare empowered the individual man. It offered soldiers a chance to fight close to home, eat home-cooked food, wear sturdy, comfortable well-fitted homemade clothes, ride a horse, choose their weaponry, and make tactical decisions for themselves. Partisan warfare was more in accord with expectations of white men in the antebellum South than "conventional" or "regular" warfare, which stripped men of their identities and rights.[10]

If Quantrill hoped someone in Confederate leadership would see things the same way that he did, he was disappointed. The first mention of the argument between Quantrill and the Confederate secretary of war, presumably James Seddon, came from John N. Edwards's 1877 *Noted Guerrillas*. Like most of his book, Edwards's depiction of this unlikely meeting is dramatic, colorful, and unreal. He claimed Louis Trezevant Wigfall, a Confederate senator for Texas, and a pugnacious, sensitive, drunken, and generally despicable character, was the source of his information, which does not instill confidence in the content this story. Edwards—himself a hard-drinking rascal—might have thought Senator Wigfall was an impressive name to attach to this interaction. It is also possible that the author of *Noted Guerrillas* created the exchange between Quantrill and Seddon out of his own imagination.[11]

Suspending our good judgment, then, perhaps Wigfall and Edwards were sharing a quart of rotgut in some musty tavern and hurling tall tales here and there when the onetime senator from Texas said that he was in Richmond in the secretary of war's office when Quantrill was there. According to Wigfall, the guerrilla chief tried to convince the secretary to make partisan warfare the preeminent form of

156 CHAPTER TWELVE

warfare across the South, an argument Seddon rejected. Quantrill proclaimed, "Barbarism! Barbarism, Mr. Secretary, means war and war means barbarism. . . . The cloud has burst. Do not condemn the thunderbolt. . . . Every struggle has its philosophy, but this is not the hour for philosophers. . . . Men must be killed. " Seddon responded, "What would you do, Captain Quantrell, were your's the power and the opportunity?" Quantrill fired away, "Why I would wage such a war . . . as to make surrender forever impossible. I would cover the armies of the Confederacy all over with blood. I would invade. I would reward audacity. I would exterminate." Quantrill concluded, "You have my ideas of war, Mr. Secretary," and "I am sorry they do not accord with your own, nor the ideas of the government you have the honor to represent so well." He bowed his head and headed back to Missouri, or so *Noted Guerrillas* tells us.[12]

Although Edwards's account sounds like a tall tale, there is some evidence that Quantrill was at least in Richmond. Biographers who followed Edwards regarded this part of Quantrill's story as a myth. The only pieces of evidence they had were the story Quantrill told his men when he returned and Edwards's yarn. However, buried deep on a back page of the March 14, 1863, edition of the *Sentinel*, a daily Richmond, Virginia, newspaper, a short blurb confirmed that Quantrill traveled to the Confederate capital. It read, "Col. Quantrell, the noted partisan ranger, who has been a terror to the Yankees in Missouri, and performed excellent service during the war, is now sojourning at the Spotswood Hotel in this city."[13]

In calling Quantrill a Partisan Ranger and a colonel, The *Sentinel* granted him a surprising amount of legitimacy. His name does not appear in the existing official Confederate records for the partisan service. Nothing in the surviving correspondence between Confederate leadership suggests he received a colonelcy. Yet during his visit to Richmond, Quantrill gave the impression he was a colonel and a Partisan Ranger, and when he rejoined his men in Missouri they referred to him as "Colonel Quantrill." We may never know for sure whether he received an official commission as a colonel, but it may not matter too much. Official or not, conferred by the Confederate government or self-assigned, Quantrill's rank transformed into that of colonel on his trip to Richmond. This status befitted the man who, within the next few months, became the most powerful partisan leader of the Civil War, North or South, East or West.[14]

Chieftain

1863–1864

CHAPTER 13: *Colonel*

Immediately upon his 1863 return from Richmond, William Clarke Quantrill's men tested his authority. As Andrew Walker recalled, "One morning Quantrill, Todd and I were in camp alone, currying our horses . . . and Quantrill, in a playful way, flipped a twig at George, taking him on the cheek." George Todd was stung, though, by the jovial assault and "threw a hard clod, striking Quantrill with stunning force in the ear." Such an escalation was dangerous in the guerrilla ranks. "Both whipped out their guns and would have fired in another breath," Walker said, "but I was quickly between them, shouting, 'Hold on here! You don't know what you are doing. . . . You ought to be ashamed of yourselves.' . . . Todd, realizing that he had acted with undue heat, turned on his heel" and "walked off in the direction of the trees." Once Todd backed down, Quantrill holstered his pistol and went to his tent. Walker followed Quantrill, who "declared that he would kill George if he wasn't such a good fighter. . . . 'It would be a pity . . . to kill such a good fighter.'"[1]

A guerrilla might gun down his chieftain after a flip of a twig or the toss of a clod. These bushwhackers demonstrated such a propensity for violence that they would just as soon blast one another full of holes as they would shoot the enemy. Anarchical and chaotic, Quantrill's guerrilla band could easily be depicted as a group of desperate gunsels let loose on society. As seen from a certain historical perspective, the guerrillas waged a war of all against all.[2]

In actuality, though, these men grew organically out of their society. The South was a region of hot tempers and bloodletting. From border ruffians to legislators, the frontier to the halls of Congress, southerners were prepared to use aggression to wrangle and subdue their world and the people in it. The same was true for the residents of Little

Dixie, Missouri. In many of these counties, half of the white householders owned at least one slave. This ratio was higher than in other areas of the South more often associated with slavery. Missourians' proximity to the frontier nurtured a sense of gun-gripping self-reliance. Geographic and historical intimacy with borderlands violence created a set of expectations for men in which they were ready to defend themselves against anything and anyone. In Missouri, young men were tormented by very real wolves, bears, scalp-lifting Indians, rebellious slaves, and slave-liberating Kansans.[3]

A fighter drawing a pistol on his commander, though, was out of step with the behavior of other southern men in the Confederate army. Authority was a fragile thing among the guerrillas. Quantrill went to Richmond and was maybe commissioned a colonel, but it is unclear how much those circumstances mattered in the Missouri brush, where the upstart southern government possessed mostly symbolic power. When challenged, there was no institutional power to buttress the status of a guerrilla chieftain, and leadership changes could be swift. Quantrill's authority was bestowed on him by the men he led. In the guerrilla community, power flowed up from the fighters: men acquiesced to proven killers, promising a speedy rise through the ranks for skilled and experienced warriors. Likewise, guerrillas could quickly revoke their consent to be led by Quantrill and offer it to a man with a greater reputation as a killer. Explicitly associated with masculine prowess, the volatile guerrilla democracy was constantly rating men as men.[4]

By the beginning of the bushwhacking season of 1863, the guerrilla power structure looked like a cosmic game of king of the hill. Skilled fighters like Todd, Bill Anderson, William H. Gregg, Dave Pool, and Cole Younger led their own bands of loyalists, and any one of them might want more power or might take offense to an exchange with Quantrill. From a cheerful jab to an ill-received prank, seemingly anything could send hands reaching for revolvers.[5]

A hub with many spokes, Quantrill sat at the center of this wild, churning war, constantly working to direct the violent energy of lieutenants outward toward those they saw as occupiers. Rather than constantly resist the ambitions of fighters, Quantrill acted with magnanimity and empowered his compatriots and rivals. He did not govern through threats, and he rarely issued orders. Instead, he used persuasion to develop a consensus. He granted his lieutenants autonomy, allowing them the freedom to lead their bands as they liked. Using this approach, he was able to stay ahead of the many potential threats that welled up from within his band, and he remained in favor with the majority of guerrillas, at least for a while.[6]

Quantrill's captains—compatriots but also potential rivals—represented the range of white men living in western Missouri at the time. They included the sons of well-to-do slaveholders, foreigners and outsiders, and ne'er-do-well rustlers. All of them were dedicated to the cause of slavery and the protection of hearth and home. Although their methods differed, the captains were each deadly—there was not a saint among them.

Frustratingly little is known about the backgrounds of a few of these men. Andrew Blunt, Fernando (or Ferdinand) Scott, John Brinker, and Bill Haller remain mysterious figures. We know that Blunt was close with Quantrill, the chief's confidant and close friend. Scott led a group north of the river in Clay County that included such bloodletting luminaries as Frank James. Brinker operated along the line between Jackson and Johnson Counties and led as many as ninety men early in the war. Haller was one of Quantrill's first lieutenants. U.S. officers recognized these notorious captains and mentioned them occasionally in reports. Guerrilla memoirists referred to these men as though readers should know who they were, and so revealed no information about them. With this in mind, it is possible to imagine the captains and lieutenants crouching beside the chief atop some ravine silhouetted against the sky, gazing down at some unlucky group of U.S. troopers. Each man was a shadowy influence on the commander and the course of the war.[7]

We know more about guerrilla captain Dave Pool (or Poole). Born Francis Marion Pool, he seemed born to be a guerrilla. This reincarnated Swamp Fox was charismatic, funny, and deadly. It is not hard to understand why men wanted to fight alongside him—the gutsy partisan possessed a disarming sense of humor and was always ready to lift a glass. There are two very different photographs of Pool from the war, and both are striking. In one he is a clean-shaven, handsome fellow with a thin face, high cheekbones, and bright eyes piercing the camera lens. The other picture shows him in full bushwhacker bloom. He is standing between a couple of seated guerrillas. Sporting a beard and shoulder-length curly hair, Pool is pictured with a cigar in his mouth, a pistol in one hand, and a bottle of whiskey in the other. A better analogy for the way he fought his war can hardly be imagined.[8]

If Pool was not an obvious threat to consolidate power among the guerrillas, Cole Younger was well positioned to do so. In the early days of the war, Younger was the golden-boy guerrilla. Scion to a wealthy and prominent family when the war began, he enjoyed a social status that placed him on a trajectory to lead during the war. His father was a distant relative to Robert E. Lee, and his mother was a member of the Fristoe clan—a sprawling kinship network rooted in Jackson County. In addition to benefiting from these connections, Younger was moved by vengeance: his father, who was a Unionist, was gunned down by northern soldiers. Younger linked up with Quantrill, but much of his time was spent leading a band made up of his own kin.[9]

William H. Gregg came from a fairly well-known family of slaveholders in their own right, and during the war he leaned closer to the seat of power than anyone. Gregg was one of Quantrill's earliest followers, being among the first eleven guerrillas in the chief's band. He appeared to be quieter and a bit more modest than some of the more flamboyant captains wreaking havoc. Gregg cozied up to Quantrill and became his right-hand man, part adjutant, part enforcer. He seemed loyal to his chief, but laconic killers are notoriously difficult to read.[10]

Of all the potential rivals to Quantrill's status as chief of the guerrillas, Todd and Anderson were the most outwardly threatening. Anderson was a horse thief whom Quantrill scolded early in the war, but Quantrill tolerated him and his gang because he valued their fearlessness, if not their honor. Born in 1839 in Kentucky, Anderson moved with his parents to the Kansas Territory, where his father set up a grocery along the Santa Fe Trail. The family did well until Anderson's mother was struck by lightning and killed, and his sister Mary was "ruined" by a neighborhood widower, A. I. Baker. Anderson's father, Bill Sr., lost his cool, got drunk, and went to kill Baker, but when he stopped off for one last topper of liquid courage, the other men at the grocery took the caps off his shotgun. While they were attempting to prevent a murder, Anderson was helpless when he confronted Baker, who shot him dead on May 12, 1862.[11]

By that point, Bill Anderson was already operating along the border. His loyalties at this stage were not altogether clear, but he seemed to be using the tumult and confusion of war to rustle horses, taking them from farmers on one side of the border and then selling them on the other. Horse stealing initially brought him to Quantrill's attention. When the chieftain sent Gregg to retrieve Anderson and his men so that he could discipline them, he possibly also offered them a chance at salvation: if they became guerrillas and focused their plundering on Kansans and Unionists, all would be forgiven. Either way, at some point in 1862, Anderson and his band—he called this unit the Kansas First Guerrillas—loosed their violence on U.S. soldiers and sympathizers mostly along the border. Perhaps more than any of the bands whose leaders originated in Jackson County, Anderson's men operated almost entirely independently from Quantrill, and they were a motley bunch. Men who were not from Jackson County kinship networks and cliques tended to fall in with Anderson and his brother Jim.[12]

Todd was an even more immediate rival to Quantrill's chieftainship. He was born in Montreal, Canada, in 1839, the son of Scottish immigrants. His father was a stonemason, and his mother kept their house. At some point in the 1850s, the Todd family moved to Kansas City, Missouri, where Todd's father and brother built sewers and bridges. The handsome Todd, said to stand close to six feet tall and speak with a bit of a lisp, assisted in the work. He was maybe apprenticing to become a mason himself, but he was not one by the time the war broke out. Just before the war, Todd watched as a loose stone fell and killed his brother while he was working in a sewer. Apparently, his dying brother asked Todd to marry his widow, which he did just as the war was beginning. He immediately left, joining the Confederate Missouri State Guard, and he subsequently fought in a few early skirmishes. Returning home after possibly being wounded, Todd joined Quantrill. Daniel Geary, a neighbor and associate of Todd's father, once said of Todd, "Why he took to the 'bresh' will always remain a mystery, as he had no knowledge of any of the issues involved in war, no grievances to redress, no wrongs to avenge nor property interests to protect." Geary concluded, "One would think from his origin he would have been an enemy of slavery, but the eccentricities of the human family are many and varied and past explaining."[13]

Whatever peculiarities Todd brought with him to Quantrill's camp, the whiskerless, handsome boy became close with his chief. Whether due to their common position as outsiders to the southern community, a shared upbringing as the sons of craftsmen, a relationship in which each man filled the role of a lost or missing brother for the other, or something else, the two bonded straightaway. Sometimes, when the guerrillas spent the night in the homes of their followers, Quantrill and Todd shared a bed while the rest of the guerrillas slept on the floor. Whatever was between Quantrill and Todd, the two recognized something of themselves in each other and remained close for much of the war.[14]

In May 1862, they disguised themselves as U.S. officers and traveled to Hannibal, Missouri, to procure percussion caps for the Colt Navy revolvers the guerrillas used. They were gone for days or even a week. Out of that story came a telling anecdote: Todd and Quantrill were both disguised as majors in the Union army. This was a mistake—above the enlisted ranks, men of the exact same rank rarely moved about together. Recognizing Quantrill's authority, Todd demoted himself. The way he put it, though, strikes a different chord than one might expect from this fearsome bushwhacker: "Too many majors traveling together are like too many roses in a bouquet. . . . The other flowers have no show."[15]

It is hard to know what to make of this story. Cole Younger was the one who reported the tale, and that fact by itself raises questions. The outlaw was known to bend the truth wherever he thought a twist of the facts might benefit him. For example, he falsely claimed that he heard Todd's comment firsthand because he had been with Todd and Quantrill on the secret mission. However, it is hard to see how the exact phrasing of the analogy benefited Younger. Possibly Younger heard the story secondhand and remembered it. The pithy expression sounds like an authentic Victorian metaphor. Flowers were bursting with symbolism. They were beautiful outgrowths of that nineteenth-century appreciation for a well-cultivated nature, and the long-defunct language of flowers provided an easy iconography through which Victorian Americans expressed themselves in veiled terms.[16]

As the type of fellows who wore flamboyant shirts decorated with colorful flowers, Todd, Quantrill, and the other guerrillas were in tune with this symbolism. If Todd was familiar with the language of flowers—as he no doubt was—then he knew that roses represented love during the nineteenth century, just as they do today. This may be reading too much into the secondhand story passed down by a known embellisher. It is wise to remember that men are not flowers, and stories are just stories—most of the time.[17]

When Quantrill left the guerrillas for the East, Todd began jostling for control of the men in his absence. Quantrill put Gregg in charge of the men, but Gregg "noticed that Lieutenant Todd was not about." "On close inquiry I found that he with eight men had left for Missouri some hour or so before I made that inquiry," Gregg recalled, adding, "Whether Todd left with consent of Quantrill or not, I was never able to learn."[18]

Todd put his stamp on the war not long after leaving the other guerrillas in Arkansas. In late March 1863, Todd and his men, a group that now numbered more than a dozen and maybe as many as forty, were operating on their own while they awaited Quantrill's return. They heard that seventy-five runaway slaves—contrabands, the U.S. Army called them—were being transported up the Missouri River to Kansas. These boats docked so often as they churned their way upriver against the current that any number of folks saw the large contingent of Black women, men, and children on the *Sam Gaty*. Todd and his men likely spotted the boat on Friday, March 27, at Lexington, a prominent river town in Lafayette County. Some of the guerrillas probably stalked the boat from the banks of the river while others rode ahead to either find a good place to waylay the boat or maybe they set up at a predetermined location.[19]

On March 28, 1863, as the *Sam Gaty* pushed past Sibley in the darkness of the small hours, a volley of pistol and rifle shots exploded high atop the bluffs overlooking the river. The flustered captain heard a voice from the heights overhead tell him to steer the ship to the shore, which he obediently—and foolishly—did. "As soon as the *Gaty* landed, a party of bushwhackers rushed on board," made a prisoner of the captain, and then killed two white soldiers. Perhaps these two men attempted to resist, or maybe Todd thought it best to make an example of them. "Todd led his assassins in person," and "the boat's money was taken, [and] every passenger who could be found was robbed of money, watches, arms and such clothing as the rebels wanted." Afterward, Todd and his men threw much of the cargo overboard. At this point, the bushwhackers turned their attention to the "contraband." "The negroes were marched off the boat and placed in line. A part of the murderers took position a few feet from the helpless creatures," and then "the order was given to fire, and fifteen fell dead."[20]

U.S. Army reports do not agree on the number of Black women, men, and children killed. One U.S. officer said that the guerrillas "murdered several soldiers and 9 contrabands." Another stated, "Meyers and Henry, of Company E, killed, others escaped. Twenty negroes killed." The *Smoky Hill and Republican Union* reported, "Thirteen of the contrabands escaped from the boat when the robbery commenced, ran up the river, and were picked up by the *Gaty* eight miles above. There was a report yesterday that the rest of the negroes were killed after the boat left." More contrabands might have been gunned down. All of them were not killed, though. A U.S. officer reported ambushing some of the guerrillas, "killing 17 and [hanging] 2 engaged in the robbery of the Sam. Gaty." The soldier continued, "[We] also recovered some of the contrabands." The inexactitude does not take away from the obvious conclusion: this was a racially fueled massacre.[21]

What happened on that moonlit gravel bar in the cold morning air was a sign of things to come. Events revealed the mindset of the guerrilla captains. Quantrill needed to account for the evolving motivations of the men under his command. If he was to stay in charge of this democracy of killers, their murderous bigotry needed to be either enabled or redirected.

When Quantrill returned from Richmond in the late spring or early summer of 1863, he went first to Todd. "One day—it was early June—those of us in camp had our attention drawn to an unaccustomed figure, on a jaded beast," Andrew Walker recalled. The mysterious man was "approaching in company with Todd." As Walker remembered, "The figure had a familiar look but a certain downcast air. Yes, it was he, Quantrill." Upon the chieftain's arrival, the men threw their hats toward the sky and hollered for joy. The enthusiastic ovation with which he was greeted did not improve Quantrill's attitude. "The look of dejection was still apparent. . . . He didn't have much to say about his trip," and "his disappointment was plain." Whether owing to his inability to secure a colonelcy, his heated exchange with the secretary of war, the ugly state of the Confederate war effort, or travel weariness, Quantrill seemed depressed.[22]

Todd worried that his chief was not himself, and the well-being of Quantrill was of supreme importance. Todd urged Walker to stay with Quantrill in camp, hoping that time, food, and rest would help their leader recover and regain his fighting spirit.[23]

During these days of physical and mental refitting, Quantrill thought about moving on from the war. This sentiment seemed out of touch with the general spirit of the white South in the spring or summer of 1863, but Walker offered a picture of a man disillusioned with the southern war effort. He recorded the following concerning Quantrill's mood:

"[He feared that] the armies of the North, dogged and well fed, would yet . . . march in triumph through the streets of Richmond. So that a slight despondency possessed him in place of his gay abandon." One day, Quantrill turned to him out of the blue and said, "Andy, it's a lost cause. . . . We'd better make preparations to get out of the country; they'll hang every one of us." Another time he confided, "Andy, Blunt and I are going to leave. I want you to know that I'm not dead, but I don't want you to say a word to anyone about it."[24]

Given his talk of a lost cause, deserting the band he helped create, and fleeing the noose, Quantrill could see the end. In the 1850s, Quantrill demonstrated the ability to forecast the coming of events, visualize an exit, and get out while the getting was good. He departed from the classroom, the farm, the teamster's wagon, the quartermaster's mess, the goldfields, and the world of the confidence man—Quantrill's impulse to slip away in the night was in step with a lifetime of similar behavior. He was ready to skedaddle, but he dragged his feet too long.[25]

One day a Confederate officer arrived in camp looking for the guerrilla chief. According to Walker, Colonel Holt "displayed his recruiting papers from General Price, and insisted on Quantrill's resuming operations." The colonel believed that "aggressive measures just at that time would arouse an enthusiasm that would induce men to enlist. Then, if enough men could be recruited, some movement of more consequence could be set on foot." It was after this interaction with Colonel Holt that Quantrill went off to meet with his captains. "Quantrill was gone two or three days," as he went to visit with "Cole Younger, Captain Gregg, Dave Pool, Bill Anderson, John Brinker, and others, with their independent bands of ten, fifteen, and twenty men each." After he made his rounds, "all declared themselves ready, and desired him as leader. When Quantrill got back he agreed to begin operations." Gregg offered a slightly different timeline of the beginnings of the 1863 campaign, suggesting that Quantrill did not take time to recover after he arrived back in Missouri. Instead, Gregg said, "On Quantrill's return to the state, military operations began in earnest."[26]

Walker's and Gregg's different perspectives on Quantrill's activities in early 1863 highlight the chief's genius. Each captain and small band possessed an independent bond with Quantrill. Todd, who was obviously special to Quantrill, provided a safe harbor. He could rest and reset his mind among Todd and his men. By the time he got to Gregg, Quantrill looked ready to go, and Gregg thought he was the first one

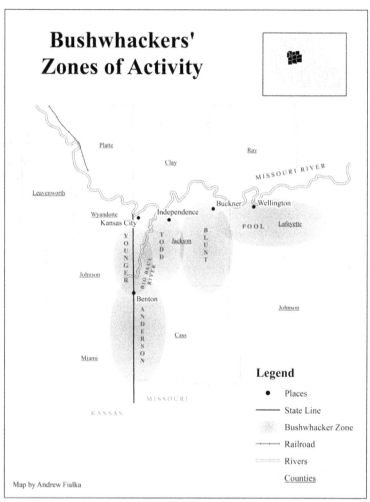

This map offers a visual representation of William H. Gregg's description of the geographic structure of guerrilla warfare in and around Jackson County in the summer of 1863. Andrew Walker referred to these regions as "zones of activity." Quantrill dispatched his lieutenants to their home neighborhoods, allowing them to fight individual little wars against the Union army and Unionists living in their region. The exact dimensions of these zones are unknown, and the fluidity of guerrilla warfare discouraged a hard, stative boundary between one lieutenant's area and another.

the chief visited. Each captain probably held that belief. Younger, Pool, and even Anderson all considered themselves precious to the chief.[27]

Regardless of when the campaign began, the guerrilla warfare of 1863 took on a new, dynamic character under Quantrill's leadership. "During the year 1862 the men were kept close together and all under the watchful eye of Quantrill. Not so in 1863." Instead of commanding all of the bands directly, Quantrill relinquished tactical control to his captains and lieutenants and oversaw their semicoordinated efforts. "There was Todd, Pool, Blunt, Younger, Anderson, and others, and each had companies and were only called together on special occasions." In any case, "all . . . recognized Quantrill as commander in chief, with Lieutenant Gregg as adjutant." Once the guerrilla band was reorganized, "occurrences were thick and fast during the summer of 1863. Todd would annihilate a party of the enemy in western Jackson County. Blunt another in the eastern portion, Anderson somewhere in Kansas or Cass County, Missouri, Pool in Lafayette or Saline, Younger on the High Blue."[28]

This new organizational structure transcended anything the guerrillas had previously done. Walker referred to a "zone of activity." Gregg's depiction of the "thick and fast" fighting from 1863 is not a series of examples of how the fighting went. Rather, this is a geographic rendering of exactly the way in which the guerrillas organized themselves. By attaching a specific lieutenant or captain to a particular landmark or area of the countryside, Gregg demarcated the defensive zones of the bushwhacking map. Quantrill sent each leader to a particular part of the countryside to engage the enemy there until he told them to relocate. The man in charge of that range chose how he and his men fought, giving each zone of warfare its own idiosyncrasies borne of the person in charge and the landscape on which the guerrillas waged battles. U.S. troopers accustomed to fighting George Todd might confront a different set of tactics when they wandered into a different township and faced off against Cole Younger and his men.[29]

It is difficult to overstate the brilliance of Quantrill's tactical approach in 1863. He effectively married the two driving forces of guerrilla warfare: personality and geography, the man and the land. Out of a wealth of emotional intelligence, Quantrill understood that his men valued independence. While they were fighting for their households, families, and rights as slaveholders, partisans chose to fight in a way that allowed them to maintain their liberty. In the formal Confederate forces, men were expected to acknowledge hierarchy and rank and ultimately yield to other men of the same social standing. In the bush, however, all the guerrillas considered themselves equal. Quantrill further promoted the ambitions of his lieutenants by letting them run the war in their home neighborhoods. Letting men fight with their brothers, cousins, and childhood friends in places where they had raced horses and hunted accentuated the home-field advantage and infused the cause of the war into its conduct. Quantrill saw his men as they wanted to be seen—honor-bound defenders of hearth and home—and he designed a war that suited that profile.[30]

This new approach accompanied another affectation of guerrilla warfare in western Missouri: wearing enemy uniforms. Although the practice began in early 1862, by 1863 every bushwhacker on the border disguised himself as a U.S. trooper. Walker did "not remember ever to have seen a bushwhacker wearing a Confederate uniform . . . [but] more often Federal uniforms." Donning a Union disguise, partisans approached and engaged their enemies, sometimes getting close enough to actually exchange words or even shake hands. To be more exact, they wore a blue U.S. uniform that cloaked the guerrilla shirts indicating their authentic selves, and that reflected on Yankee soldiers an image of their own selves rather than of the secesh enemy. Once the ruse worked, the U.S. troopers let their guard down, and the guerrillas pulled their pistols and fired away.[31]

Charley Hart inspired this tactic. As Hart, Quantrill masqueraded as a farmer, detective, surveyor, and jayhawker. Shifting shapes before the war, living inside and outside society, Quantrill could see—or at least perceive—the lines that were invisible to others. When the war came, he saw the potential of a performative turn in adopting the blue uniforms of his enemies. This practice transformed the guerrillas into a legion of confidence men. Guerrillas dressed as Union soldiers. Irregulars acted like regulars. Troopers from Iowa or Ohio or Colorado and officers from the Upper Midwest or the East were blinded by their own military culture as expressed in things like a coat, a color, a style of salute, a few brass buttons, or a chevron. This dark charade was a radical tactic that not only broke the norms and rules of convention but used convention against itself.[32]

Todd seemed to revel in this masquerade more than any of Quantrill's other lieutenants. The only guerrilla photographed wearing a U.S. uniform, Todd had his likeness made in Independence, Missouri, striking a common guerrilla pose. In this image, he sits with one leg over the other, showing off his hip-high riding boots. He holds a plumed cavalier's hat in his lap while resting his other arm on a table. Todd's shirt is buttoned all the way to his neck and is neutral in color, perhaps gray or butternut. Over that he wears the blue coat of a Union officer, signified by the gold patches sewn on his shoulders. Clean shaven and wearing his hair combed over, the handsome guerrilla purses his lips, barely holding back a grin. Todd wants to let the camera in on the deception, but he just cannot bring himself to do it. That would ruin the fun.[33]

Wearing blue uniforms and organized in "zones of activity," Quantrill's guerrillas gained the upper hand in the war on the ground in western Missouri by July 1863. Tactically speaking, the U.S. Army was no match for this new shape of warfare. Commanding the newly created District of the Border, Brigadier General Thomas Ewing reported, "From the character of the country and the people, and the great vigilance of the enemy, and the secrecy of their movements, it is rarely practicable to surprise them, and they will never fight unless all the odds are on their side, and they are too well mounted to be run down." Unaware of the guerrillas' new geographic divisions and making no mention of the partisans' disguises, Ewing was nevertheless sure of the difficulty of this task. "The country is rich and supports them well," he reported, "but it is so rugged and heavily timbered, and full of places of concealment and ambuscade, that these bands could not possibly be expelled from it with forces in the field less than three times their own."[34]

Incapable of combating the guerrillas, U.S. officers were also beginning to realize that their larger strategy for defeating the insurgents was failing. They simply could not kill enough guerrillas to win the war. Henry Halleck's General Order No. 2 backfired, driving peaceful men to become bushwhackers. Lamenting the state of the war, Ewing noted that the southern white men in his district were "unable to live at their homes if they would." "They have gone to bushwhacking [instead]," Ewing pointed out. The Union policy of no quarter proved detrimental to winning the hearts and minds of the white southern populace. Each unarmed southern man killed by Union troopers created at least one new guerrilla. In this honor-based society, the killing or injury of a father, brother, cousin, or friend evoked bad feelings among their kinsmen and drove men who had been on the fence into the war. Gregg recalled one such instance: when Jeptha Crawford was killed, his wife dragged their young son Riley out into the brush to join Quantrill's band.[35]

Quantrill's power increased by the day. By twos and threes, young men were seeking out one of the bands under his leadership. His captains were impossible to catch, and when they had the opportunity, they cut U.S. patrols to pieces. While the formal Confederate army was on its last legs in the Mississippi River valley, Quantrill's guerrillas were holding down the fort along the border. Perhaps the Confederate high command regretted not giving Quantrill a partisan colonelcy. By this point in the war, he seemed to deserve it. While his men were riding soldiers in the U.S. Army out of their saddles, Quantrill did something even more impressive: he held together a volatile group of passionately independent and deadly men without getting himself shot.

CHAPTER 14: *Gambler*

In late July or early August 1863, Quantrill conceptualized a raid on Lawrence. Building on the guerrillas' momentum gained on the battlefield, he sent word to his captains and other independent guerrillas in the region to resupply. Anderson, Todd, Younger, and the other captains told their fighters to lie low and refit themselves for battle. The bands would then reunite at some familiar haunt in the next few days.[1]

Complying with the captains' instructions, a young bushwhacker might have ridden all the way to his family household on game trails through the dense brush, crossing creeks and keeping clear of those well-beaten roads between Kansas City and Independence or Sibley and Napoleon. Once there, he left his horse in the woods, and on a moonlit night he crept up to the back door and gave Ma or Little Sis a whistle through the open window. For the next few days, he hid out in a gulley some distance from the house, resting his mount. Sitting by the fire, he molded bullets with the block of lead his womenfolk hid for him, along with some dry powder and a few percussion caps. Meanwhile, those guerrilla women were in and out of the kitchen, cooking up bread and biscuit and smoking a side of beef. His aunt sat in her chair and mended a shirt or pants and finished sewing a pair of socks. In a few days, he would be ready for whatever fight was coming.[2]

As the guerrillas resupplied, Quantrill held a council of war with his commanders on August 10. In his account of the meeting, Gregg recalled, "Quantrill said 'lets go to Lawrence,' and in support of this proposition he said, 'Lawrence is the great hotbed of abolitionism in Kansas, and all the plunder, (or the bulk of it) stolen from Mo. will be found stored away in Lawrence.'" The guerrillas were going to Lawrence to avenge the jayhawkers' years of raiding on the Missouri side of the border, and to take back stolen goods as well as anything else of use. However, the timing of the attack suggests that U.S. efforts to enlist Black men as soldiers and put them in the field played a role in the planning of the raid on Lawrence. Earlier that summer, Black troops in the U.S. Army had made headlines for their actions in South Carolina. In early June, several hundred Black troops of the Second South Carolina under the leadership of Colonel James Montgomery, a former jayhawker whose name would have been familiar to many Missourians, raided up the Combahee River. They destroyed millions of dollars' worth of property and liberated hundreds of slaves. In July, the Fifty-Fourth Massachusetts took part in the brutal assault on Fort Wagner outside Charleston. Given the wide coverage of these events in both northern and southern newspapers, Quantrill and some of his men likely read about them.[3]

Although the guerrillas could do little to change the direction of the entire war, Lawrence provided an opportunity to strike at a prominent abolitionist symbol. Quantrill had lived in Lawrence before the war, and he knew that it was a large station on the Underground Railroad for runaway slaves and the home of the most prominent abolitionists. Now, he and the guerrillas had reason to believe that Black men were being enrolled in the U.S. Army in the free state's capital. Quantrill did seem to possess some intelligence of the U.S. Army presence in and around Lawrence, and he might have been tipped off to the fact that there were Black troops camped there. The guerrilla captains likely issued bloody curses as they thought about the possibility of catching a company of Black troops unawares.[4]

The chance to strike at the heart of abolitionism was not enough to entirely convince Quantrill's men of the proposed attack on Lawrence. The mission would be incredibly dangerous. Not only would the men be exposed for days in enemy territory, but they would also be leaving their homes defenseless. Indeed, it appeared to many of the guerrillas as well as their enemies that such a raid was suicide. Ever the card sharp, however, Quantrill gambled that they could pull off the raid and make it back to Missouri alive. He parlayed this bet into the wager that whatever damage partisans did to abolitionists would outweigh any retribution for the raid aimed at southerners in western Missouri, a bigger risk than he probably imagined. Quantrill finally won his captains over by using language that spoke to the wagering nature of the guerrillas, saying, "If you never risk you will never gain."[5]

While Quantrill egged on his men, he was unaware that U.S. general Thomas Ewing was looking to strike at the foundations of the guerrillas' identities. Proclaimed on August 18, about a week after the partisans' council of war, General Orders Nos. 9 and 10 respectively liberated the slaves of disloyal slaveholders and banished the women of known guerrillas. General Order No. 9 authorized Lieutenant Colonel Walker King to go to various posts in the District of the Border and survey the state of enslaved African Americans: "[King is to] ascertain what negroes are there who desire escort out of Missouri, and were they slaves of persons who . . . have been engaged in the rebellion, or have in any way given aid or comfort thereto." If some of these "negroes" were "fit for military duty and willing to enlist," they would be enrolled in the Union army, which amounted to a nightmare come to life for the bushwhackers.[6]

In General Order No. 10, Ewing instructed his officers, "The wives and children of known guerrillas, and also women who are heads of families and are willfully engaged in aiding guerrillas, will be notified by such officers to remove out of this district and out of the State of Missouri forthwith." Ewing knew that any woman willing to assist the bushwhackers in their war effort might be inclined to put up a fight, so he added, "If they fail to remove promptly they will be sent by such officers, under escort, to Kansas City for shipment south." U.S. officers would arrest these female bushwhackers, haul them into headquarters, and hold them until Ewing could send them downriver. The women whom the bushwhackers sought to protect became the sanctioned targets of the Union occupying force.[7]

During the summer of 1863, Ewing began identifying the female supporters of the most infamous guerrillas in his district. He compiled a list of these feminine targets, writing their names on a sheet of paper beside the names of their male kin. Before he could arrest them and remove them from the guerrilla theater, Ewing needed approval. However, even before he received permission from General John Schofield, commander of the Department of the Missouri, Ewing went ahead and ordered the arrest of some of these women. He housed them in a makeshift prison in Kansas City that had once been the home and studio of Missouri artist and U.S. officer George Caleb Bingham. The house was not as sound as it looked, and when U.S. troopers removed a weight-bearing pillar in an adjoining row house while making room for barracks, both houses crumbled. The August 13 collapse killed a handful of the rebel women—sisters, wives, and cousins of Quantrill's most noted men. The death of their women and the arming of Black men caused guerrillas' collective emotions to rise up, shaping their raid on Lawrence and catalyzing an acidic chemistry that ultimately destroyed Quantrill's Raiders.[8]

As the guerrillas came together at the assigned rendezvous in Johnson County, Missouri, their minds were on the death of the girls in Kansas City and their disgust over their former slaves taking up arms against their families. Quantrill attempted to focus and harness the rage of his men. Unsurprisingly, all of these new developments changed the way that some of the guerrillas thought—and felt—about killing. The August 21, 1863, raid on Lawrence presented the first example of the collective change in life taking among the raiders. McCorkle remembered Quantrill shouting, "Boys, this is the home of Jim Lane and Jennison; remember that in hunting us they gave no quarter. Shoot every soldier you see, but in no way harm a woman or child." The guerrillas made killing of soldiers and abolitionist men their primary focus, with the idea of plunder now secondary. Decades later, Gregg recalled Quantrill's new order: "Kill, kill, and you will make no mistake, Lawrence is the hotbed, and should be thoroughly cleansed, and the only way to cleanse it, is to kill."[9]

Although the guerrillas targeted every man or boy big enough to carry a gun, they took special care to kill any Black men they found in Lawrence. While many African Americans in the town fled or hid and escaped the wrath of Quantrill's men, the guerrillas discovered and gunned down twenty or so men, and a few more probably burned to death inside one of the dozens of buildings put to the torch. What relief or joy these violent acts brought to the guerrillas cannot be known, but if they sought to deaden the fear or obliterate the nightmare stalking them, it seems unlikely that the blood, the fire, and the howling screams of their victims did much to help them sleep. That said, none of these men expressed regret over their wartime deeds, and a survey of guerrilla memoirs will show that they were proud of events in Lawrence.[10]

While his men littered the streets with the bodies of Black and white men, Quantrill expended much of his time and energy at Lawrence saving lives. He made his base at the Eldridge House Hotel and spared everyone inside, perhaps because he knew they were not residents of the abolitionist "hotbed," or because he could not bring himself to personally participate in the massacre. Eventually, however, a group of drunken, uncontrollable guerrillas began to loiter in the streets around the hotel and even spill into the building, forcing Quantrill to move the residents to a safer location. He took them to the Whitney House Hotel, operated by his old acquaintance Nathan Stone, where they stayed safely for the remainder of the raid.[11]

Quantrill's attempts to spare a few lives challenge a preexisting interpretation of his life and role in the war. For several biographers of the guerrilla chief, the raid on Lawrence represents the realization of their subject's desire for revenge. Castel says that the raid "was the moment he had been waiting for—this was vengeance. Charley Hart, the man whom Lawrence had scorned and outlawed, had returned." Yet Castel does not explain why this desperado did not kill a single man. Instead, Quantrill stood between his bloodthirsty men and their potential victims. The raid hardly seemed as personal as Castel makes it. While Quantrill possessed the intimate knowledge of Lawrence to design the raid, it was evidently something that fit with the will of the guerrilla community.[12]

Regardless of his mercy, Quantrill led his guerrilla company to Lawrence and let the men loose with orders to exterminate the soldiers and abolitionist men. They killed between 150 and 200 men and boys in the raid on August 21—some of them soldiers, but most of them unarmed men. A much smaller number of men were saved or spared by Quantrill, and even his attempts to protect a chosen few were ineffective. Although it is unclear whether Quantrill ever learned of it, a drunken guerrilla shot and killed his old acquaintance Nathan Stone after the bulk of the company of raiders left the town.[13]

By not killing, Quantrill weakened his position as the chief of this band of killers. While he spared lives, other guerrillas, particularly Bill Anderson, made their names at Lawrence for their bloody acts. Some guerrillas and scholars claim that Anderson chafed under Quantrill's discipline in Texas during the winter of 1863–1864, or that the seed of his rebellion against the guerrilla chief was planted at the Battle of Baxter Springs in October 1863. At Lawrence, though, some guerrillas saw Anderson as ascendant. McCorkle remembered, "We were determined to have revenge, and so, Colonel Quantrill and Captain Anderson planned a raid on Lawrence, Kansas," and he also asserted, "Colonel Quantrill and Captain Anderson were getting the boys together for the raid on Lawrence." Although Gregg's account was the most accurate of the remembrances of the days leading up to the raid, it is nevertheless important that in McCorkle's mind Anderson was a cocommander with Quantrill rather than a subordinate.[14]

Anderson moved up in the minds of many guerrillas because of his deeds at Lawrence. Although an accurate number is impossible to verify, sources report that he killed around fourteen men on the raid. Quantrill's attempts to intercede on behalf of a few old friends and innocent out-of-towners represented one pole of behavior during the raid, Anderson's prolific killing stood at the other pole. For those men who were so enraged by the prison collapse, General Orders Nos. 9 and 10, or some other personal tragedy wreaked by Union troopers, Anderson's bloodlust was attractive. In following him, these partisans might be able to "glut" their vengeance. At the beginning of the war, Quantrill was the killer among novices, but now other men were spilling more blood than he was, and the same rules applied. Anderson was marking himself as *the* killer among killers.[15]

Even if men like Anderson became more powerful because of the killing they did at Lawrence, Quantrill remained in command long enough to achieve another battlefield victory. Immediately after their return from the raid in Kansas, the partisans scattered into the brush. For weeks, they stayed on the run, trying to avoid the persistent, aggressive U.S. troopers and Kansas militiamen seeking to punish them for the bloodshed at Lawrence. Ewing also issued General Order No. 11 depopulating the guerrillas' haunts along the border, making it harder for supporters to provide them food, shelter, and intelligence. It was a difficult time for the partisans, who were now reaping the harvest of destruction from the seeds of bloodshed sown in Kansas. On October 1, Quantrill called the men together once again and led them south for the winter. Five days later, as they made their way to Texas, the lead elements of the band stumbled on Fort Blair near the settlement of Baxter Springs in southeastern Kansas. Led by Gregg and Dave Pool, the guerrilla vanguard made several unsuccessful charges against the U.S. fortification.[16]

While the action around the fortress settled into a stalemate, a U.S. force approached unaware of the fighting at Fort Blair. As he rode at the head of a column toward Baxter Springs, U.S. general James G. Blunt saw a regiment of cavalry riding out of the timber to greet him. The riders "were some 500 yards on our left," Blunt recalled. He continued, "When within 300 yards, they halted; and they being all dressed in Federal uniform, I supposed them to be Lieutenant Pond's cavalry (of which he had two companies)." Continuing to ride toward the welcoming party, the general began to doubt his eyes; there was something off about the way the body of blue-clad men moved. Still, Blunt rode closer, his escort in tow. When he filed his official report nearly two weeks later, he remembered, "My first suspicion of their being an enemy was aroused by seeing several men, supposed to be officers, riding hurriedly up and down their line." Now unsure of who was in front of him, the curious if not careful Blunt nevertheless "advanced toward their line to satisfy [himself] as to the character of the force." Before long, he was a mere fifty yards from the cavalry there to greet him.[17]

Unlike Blunt, Quantrill knew the enemy when he saw them. Wearing his blue cavalry jacket as he rode out of the trees, he looked across the field and saw a group of U.S. troopers preparing to parade into the nearby fortress. John McCorkle, who was with Quantrill at the time, recalled, "[The chief] turned to me and told me to get the boys away from the fort and to form in line." Quantrill, McCorkle, Todd, and other officers rushed about shouting orders. According to McCorkle, "Quantrill then rode behind the lines and when he reached the center, rode out in front, taking off his hat, placed it in the bosom of his coat, touched his horse with his spur and said, 'Come on, boys.'" Following their commander's lead, the guerrillas trotted toward the U.S. column.[18]

Quantrill duped Blunt. While there was little agreement about who shot first, by the time the exchange of lead began, the outcome of the fight had been decided. When they recognized their mistake, the members of Blunt's escort fired a volley, then immediately turned and ran pell-mell across the prairie away from the guerrillas. Seeing the Yankees stricken and fleeing, Quantrill's men pursued them, firing their pistols into the backs of their enemies. When it was all over, eighty-five U.S. soldiers were dead and only two guerrillas killed. Despite leading his men into the trap, Blunt escaped with his life, but he lost most of his escort, his band, his baggage, and his colors. For his part, Quantrill won his greatest victory against conventional army troopers by winning their trust, a triumph that was the pinnacle of his power as a guerrilla chieftain. Unlike the assault on those unarmed, sleeping men at Lawrence, this battle was one he enjoyed. Riding out front—rather than hiding away—Quantrill proudly brought the fight to the enemy on that Kansas prairie. If the raid on Lawrence was necessary as an outlet for the vengeance and bigotry of his men, this accidental meeting was the thrill that Quantrill quested after and proof of his standing as a warrior chieftain.[19]

After he tricked Blunt, Quantrill allowed his men to wreak havoc on the outmatched U.S. troopers running for their lives. The guerrillas killed most of the Federals as they ran or were trying to surrender. The majority of corpses had bullet holes in the middle of their foreheads, as if they had been executed. Quantrill's partisans then stripped most of the bodies and took the uniforms as trophies of a great victory, but the blue jackets and coats would be used as disguises against the next batch of U.S. troopers the guerrillas met.[20]

The guerrillas next confronted an enemy not so easily tricked. Quantrill conferred with Pool and Gregg, then reconnoitered the new fort. It contained multiple companies of men armed with rifles and smoothbore muskets, as well as artillery protected behind breastworks. The guerrillas could not approach Fort Blair without crossing an open field that was an excellent killing zone. Despite these detriments, the battle-happy Todd and Anderson demanded that the guerrillas assault the fort and kill everyone inside. Knowing that such an attack would lead to the deaths of many of his own men, Quantrill refused. He did so in part because he recognized dynamics of the battlefield that are obvious in hindsight but maybe escaped the intellectual grasp of some of his partisans. He seemed to possess a spatial understanding of tactics that exceeded his subordinates' view of warfare. Looking across the open prairie, Quantrill was able to quickly estimate the distance to the fort and the ballistic range of those muskets, and he figured that an attack was foolhardy.[21]

In addition to understanding the strength of Fort Blair, Quantrill found that his strategic philosophy collided with the guerrillas' belief in white supremacy. When Gregg and Pool launched their initial assaults on the fortification, they noticed that they were going up against Black soldiers, a company of the Second Kansas Colored Infantry numbering about seventy men. Todd, who was tasked with riding under a flag of truce to Fort Blair to demand its surrender, must also have seen

Black faces peering back at him from behind the breastworks. Informing Quantrill that the Union commander would not surrender, Todd probably voiced his observation that there were "negro" soldiers in the fort—or he more likely called them "niggers," "darkies," or "runaways." Still, Quantrill told Todd and the men gathered around him, "I would not give the life of one of my men for the whole business."[22]

This event anticipated a much more infamous episode, the Fort Pillow Massacre. On April 12, 1864, Confederate general Nathan Bedford Forrest besieged Fort Pillow on the Mississippi River, assaulted it, and routed the garrison down the bluff toward the river. As the U.S. troops realized their fate, they began to throw down their arms and surrender, but the attackers did not heed their pleas for quarter. Instead, the Confederates gunned them down. At first, the massacre included both white and Black soldiers, but soon after it began, Confederates focused their rage on Black soldiers and the white officers of the USCT for especially rough treatment.[23]

James R. Bingham, a civilian clerk in the fort's general store, bore witness to the brutality. After fleeing the fort and returning two days later, he saw "the remains of Lieutenant Ackerstrom. He had been nailed to a house, and supposed burned alive." The clerk also recalled, "There were the remains of 2 negroes lying where the house burned. I was told they were nailed to the floor." Of another, perhaps more impactful, memory, Bingham stated, "[I] found a negro partially buried with this head out of the ground alive. I went for assistance and water for him," but "he was so near dead that no assistance could save him. We sat by him till he died." Bingham could not "recount but a small part of the barbarities [he] saw on that fatal day, when hundreds of loyal soldiers were murdered in cold blood."[24]

Fort Blair and Fort Pillow, both engagements between white southern horsemen and Black Union soldiers, revealed deep racial hatred. Quantrill's views on race might have been more ambivalent than Forrest's, but white supremacy informed his decision to restrain his troops at Fort Blair. He saw the lives of his white soldiers as more valuable than those of the Black men behind the fortifications. Even if Todd and Anderson had had their way and murdered them all, losing a single white guerrilla in the process would have made it an unacceptable loss in Quantrill's eyes. He would not risk his men's lives to kill some Black U.S. soldiers in an otherwise worthless fortress in that empty stretch of borderland known as southeastern Kansas.[25]

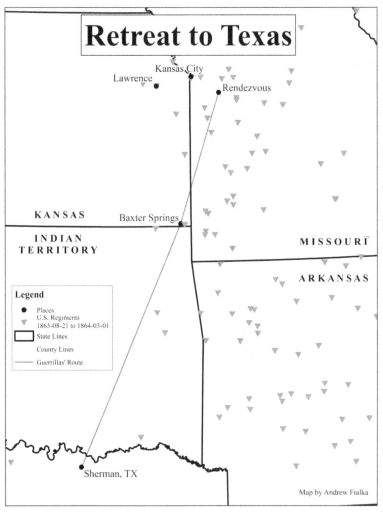

Following the raid on Lawrence and General Order No. 11, Quantrill and his men rendezvoused in Johnson County, Missouri, and marched to Texas to spend the winter behind Confederate lines. Along their march they skirted Union patrols and outposts, slipping past thousands of Union troops. At Baxter Springs, however, the partisans ran into a fort they had not known about. While the Union soldiers in the fortress successfully repelled the guerrillas, Quantrill and his men ambushed a column led by Union general James G. Blunt, massacring around one hundred soldiers, most as they ran away or tried to surrender. The guerrillas then continued their passage south through Indian Territory to Sherman, Texas, where they established a camp some miles outside the town.

After he refused to let his men loose on Fort Blair, Quantrill's chiefdom fell apart, and his men fell into cliques. Some of them gathered around "Bloody Bill" Anderson, others around Todd, and so on. Far removed from their true enemies—U.S. troopers and jayhawkers—these groups took on a clannish quality with petty arguing and infighting among themselves. Small feuds tended to escalate, and more than one man found this environment corrosive. Gregg, who believed his life was threatened by fellow guerrillas, decided to leave. He joined the Confederate army. Younger also departed from the company for a more conventional role in the war. Dave Pool headed out too.[26]

Many of the men who left were Quantrill's allies, and in their absence he struggled and failed to maintain discipline. Men of the wilder sort who gravitated to "Bloody Bill" Anderson were drinking and carousing, thieving, and even murdering. Quantrill scolded men who went into town and raised hell. He even arrested a few guerrillas for murder, tried them, and executed them.[27]

In Texas, the greatest struggle for Quantrill might have been the bawdy behavior of his men. The guerrilla Fletch Taylor remembered drinking and whoring being *the* source of the falling-out among and the dissolution of Quantrill's Raiders. Of Quantrill, Taylor said, "While quartered in Sherman Texas he staid in camp almost all the time while the rest of his officers were having a good time." In an undated letter to W. W. Scott, probably written in the late 1870s or early 1880s, Taylor offered an even more illuminating sentiment regarding his commander's resentment. After all these years, though, the letter is in bad shape—looking worse than an ancient document dislodged from a cave in the Middle East. In its current state, it is only partially legible, but it includes a particularly intriguing sentence: "He never —— after the women, but —— them."[28]

A cipher exists that can help us restore the illegible parts of this sentence and offer further context for Taylor's message. As a journalist, Scott wrote up and published some of his findings on Quantrill. In 1881, he penned a story for the *Cincinnati Enquirer* that was later picked up and printed by the *St. Louis Daily Globe-Democrat*. Scott filtered and summarized the materials at his disposal—including his correspondence with Taylor—and offered insight into what was written on the papyrus before it deteriorated. Scott reported that Taylor told him, "Kate

Clark, who is now proprietor of a bagnio in St. Louis, accompanied the guerrilla on many of his expeditions, but she was the only woman he ever had aught to do with." "Taylor says of Quantrill that he never married," Scott added, and "that he shunned women."[29]

Quantrill *shunned* women. Not all women, as Taylor noted that Kate was his companion, but apparently most women. Taylor's claim might be read as evidence that Quantrill was a loyal man, true to his one and only. Still, "shunned" is a strong word, and it was an even more potent in the nineteenth century, when Taylor used it. Today, "shunning" is synonymous with "spurning" or "shaming." In the 1800s, though, the word meant something closer to its original definition. To shun was to avoid someone out of fear. Taylor implied that Quantrill did not like women because he was afraid of them.

In another letter, this one dated 1879, Taylor elaborated a bit more, claiming, "Quantrill was of a jealous nature." This jealousy was not in regard to Kate Clark. Rather, the envy Taylor observed was in the context of Quantrill's male friends and his officers. Taylor said, "He fell out with several of his officers through one cause and another . . . at different times and we all had a falling out with him and had to quit him." For instance, Anderson quit the chieftain because of numerous disagreements, but especially after Quantrill protested Anderson's proposed marriage to Bush Smith. Anderson had met Smith in Texas that winter, and he married her and then broke with Quantrill.[30]

Annoyed by Quantrill's jealousy and persistent attempts to discipline him and his men in Sherman, Anderson surreptitiously visited Henry McCulloch's headquarters in Bonham. He played the role of innocent informer and told the Confederate general exactly what he wanted to hear: Quantrill, the infamous raider, was to blame for the thievery, murders, and chaos that now reigned in his district. In response, McCulloch called for Quantrill to visit his camp and arrested and disarmed him upon his arrival. The general asked Quantrill to dinner. Quantrill responded, "No, sir, I will not go to dinner. By G——d, I do not care a G——d d——n if I never taste another mouthful on this earth."[31]

After rejecting McCulloch's invitation to dinner and essentially denying the authority of the Confederate government, Quantrill was left with a couple of guards. Pretending to be thirsty, the prisoner asked whether he could pour himself some water from a pitcher nearby. Walking over and reaching down as if to pick up the decanter, Quantrill quickly lunged for his nearby revolvers and swung them toward his guards, catching them unawares. He unshackled himself, fastened his gun belt over his hips, and backed out of the room. Then he mounted his horse and rode out of town before the alarm could be sounded.[32]

Quantrill rode after Anderson, who had convinced dozens of the rowdiest, drunkest, and bloodiest guerrillas to break with their old commander and follow him back to Missouri. After they fled camp, Quantrill arrived, and he and Todd organized a group to go after the breakaway sect of bushwhackers. A brief firefight broke out between the two groups, but no one was killed or seriously wounded, and after they all returned to Missouri, the groups came together again to fight the Yankees. However, Anderson effectively usurped a significant portion of Quantrill's power and made him appear vulnerable.[33]

After Anderson rode back to Missouri, Quantrill stayed on edge, even responding to indirect challenges. During their last few days in Texas, "Todd began to boast of his superior prowess and courage, saying in the camp in Texas one day that he was not afraid of any man on the planet." Any man with planetary confidence was dangerous, but Quantrill called his bluff. "How about me?" the chief said. Todd was taken aback, replying, "O, well, you are the only d——d man that I ever was afraid of." The near shoot-out over a tossed twig and the hurled clod and now this—twice Quantrill called Todd out, and twice Todd gave way to his chief.[34]

Quantrill and Todd left Texas with a group of over sixty men and rode toward their old haunts in Missouri, reaching Lafayette County on the southern bank of the Missouri River by April 1864. There the guerrillas waited until the flooded rivers and streams went down and the foliage filled out so they could return to bushwhacking. They passed the days in their wooded camp lying low and playing cards. On one such day, Quantrill, Todd, and a few other men were playing seven-up, with the pots consistently growing to over $100. Todd was on a streak, winning hand after hand. It became clear to everyone in the game that he was cheating, but nearly all of the men at the table were afraid of the wild-eyed Scotsman with his volatile mood, quick trigger, and lust for blood. Not Quantrill, though, who called him out. Anticipating the challenge, Todd quickly drew his pistol, got the drop on his commander, as well as the upper hand. Todd baited Quantrill and held his fate in his gun hand.[35]

Staring down the barrel of a Colt Navy revolver and seeing the face of death, Quantrill flinched and failed to draw his pistol. The original confidence man was conned, and Todd reveled in the moment, gloating and goading him. In a scene that recalled Charley Hart's confrontation with White Turkey, Quantrill slowly rose to his feet and backed through the crowd of guerrillas toward his horse. He hopped astride Charley, turned his back on Todd and the men he had once led, and rode away into the woods, a chieftain no more.[36]

Wanderer

1864–1865

CHAPTER 15: *Outcast*

Spring rains soaked the earth and swelled the creeks as Quantrill rode deep into the budding wood of Little Dixie. Shamed and threatened, he entered a nether region of a world at war. Quantrill had spent other stretches of the Civil War away from the protection of his men, but this was the first time the decision to leave was not his own. He could not return to the band, not without seeking the permission of George Todd. Alone except for Old Charley, he made his way between the killers he had once led and the men in blue who sought his life, and the horse chose carefully their path through the muddied landscape.[1]

Quantrill might have met up with a female companion. Evidence indicates that he went looking for and found Kate Clark—a fifteen- or sixteen-year-old girl rumored then and now to be his child bride. Quantrill had met Kate as early as the late fall of 1861. As the leader of the patrol that tried to defend the area around Independence in the Sni-A-Bar Township, he visited the farms of that neighborhood, including the home of Robert King. King was fifty-one when the war began. Like his neighbors, he was a native of the border South, born in Kentucky just before the outbreak of the War of 1812. He and his wife, Malinda, moved to Illinois for a bit and then on to Jackson County, Missouri, nearly twenty years before the Civil War. Robert was fairly wealthy, owning $2,500 worth of land and over $1,000 worth of personal property. However, that property ownership did not include slaves, at least according to the 1860 Slave Schedule. Malinda and Robert had five children: Jasper, Martha, Marion, Sarah, and Samuel. Sarah, listed by the census taker as just twelve years old in 1860, was the girl whom Quantrill called Kate.[2]

Quantrill left no record of his feelings about the girl. Nothing. Like so much of his biography, his relationship with Kate is interwoven with

189

the invisible strands of mystery. While she was mentioned here and there by a few of Quantrill's men, the most talkative informant concerning the nature of their bond was Kate herself. In old age she sat for an interview and offered the most vibrant picture of their romance. Her account is also shot through with aggrandizement.[3]

Kate remembered her meeting with Quantrill as love at first sight. According to the story that ran in Missouri's *Kansas City Star* in 1926, she came walking home "from a schoolhouse one mile away, [and] saw a young man talking to her father on the King's front porch." Kate "was struck instantly with the young man's straight and graceful stature. As she entered the yard carrying her lunch pail and books, her eyes were riveted upon the tall young man who, she later learned, was William Clarke Quantrill." Kate was described as "a buxom girl, of sturdy build and well developed for her years . . . She was lively and jolly." It seemed that she was full of life, which the newspaper attributed to the "farm life, spent mostly outdoors and [to] a great deal of time on horseback," which "had given her health and vigor and rosy cheeks." Going on and on about her physical attributes, the paper finally assured its readers, "Old-timers who knew her say she was pretty beyond question." Kate claimed that when she walked up the steps of the porch, Quantrill brazenly turned to her father, and "the young gallant complimented her looks." Robert King's reaction to this stranger's comment was not recorded.[4]

Quantrill's reputation as a warrior deepened Kate's attraction to him. According to the *Kansas City Star*, she heard his name before she ever laid eyes on him. Her father's farm was "close to the Morgan Walker farm, where Quantrill's name first had been brought into prominence." Like so many of her neighbors, "she had heard how this dashing young man had brought three Jayhawkers along with him from Kansas to raid the Walker place and liberate the slaves," the *Star* reported. Kate was also aware that Quantrill "had informed the Walkers of the Jayhawkers intentions so that the three men might be clipped off." Clearly, she "admired the young man's daring deed." She remembered that "she idolized the young Southern hero more than ever."[5]

Kate recalled the unique friendship that commenced. The *Star* reported that the closeness developed "after a few weeks of acquaintance, when the two began riding around the country on horseback." Perhaps "her daring astride a horse as well as her beauty . . . charmed the young outlaw." According to the article, "Kate never hesitated to take a fence or jump a creek." She recalled that "he [Quantrill] was uneasy about her ability in the saddle when she spurred the horse on daringly. . . . He would dismount to keep her horse from rearing, a trick Kate delighted to do to receive her suitor's attention."[6]

Kate's friendship with Quantrill became a source of consternation for her parents. While it was unclear whether the mysterious captain of the patrol was courting her, there was a significant age difference between them. The *Star* recounted, "There came a day when Kate's parents objected to her growing familiarity with the raider. Their daily rides were stopped by her father and she was forbidden to go anywhere with him." Despite her father's reprimand, Kate went to visit the bushwhacker camp. This act of rebellion was discovered, and "Mr. King was told about it and the girl received a severe scolding." Again, though, she took a horse and rode among the other rebels.[7]

Kate said that she married Quantrill in secret. Exactly when or if the two really tied the knot remains a mystery. There is no record of the ceremony. Kate said that they were married early in the war: as early as the winter of 1861–1862, or perhaps a bit later in 1862. Fletch Taylor, a guerrilla riding with Quantrill, claimed his captain wed later in the conflict. In an 1879 letter to W. W. Scott, Taylor asserted, "He [the guerrilla chieftain] took Kate Clark in the summer of 1863." Although Taylor did not witness the ceremony, he was certain of the date, stating, "[Quantrill] borrowed my grey mare for her [Kate] to ride on to a place some 5 miles from camp [where the two were to be married]."[8]

On the day of her wedding, Kate rode out to the brush on her own. She was hiding at a friend's house, afraid to go home and face her father, who was upset with her for continuing to ride to the guerrilla encampment. In the morning, Kate "returned home, took her horse and told her folks she was off for school. Instead of going there she rode into the guerrillas' camp and told Quantrill she feared to meet him any more." Quantrill gave her a new saddle and asked her to go for a ride. Then "he induced her to go with him to a country preacher's home six miles away." Years later Kate explained she was "too young to know what marriage meant. She only knew that she had a blind worship for the young gallant." They found "a vacant shanty by the wayside" where, "Still trembling[,] the young bride prepared a meal." Then, "Quantrill and his bride slept on the floor that night."[9]

After their first night together, Kate realized that intimacy with Quantrill was nothing to fear. "The first day of her married life found her shorn of all timidity"; she realized that "she was no longer the trembling girl of the day before." Furthermore, "as Quantrill's mate she was ready to follow fearlessly wherever he led." Marriage to the chief guerrilla empowered Kate and revealed to her new possibilities she did not see before they were wed. With Quantrill, she could ride her horse, sleep on the floor, and otherwise run wild, free from her parents and free from the expectations that restricted her activity in her rural agrarian community.[10]

Kate claimed she was present for some of the most significant decisions of the war. She lay inside their tent in the guerrilla camp, listening to her husband, Gregg, and Todd as they sat around the fire arguing about the raid on Lawrence. Her recollection in the *Kansas City Star*'s article is the only one that places her in camp during the planning of the raid. There are few other reports of Clark being anywhere near the partisan camp at any time during the war. Kate also claimed that she rode out to meet the guerrillas as they left Lawrence and partook in the retreat, and that she was with Quantrill during the frantic few days of being chased by thousands of troopers and militiamen after they made their way back into Missouri.[11]

However, scattered among these fabrications are a few moments that sound real. For example, in the wake of the raid, the guerrillas and their supporters were looking for places to escape the redemptive violence of jayhawkers and U.S. troopers, as well as the upheaval wreaked by General Order No. 11. During this time, Quantrill and Kate found their way to "a safe Missouri haven." There, in some hollow or some moss-covered hunting cabin far from any road, Quantrill presented his companion with "seven diamond rings, three pins and four sets of earrings out of the loot." Kate readily accepted these spoils of war.[12]

When the guerrillas headed to Texas in the fall of 1863, Kate might have taken up residence in a St. Louis boardinghouse. As the Provost Marshal in charge of St. Louis pursued a case against the famous mail runner and boat burner Robert Louden, he questioned a young woman who gave her name as "Kate Clark." Given the commonality of such a name, and the fact that this document is the only piece of evidence to suggest that she lived in the River City in the fall of 1863, this might be coincidental. Perhaps it was a strange accident that a woman with the same name as the companion of the Trans-Mississippi's most notorious southern guerrilla rented a room in the same house as a "Miss Barry," the apparent love interest of the most renowned Confederate spy in the

West. If this woman was not Quantrill's Kate, she might possibly have moved to central Missouri with her family like so many thousands of refugees whose houses were destroyed in the wake of General Order No. 11.[13]

The next time the two saw each other was in the spring or summer of 1864, when "Quantrill joined Kate, and they went to Howard County," where she looked after him. Kate Clark remembered that summer as their happiest time together, a sort of bushwhacker honeymoon. Once the couple was far enough from the hottest parts of the war, "[Quantrill] put up a tent and Kate had a kitchen built onto the place. It was as near a permanent home as the two ever had." "He had taught her to smoke," Clark recalled, and with little else to do, "they wiled away many hours beside the stove, planning the future while he puffed a cigar and she a pipe." Just the two lovers living under their canvas roof tucked away in the central Missouri woods, a swashbuckling man and renegade girl, an iconic picture of love in the guerrilla war.[14]

Connelley was suspicious of Quantrill's relationship with Kate Clark. Biographies of the guerrilla chief do not allow Kate any agency. Instead, these works present her as a passive victim of Quantrill's depraved sexual desires. Connelley, who was unable to dig up much information on the couple's relationship, nevertheless claimed that the partisan "kidnapped a girl named Kate Clarke and made her his mistress, and spent most of his time with her in the brush." In a footnote, Connelley said, "Others say he kidnapped this girl and that it took her some time to become reconciled to the life to which he doomed her, but that she became infatuated with him, even wearing a man's clothing and riding in the ranks near him."[15]

However, reading Kate's account without gendered stereotypes, it looks like she pursued Quantrill. She was evidently enamored with him. She "admired the young man's daring deed" and "idolized the young Southern hero"; he was "dashing," a "young gallant." Kate's actions, too, revealed her pursuit of the guerrilla. When they went riding, she showed off for him, jumping fences and logs. When he did not come by her parents' house, she took a horse and rode out to see him in the bush. Kate did not sit at home like a delicate flower waiting to be plucked by a suitor of her father's choosing. She hunted her quarry.[16]

Although Kate asserted her presence with Quantrill during the summer of 1864, a couple of guerrilla memoirists believed that the partisan chief was actually joined that summer by a handful of men. Gregg explained what he had heard at that time: "[Quantrill] with a few chosen friends spent the summer in Howard County, Missouri—you might say, dormant." Similarly, someone told McCorkle, "Colonel Quantrell, soon after we had returned from the South, had taken with him Jim Little, John Barker, Tom Harris, Dave Hilton and Tom Evans, and, crossing the Missouri River at Arrow Rock, in Saline County, went into Howard County, where he remained all summer until after Price's raid." Neither Gregg nor McCorkle, who were both otherwise reliable in their recollections of the war, mentioned Kate Clark or any other girls or women in the camp.[17]

Quantrill surrounded himself in the summer of 1864 with the people he loved and who cared for him, whether these individuals included one woman, some men, or all of them. Together, they retired from the war, and as Gregg said, "It really began to look as though Quantrill's military sun had set to rise no more forever."[18]

In the summer of 1864, the sun set across the white South. In Virginia, General Robert E. Lee engaged in a campaign for the survival of his army and the Confederate government. To the south, Major General William Tecumseh Sherman's armies—the Army of the Tennessee, Army of the Ohio, and Army of the Cumberland—pushed into Georgia from Chattanooga, Tennessee, in May 1864. Sherman took Atlanta on September 2, doing unmeasurable damage to the Confederate infrastructure and helping to secure Lincoln's reelection. John Hunt Morgan attempted one last-ditch, ill-fated attempt to retake Kentucky, but he was easily dispatched back across the mountains. In Missouri, with Quantrill in exile, the war turned bloodier, more gruesome than ever before.[19]

While the sun went down seemingly everywhere else, Quantrill was lounging in the warm sunlight of some lush glade. Whether he was sitting beside a furnished tent with an infatuated girl waiting on him, or he was bivouacked with a few old friends, he was away from the killing, and it looked like he got out at the right time.[20]

CHAPTER 16: *Vagabond*

John McCorkle, who was riding with George Todd, recalled a rendezvous of several bands of bushwhackers in September 1864. Somewhere between Franklin and Rocheport, the commands of Todd, "Bloody Bill" Anderson, Tom Todd (no relation), and John Thrailkill came together and began plotting their next move. The guerrillas were on the offensive in an effort to help Sterling Price's invasion into Missouri, and it seemed that even reluctant killers were pulled back into the fray. As the groups greeted one another, some of the men looked up to see a small band of wayward friends riding toward them. McCorkle remembered the moment thus: "To our delight, Colonel Quantrell, with his friends who had been with him in this country, came to us." McCorkle and most of the other guerrillas held a deep fondness for Quantrill and he for them; it was the only way to explain his return to the war.[1]

Now that Quantrill was no longer in charge, Todd and Anderson sat at the head of this combined company of guerrillas. They wanted to assault a fortified group of U.S. troopers, and nothing their old commander said would stop them. After offering salutations, Quantrill rode off with the other captains, who "held a consultation in regard to attacking Fayette," a town just to the north. Quantrill "told the other officers there was no use in attacking men in brick houses and log cabins with only side arms; that if [they] did, [they] would only succeed in getting some of [the] men killed . . . and [he] insisted that [they] let Fayette alone." The other captains did not listen, so Quantrill rode with his men toward the blockhouses bristling with rifles.[2]

The attack on Fayette went as Quantrill feared. U.S. soldiers blasted the guerrillas to bits with aimed rifle fire as they charged toward thick-walled buildings looped with holes. Horses spun about, men and beasts crashed together in heaps, dust rose, and combatants spat in anger and whimpered in pain. Jim Little, who had been with Quantrill since the first ride of Andrew Walker's patrol, was shot through the arm. Riding beside him, Quantrill grabbed Little and pulled him to safety. McCorkle helped Lee McMurtry out of the fight and remembered, "When I reached the pasture I there found Colonel Quantrell with Jim Little, who had received a bad wound in the right arm." Leaving McMurtry in Quantrill's care, McCorkle tried to ride back into battle, but Quantrill stopped him. "Quantrell called to me and asked me where I was going," he recalled, "to which I replied, 'To help the boys.' He said, 'Come on back, there's no use trying to shoot through brick walls and logs with pistols.'" McCorkle heeded Quantrill's advice and stayed put until what remained of the company limped out of the town. Describing the wake of the fight, McCorkle remembered, "Quantrell left us at Fayette, going back into Boon's Lick Township and taking Jim Little with him." Enough was enough.[3]

Quantrill was primarily motivated by his affection for men like Jim Little. He could not stand by and watch his friends and comrades be slaughtered. Whether the product of Todd's and Anderson's combined bloodlust or tactical shortsightedness or both, the attack on Fayette resulted in the needless deaths of more than a dozen guerrillas, with dozens more wounded. Each dead or wounded friend chipped away at Quantrill's will to fight. While he shared the Missourians' proslavery views and probably would have fought for the South in some other capacity during the war, Quantrill's bonds with other young men kept him fighting as a bushwhacker. In a war effort without enlistments or contracts, a conflict where commissions were more of a suggestion of authority than anything else, human relationships—whether brotherhood, kinship, or, for an outsider like Quantrill, friendship—made him a part of the company. The Walker men were his first friends, and when the war began he rode side by side with Andrew Walker into combat. When Quantrill returned from Richmond, he sought out his close companion Todd. Before Fayette, Quantrill rode back into the fray to be with old friends and to advocate for them. Once it was clear that he could not protect his pals, Quantrill again wandered away, a warrior without a home, but he would try once more to save some old friends and maybe even himself.

After Quantrill retreated to the no-man's-land between the bushwhackers and the U.S. Army, Sterling Price's raid was just beginning. With twelve thousand men, Price's Army of Missouri invaded the southeastern corner of the state on September 19 and moved slowly northward in the general direction of St. Louis. The invasion was ill-fated from the start. Some men rode mules, and other men in the poorly equipped Army of Missouri did not possess firearms. In addition, the army did not have much artillery. Worse, Price showed poor judgment in leading this hardscrabble group of diehards. On September 27, he wasted precious men and resources attacking Fort Davidson near Pilot Knob. Although U.S. commander General Thomas Ewing, who had been reassigned from the border, gave up the fort after blowing up the powder magazine and escaping with the garrison in the middle of night, Price wasted enough time that his goal of taking St. Louis became unattainable. At this point, Price turned the Army of Missouri toward the state capital of Jefferson City.[4]

On the same day as Price's disastrous assaults against Fort Davidson, Anderson, Todd, and several other guerrilla captains with their respective bands orchestrated the bloodiest ambush of the war outside Centralia, Missouri. In the morning, Anderson and his men raided the town and ended up executing twenty-four unarmed U.S. troopers. A few hours later, a Union patrol under the command of A. V. E. Johnston discovered the bodies and rode into the countryside to kill the guerrillas. About two miles from town, Johnston and more than 130 men rode into an open field surrounded on three sides by woods that hid hundreds of bushwhackers. After Johnston dismounted his men and walked them some distance from their horses, the guerrillas burst out of the tree line and attacked the outnumbered, outgunned, horseless troopers. The partisans killed nearly every man, executing most of them as they ran or tried to surrender. More than a few guerrillas also mutilated the corpses, taking scalps, severing fingers, noses, and ears, and even cutting away genitalia.[5]

After the Army of Missouri entered Little Dixie and was rebuffed by the U.S. Army outside Jefferson City, many guerrillas joined the rebel unit, including many of the men who participated in the gory bloodletting of Centralia. Both Todd's and Anderson's men met with Price. The Confederate general assigned the guerrillas special tasks, like the destruction of railroad bridges, the cutting of telegraph wires, or the performance of diversionary raids. Eventually Todd and his men served as scouts for the army. On October 21, 1864, a Union soldier shot and killed Todd while he was riding out in front of Price's army, not far from Independence, Missouri. While the loss was significant, Todd's death did little to change the fate of Price's raid. Over the next few days and weeks, the Army of Missouri lurched west a few more miles, then turned southward and crept its way toward Arkansas while U.S. forces battered its flanks and rear guard. In early December, Price made it back to Confederate territory totally defeated; he had less than half the men with whom he had begun the raid.[6]

Not every group of guerrillas followed Price's path out of the state. "Bloody Bill" Anderson and his men continued to bushwhack across Little Dixie. On October 26, U.S. troopers gunned Anderson down in an ambush. The victorious U.S. soldiers then took Anderson's body to Richmond, Missouri, and photographed the corpse, generating a gruesome and iconic image that announced an end to the most brutal chapter of bushwhacking in the state.[7]

After Anderson and Todd were shot down in the fall of 1864 and Price's raid inevitably fizzled, a few aimless bushwhackers made their way back to Quantrill. McCorkle was one of these wanderers. Upon getting back with his old commander, McCorkle remembered, "[Quantrill] told us that he intended to . . . go across the State of Missouri into Illinois, then into Kentucky and thence into Virginia, [and] that we were all to wear Federal uniforms and to pass ourselves as Union soldiers." The fighting in Missouri was on such a path that none of them were going to live to see peace.[8]

It was around this time that Quantrill took Kate Clark away so he could tend to his men. According to a story about Clark in the *Kansas City Star*, "Before Quantrill made the fatal expedition into Kentucky he took his bride to St. Louis." "When he left Kate in St. Louis," the article noted, "it was in the expectancy that he would be back in two months." Clark recalled, "Some of the men who broke with him after the Todd dispute, also joined the party. Quantrill seemed to possess a hypnotic influence over them and they were ready to lay down their lives for him." She thought that this influence was the result of "his personal supervision of them." Specifically, Quantrill "was known to go among them at night to see if all went well and at times even to stand guard over the sleeping men. Such faithfulness endeared him greatly [to the guerrillas]."[9]

Now Quantrill sought to get them out of the war with their lives. There is now and will remain speculation over the partisan chief's decision to shift theaters of war. A rumor arose in the postbellum years that Quantrill was on his way to Washington to assassinate President Lincoln, but nothing substantiates this speculation. Instead, Quantrill's primary motivation was to continue to fight as the guerrillas had done in the first two years of the war, and to link up with a formal Confederate army so that he and his bushwhackers could surrender without forfeiting their lives.[10]

Quantrill saw promise in Kentucky. The guerrilla fighting there was only beginning to take hold on the systematic level that Missouri had witnessed earlier in the war. Although the U.S. occupation force administered some draconian measures there, the brutality was not as extreme. There had been no General Order No. 11, rebel women were not imprisoned or killed, and guerrillas and male southern sympathizers were not being shot down without restraint—or, at least, Quantrill did not hear of any such things happening in Kentucky. Furthermore, it likely occurred to him that Kentucky was close to Ohio. Perhaps Quantrill dreamed that once the war ended, he would make his way home to see his mother. Whatever his motivations, Quantrill and a couple of dozen men swam their horses across the Mississippi River and slipped into Kentucky in January 1865.[11]

Not long after Quantrill and his Missourians entered the Bluegrass State, the U.S. Army made sweeping changes to its counterinsurgency policies. On February 10, 1865, the War Department issued General Order No. 21. The order redrew the military map, proclaiming, "The State of Kentucky will constitute the Military Department of Kentucky. Major General J. M. Palmer, U.S. Volunteers, is assigned to the command of the Department of Kentucky." Kentucky had been a military district within the Department of the Ohio, but with the increasingly intense guerrilla violence that began in the fall of 1864, the state's situation required a greater influx of military resources. News of the arrival of guerrillas from Missouri was probably a significant factor in the reorganization of the U.S. Army.[12]

At the time that Quantrill and the bushwhackers arrived, Sue Mundy and her band were the most notorious southern partisans in the Bluegrass region of Kentucky. Mundy was originally the creation of an embittered newspaperman who sought to shame the guerrillas for their unmanly ways of war, but the guerrillas recognized her as one of their own. Jerome Clark, a small, beautiful young man possessed of feminine features, long hair, and style that rivaled Quantrill's, came to embody Sue Mundy. The men who rode with Jerome Clark, most notably Sam "One-Armed" Berry and Henry C. Magruder, proudly claimed to ride with Sue Mundy.[13]

Colorful and flamboyant, Quantrill knew his people when he met them. In early February 1865, the Missourians, bedecked in their blue Union uniforms, were resting at the home of an acquaintance—Dr. Isaac McClaskey—when Quantrill looked out on the snow-covered landscape. A vibrant burst of colors exploded out of the white-and-black backdrop and came galloping toward him like a band of circus riders. The raw, unrestrained, gaudy, dashing style of Sue Mundy's gang must have reminded Quantrill and his men of that wild, free-flowing, dashing brand of fighting that let each man feel fully himself that they had waged in 1862 and 1863.[14]

While we know little about the meeting between these kindred spirits, they seem to have discussed a sort of strategy. The Kentuckians and Missourians fought as independent bands in league with one another. Clark, Magruder, and Berry shared with the new arrivals their logistical backbone—the rebel households and southern-sympathizing women of the Bluegrass.[15]

The alliance did not last long. In early March, Union militiamen ambushed Sue Mundy's gang and wounded Magruder in the chest. Clark took hold of his friend and led him to safety at a nearby farm. After resting there, they moved on to another house and then another, staying ahead of the swarming patrols. On March 12, though, U.S. troopers and militia located Clark and Magruder and surrounded them in a barn. These opponents engaged in a shoot-out until Clark agreed to talk about surrender—something he was reluctant to do, for he knew that his life was forfeited one way or another. Nevertheless, he gave himself up for the sake of his wounded friend Magruder, and the U.S. officer promised Clark a trial rather than just an execution. U.S. officials tried Clark, found him guilty of various crimes, and sentenced him to hang. They allowed Magruder to recover before he experienced the same fate in the fall of 1865.[16]

While the Missourians spent the next few months ambushing and raiding U.S. outposts, Quantrill connected with a woman. Many guerrillas from the western side of the Mississippi had cousins on the eastern side of the river who helped them while they familiarized themselves with the landscape—both geographic and social. The Dawsons were cousins to John Jarrett, a longtime Jackson County, Missouri, bushwhacker, and Quantrill was sweet on one of their daughters—Nancy, or "Nannie." When the guerrillas visited the Dawson place, Quantrill wrote a poem for Nannie. It reads,

> My horse is at the door,
> And the enemy I soon may see;
> But before I go Miss Nannie,
> Here's a double health to thee!
>
> Here's a sigh to those who love me,
> And a smile to those who hate;
> And, whatever sky's above me,
> Here's a heart for every fate.
>
> Though the cannons roar around me,
> Yet it still shall bear me on;
> Though dark clouds are above me,
> It hath springs which may be won.
>
> In this verse as with the wine,
> The libation I would pour
> Should be of peace with thine and mine
> And a health to thee and all in door.

The poem is signed, "Very respectfully your friend W. C. Q." and dated February 26, 1865.[17]

This poem seems to be the work of an itinerant hotspur steeped in the popular culture of yesteryear. With lines like "Here's a sigh to those who love me, And a smile to those who hate," this poetry conveys the worldview of a rake who sees himself as the center of the action. Indeed, the author thinks a lot of himself; he is a man whose sighs and smiles carry weight. This libertine-warrior-poet laughs in the face of death. The swagger is propped up by the inner feelings of the classic, even cliché, lothario—a role the author seeks to inhabit. On the outside he is a killer, but on the inside he is a lover. Out there fighting, he is tough, but with the one he loves, he is soft. It is a poem about two men in one. The poem establishes the author's mask and hints at what lies behind it.[18]

Nannie might have been disappointed to learn that the poem her bushwhacking beau scribbled down was not borne of his heart for her. The author was a hack. He plagiarized the work from Lord Byron, who penned a similar poem that begins with the act of toasting for compatriot and fellow poet Thomas Moore. The first two stanzas of Byron's poem read,

> My boat is on the shore,
> And my bark is on the sea;
> But, before I go, Tom Moore,
> Here's a double health to thee!
>
> Here's a sigh to those who love me,
> And a smile to those who hate;
> And, whatever sky's above me,
> Here's a heart for every fate.

Quantrill's decision to crib this poem—one that articulates Byron's love and appreciation for another man and focuses on the consumption of alcohol—was an interesting choice for a teetotaler who was writing to a woman.[19]

A couple of months after he left the poem for Nannie, Quantrill fought in his last skirmish. On May 10, 1865, Terrell and his hunters caught the Missourians off guard in the barn of James Wakefield. When the guerrillas saw the hunters come riding into the yard, someone sounded the alarm, and most of them mounted and rode to the safety of the brush. Quantrill was not one of them. Ducking, firing, and sprinting, he made his way to Clark Hockensmith, but one of the hunters shot him in the back.[20]

Quantrill revealed his thoughts in the day or two he spent at the Wakefield farm. Wakefield recalled, "While he was lying wounded at our house . . . he told me of some money he wanted to leave for his mother and sister." Like wounded boys across the Civil War who wallowed in pain for hours or days in the field, Quantrill thought of his mother. Before he was moved from the farm, he made his wishes for her clear. Wakefield remembered, "[He said] he would write me about [the treasure] when he got to Louisville. He told me who had it and how much but I never got any word from him about it."[21]

John N. Edwards, the hagiographer, claimed that during one of the nights spent at the Wakefield farm, the dying chieftain gave a farewell speech to the guerrillas who gathered around him. Quantrill said, "I cannot live. I have run a long time; I have come out unhurt from many desperate places; I have fought to kill and I have killed; I regret nothing." "The end is close at hand," he resolved. Protesting any attempt by his men to move him, Quantrill then said, "I am resting easy here, and will die so." He turned his attention to his men, telling them, "You do not know how your devotion has touched my heart, nor can you ever understand how grateful I am for the love you have shown me."[22]

There was little doubt that Quantrill and his men exchanged heartfelt sentiments. Perhaps, though, these feelings were more complicated and one-sided than previously thought. We know well enough the depth of Quantrill's affection for his partisans. It helped him ingratiate himself to strangers, bonded him to his men, and made him a guerrilla commander. Quantrill knew, however, that his bushwhackers' love for him was limited. Most of his men deserted him at one point. Either they lost sight of their wartime duties and became entangled with booze and whores, or they jumped on the coattails of other men. When Quantrill was staring down the barrel of a pistol, none stood up to defend him. If the guerrilla chief reflected on his last few years in the brush with these men, then he almost certainly felt the same way Lord Byron did when he wrote,[23]

> This much and more; and yet though lov'st me not,
> And never wilt! Love dwells not in our will.
> Nor can I blame thee, though it be my lot
> To strongly, wrongly, vainly love thee still.

CHAPTER 17: *Quarry*

William Clarke Quantrill was as elusive in death as he was in life. Ever the confidence man, he cloaked his departure from the American drama in mystery, false leads, masks, and obscuration. His coconspirators were many—witting or otherwise. With the help of these mourners, hoarders, grave robbers, charlatans, and deniers, Quantrill left questions and befuddlements. Still, the hunt for this enigmatic bushwhacker through this fog of mystery offers a new perspective on some long-standing themes of post–Civil War America.

Quantrill's final act was to hide himself away. As the end neared, he handed his confessor, Father Powers, $800 in gold and whispered instructions for the treatment of his corpse. When Quantrill died on June 6, the priest prayed over his body. A day or two later, Father Powers and cemetery sexton Patrick Scully placed Quantrill's cadaver in a coffin hewn from Walnut and loaded the box into a hearse pulled by a single horse. They transported the body to St. John's Catholic Cemetery in the neighborhood of Portland. Putting the casket in the ground not ten feet from the residence of Scully and his wife, Bridget, Father Powers relayed Quantrill's instructions to the sexton. The guerrilla had asked "that no mound be raised over the grave . . . and that they should throw their dishwater and other slops over the spot so as to obliterate it as much as possible to keep the body from being stolen." Patrick and Bridget Scully did as the priest told them and erased any trace of Quantrill's physical existence. He was buried under a muddy pile of kitchen scraps near the entrance to the cemetery.[1]

Quantrill was right to think that people would want to dig him up. Not long after his death and burial, a mysterious lady came looking for him. A local story that circulated around the neighborhood of Portland and filtered down through the years recalls the arrival of this figure. According to this legend, Quantrill's "body was disinterred in the presence of Mr. [Scully] the sexton, and a lady who was supposed to be his fiancé." Although there was no name attributed to this lady, after the coffin was opened and his face revealed, "she wept at the sight of his still, pale features." Then the lid was nailed atop the box once more, and "after the second burial the lady passed out of the cemetery declaring the body to be that of Quantrill."[2]

Kate Clark might have been this veiled figure. If so, the story contradicts her own recollection of the guerrilla chief's final days. In 1926, Clark recalled that while she was in St. Louis in the spring of 1865, "she was stopping at a boarding house, where a priest brought word one day that the guerilla chief had been wounded in a scuffle on a farm and was not expected to live." "She hastily prepared for the journey to him," learning that "he had been moved to a government hospital in Louisville." She "arrived at his bedside three days before the end and she stood beside her husband as he breathed his last." Although the church officials who saw Quantrill out of this world and took care of his burial did not mention the arrival of a woman, Clark was possibly at his bedside to hold his hand as he accepted the last rites.[3]

It is also possible that the mysterious figure was not Clark. Maybe it was Nannie Dawson or another mourner. Whoever was looking for Quantrill on that hot summer day in 1865—a grief-stricken fiancé, a despairing friend, a painted woman in black, or someone altogether different—she glided over that hallowed ground like the very specter of mourning.[4]

Across the country, northerners and southerners were in mourning. From Maine to Florida and the Atlantic to the plains, parents, siblings, and sweethearts of soldiers learned of the death of their loved ones from a letter sent by a stranger or a casualty list published in a local newspaper. Many struggled to accept the truth. Americans knew well the reality of war and the possibility of losing a child, brother, or husband, but they wanted proof of their loved ones' demise. The bereaved left their homes and went looking for the corpses, not only to move them to family plots, but also to put to rest that debilitating sense of hope. Quantrill's visitor was one of these seekers. There was little doubt that she was crushed upon seeing the body. Only through this acceptance of his demise, however, could she begin to grieve and mourn. For that lady in black, her trip to the Portland cemetery was just the beginning of a process of coming to terms with loss, just like the several millions of other Americans who confronted the absence of a loved one in the wake of the Civil War.[5]

There is a deceptive element to this story of the stricken maiden, however. It promotes the idea that Quantrill was a dashing lothario of yesteryear whose death sent women into fits of despair and weeping. We know that women admired him. They sent flowers to his hospital, and they cherished the poems he wrote. But the long black veil of that mourner did not just cover the face of a woman. It also obscured the faces of all those men who wept when they heard about the death of their captain, or who read about the demise of the boy they had known in the settlements, on the plains, or in the mountains years before the war.

The next person who came to find the bushwhacker's body did not travel to Louisville to mourn, but to own a piece of Quantrill. In 1884, W. W. Scott, Quantrill's childhood friend, disembarked in the Falls City and went looking for a Father Brady. In his pocket, he held a letter of introduction from Father H. B. Dues, a priest from Canal Dover, Ohio. The missive detailed Scott's mission: he was in Louisville to find the grave of Quantrill and learn anything about his final days that might give the dead man's mother closure. With the help of Brady, Scott was apparently successful. He noted that he "found [the] grave of W. C. Quantrill on this visit . . . talked with Mr. Scully, the sexton, and Bridget Scully his wife. Both were there when Quantrill was buried, within 10 steps of the cemetery lodge, where they lived." Scott jotted in his notes Father Powers's role in the secret burial and the gift of $800 from Quantrill to Powers. If he sought information about the end of the partisan's life, Scott hit the jackpot. It was not enough, though. Three years later Scott came back to Louisville, this time with Quantrill's mother in tow.[6]

On December 8, 1887, under the darkening sky and falling rain, and exposed to the wind that blew along the bank of the Ohio River, two men and a woman assembled near the cemetery in Portland. They looked like any other grave robbers. The woman, Bridget Scully, begrudgingly led the two men across the cemetery to an area of the lawn where she said the prize was buried. For her trouble, Scott handed her one dollar. Louis Wertz, the gravedigger, was with Scott and Scully. Wertz and Scully were unenthusiastic about the idea of disturbing this sacred ground. As they stood over the unmarked grave, Scott suborned Wertz with two and a half dollars for getting his hands dirty. The sexton turned the other way, and the gravedigger took up his shovel and buried it in the turf.[7]

After Wertz had worked for one hour in the rain, his spade reached a human skeleton. The bones were bare—no coffin survived the decades in the ground. Hardly any clothing remained. Most of the organic fibers had deteriorated and been absorbed by the earth, leaving a few buttons and a sock. The buttons were plain with no sign of their origin, at least none worth recording, but the sock was standard issue for U.S. Army soldiers. Because bushwhackers were known to don the clothing of their enemy, the sock did not automatically disqualify this corpse from being that of a southern guerrilla. When the skull was retrieved from the ground, a ring of nearly white hair slipped from it. Standing in the rain, holding the skull, and staring into the voids where eyes once were, Scott believed he had found Quantrill. Scott told Scully he wanted to bring the skull to Mrs. Caroline Quantrill so that she could identify it, but he promised to return the skull to the hallowed ground afterward.[8]

Scott hustled the skull back to the hotel. Caroline, who was not well enough to venture out in the cold, was horrified when she saw it. Even so, she thought she recognized a chipped tooth as that of her boy. After she identified her son's skull, Caroline Quantrill absconded to Ohio with Scott and the skull and bones. Once back in Canal Dover, they interred in the family plot a box that was supposed to contain the remains found in Kentucky. However, Scott lied to Quantrill's mother about the contents of the box, secretly keeping the largest bones and the skull.[9]

Scott's exact plans for the bones are unknown. Perhaps he thought he would sell them or display them to a paying audience. Whatever he was thinking, he was not going to disclose that he possessed them until after Quantrill's mother died. When Caroline Quantrill outlived Scott, William E. Connelley acquired the arm and leg bones and peddled the trophies but found no buyers. Meanwhile, Scott's son and his fraternity brothers used Quantrill's skull as a beer schooner—an ironic turn for the head of a teetotaler. All of these shenanigans were eventually discovered. The bones were put in the ground in Higginsville, Missouri, in a cemetery for Confederate veterans, and the skull was finally buried in Canal Dover, but not until 1992.[10]

208   CHAPTER SEVENTEEN

❧

Men who could not release their grip on the past tainted the modern, parallel burials with contrived memories and misunderstandings of the past. Robert L. Hawkins III—the commander of a chapter of Sons of Confederate Veterans for Jefferson City, Missouri—gave the eulogy for Quantrill before his burial at Higginsville. He told the *New York Times*, "We do not wish him buried where people are ashamed of him, where no one remembers or cares to recall the brutality of a partisan warfare that created men like Captain Quantrill and those who rode with him." Rather, Hawkins stated, "He belongs here, here with those who were truly his people." [11]

Perhaps, or perhaps not. Although Hawkins's sentiments are heartfelt and on a certain level true, they are like so many presumptuous statements made by the living about the dead. The memories of Civil War soldiers and leaders are frequently hijacked by modern commemorators, buffs, and politicians who use their vision of the past to confirm their view of the present and vice versa. Not surprisingly, these assertions of the past's meanings miss the point and often minimize the humanity of the dead. Hawkins clearly sympathized with Quantrill. But for him to deny Quantrill the kinship of his mother or his sister—the very people he was most concerned about in the hours and days after he was mortally wounded—and to declare that those Ohioans were not his people seems opposed to what the guerrilla chief likely thought.[12]

The Sons of Confederate Veterans sought to reclaim Quantrill's skull from Dover Historical Society before the reburial in Missouri, but the organization was rebuffed. In addition to the skull being in Dover, there were already bones in the ground in the old cemetery in Canal Dover. Responding to the Missourians, Les Williams, the chair of the Dover Historical Society at the time, said to the *New York Times*, "I think they are going overboard in Missouri, with 200 people and a big ceremony over a hank of hair and five bones. I think all the bones should be buried in one place, and the largest part of the Quantrill bones are here." Even if Williams thought it was wrong to lionize Quantrill, there was no way Dover was giving up the skull.[13]

Others in Dover were more straightforward when discussing what to do with Quantrill's skull. Jim Nixon, who was the president of the Dover Historical Society in 1992, could not hide his ambivalence. He told the *New York Times*, "Our intention is just to get it over with," and the newspaper quoted him as saying he "could not care less" about the matter. Nixon was apparently annoyed by all of the free attention Quantrill's skull brought the historical society. While his feelings about presiding over a funeral for a long-dead proslavery raider are understandable, it was a rare and easily marketable opportunity for a local history society to be given so much attention, not only by the local or regional newspapers but also by the national media. To cast the subject aside and shrug off journalists' questions with responses like "It's way down my list of priorities" or "It is nothing more than a curiosity" seems shortsighted.[14]

More than one hundred years after Scott had pillaged the grave and begun dispersing Quantrill's skeleton from Ohio to Missouri, a group of admirers came looking for the original resting place of the bushwhacker. In 2008, members of various chapters of the Sons of Confederate Veterans and the United Daughters of the Confederacy met in Louisville at the cemetery where Quantrill had originally been buried. Part burial ceremony, part commemoration, the occasion combined a bit of religiosity with the pomp accompanying the celebration of a Confederate martyr of the Civil War. There were Christian prayers, hymns, a poem, a volley salute, Confederate flags, and the singing of "Dixie." The gist of the speeches and eulogy was that Quantrill was a hero, and that the true history of the war and his role in it had been suppressed to demonize him and keep him from receiving the proper memorialization due to him. Portraying the guerrilla chief as a victim was not the only bit of irony to surface during the ceremony. The SCV and UDC members set a burial stone over the place they presumed to be the ground where Quantrill's body had once moldered. By advertising the presence of his remains under that turf, they undid his last wish.[15]

There were other layers to the irony of this marker. The stone reads thus: "In Memory, Col. William Clarke Quantrill, July 31, 1837–June 6, 1865." Below his name is chiseled an epitaph, a stanza of the poem the partisan wrote for Nannie Dawson—the poem he borrowed from Lord Byron. Given his interests, Byron—had he lived long enough to see the Civil War—would have been more likely to celebrate abolitionism and the arming of Black men in the service of that cause than the war that Quantrill waged in defense of slavery.[16]

Depending on the last time the grass was mowed at the cemetery, it can be difficult to find the marker placed there by the Sons of Confederate Veterans. While Confederate flags almost certainly decorated the site at one point or another, there are none there now. Someone—perhaps a local—pulled up those symbols of white supremacy. No doubt, more of those tiny battle flags of the Army of Northern Virginia will be placed at the burial site. Regardless, a gravesite tourist had best presume that there will be no obvious indication of the stone. In this sense, something of the anonymity desired by Quantrill is maintained.

It is unknown how the Sons of Confederate Veterans and the United Daughters of the Confederacy decided on the spot. The cemetery lodge where Mr. and Mrs. Scully lived is no longer standing. An image in the *Louisville Courier-Journal* from 1888 purports to show "Quantrill's Grave Beneath The Tree In The Cottage Yard At St. John's Cemetery." However, there are three trees in the image. A grave marker sits below one large tree, but we know that Quantrill's grave was not marked. A young tree is pictured beside the cottage, and then another tree stands on the other side of the cottage. Perhaps the SCV and UDC deduced that the smallest tree sprang up near Quantrill's grave. Then they only needed to find the large visible gravestones to get a general sense of where the guerrilla's grave was. The organizations no doubt did their research.[17]

However, this is all assuming that Bridget Scully led Scott to the right body, and not to the corpse of an anonymous Union soldier. Maybe Quantrill—all of him—is still in that graveyard in Kentucky, lying a good distance from the stone put there by the Sons of Confederate Veterans. What a trick that would be. Perhaps he lies beneath undisturbed grass, his skull grinning in perpetual slumber as he enjoys the same anonymity that covers the other deceased men and women in that burial ground. If he is still there, then he is like the thousands of soldiers and noncombatants who died in the Civil War and were buried in unmarked graves. Like them, no one visits him. No tiny flags cover his grave, and the only flowers that decorate the ground over his slumbering bones are dandelions that pop up each May with the spring rain showers.

ACKNOWLEDGMENTS

The bulk of *A Man by Any Other Name* was written during the pandemic. It felt indulgent, misanthropic even, to hole up and write while the rest of the country descended into chaos. That's what I did, though. Write and teach and live with my chosen few. As perverse as it might sound at this particular moment, I think I'll look back fondly on this time.

I incurred many debts while writing this book. Many of the people that make up Penn State Erie, The Behrend College, especially my colleagues in the history program and friends like Tom Noyes and Matt Levy, provided outlets and support. Along with some money from the School of Humanities Endowment Fund, the college granted me a sabbatical during the fall semester of 2020 that allowed me to extricate myself from the classroom and the committee work. It was a time of great productivity, and I appreciate it.

In the early stages of writing, I drove to Canal Dover, Ohio, to see whether there was anything there that might help me put this book together. There was. I found Quantrill's grave, and saw the wax bust of his head and his powder horn at the Reeves Mansion. As importantly, I met some very generous and helpful people. Jim Gill, Kim Jurkovic, Shelagh Pruni, and a host of other locals helped me in different ways at various stages. I also met fellow Civil War scholar Kelly Mezurek during the first Quantrill Symposium in Canal Dover. She had her students transcribe all of Quantrill's letters to his mother, and she produced a nice little volume that was a great help to me as I wrote this book.

When I was looking for a place for this book, I kept returning to UnCivil Wars. The series has produced some of my favorite books. To me, it was apparent that an impressionist biography of Quantrill would be a good fit among those titles. Steve Berry and Amy Murrell Taylor were helpful from the word "go"—even before the word "go"—in shaping the book and making it better. As usual, Mick Gusinde-Duffy made the process a pleasant one. My thanks to all of you and the many other people at UGA Press that helped make this book real.

There were a handful of people who helped in small but important ways from a distance. Because there were no conferences and archives were shut down, I reached out to several scholars and archivists via email, and each query received a helpful response. Trae Welborn helped me track down some of Louis T. Wigfall's papers. Megan Kate Nelson helped me understand the routes Quantrill might have taken through the mountains. Barton Myers fielded a question about the Partisan Ranger Act and the list of commissioned officers. Patrick Lewis at the Filson Historical Society was nice enough to assist in the search for a needle in a haystack, as was Stephen Towne at IUPUI. That needle is still out there. James M. Prichard, also at the Filson Historical Society, hunted down a few things related to Quantrill's grave. I was actually able to talk to Trevor Plante at the National Archives in person about the potential of records related to Quantrill in the collections at NARA while I was there, and he was kind enough to respond to an email while NARA was closed to the public, a time when I'm sure he was incredibly busy.

I can only take credit for a few of the ideas and themes presented here. Many different people contributed in a variety of ways, direct and indirect, to the creation of this book. Some of these people I met decades ago, before this book was conceptualized. Professor Will Scott—a saint to wayward history majors—led an independent study during my undergraduate years in which I produced a paper with a curious topic having something to do with Quantrill (and Samuel Clemens, if I remember correctly). It was a forgettable paper, but it seems that something from that semester planted itself in my mind. I was also lucky to take one of the first courses Professor Glenn McNair taught. It was a seminar on Jim Crow. Of all the things I learned in classrooms in Gambier, I probably took the most from that class. Thank you both.

Other ideas come from the many people who read part or all of this manuscript as it made its way toward publication. LeeAnn Whites and Jason Phillips each read this work when it was in its earliest, loosest, and roughest form, and both of them gave me excellent advice and encouraged me to continue onward. Judith Giesberg read a part of this book in its unvarnished stage and helped a great deal, suggesting readings and offering helpful notes. Many thanks.

As I neared completion of this project, several others read it. Daniel Miller, my oldest friend, nearly set his printer on fire printing this manuscript out so that he could read a hard copy and mark it up properly. Daniel has the sharp eye of an editor. He saw things that no one else did and gave me ideas that no one else thought of, and my book is much better for it. Michael E. Woods read through this project with the energy and incisiveness that make him the great historian that he is. He provided thoughtful ideas for improvement and correction, as well as a short list of readings that proved helpful. Paul Quigley, who was working on a biography of Preston Brooks at the same time that I was working on this book, read significant pieces of my manuscript, and with overwhelming positivity, he shared several helpful notes and ideas. Matthew C. Hulbert, my old partner in crime, read the introduction and offered some useful tips regarding my voice and tone. Hulbert also suggested that I write this book in the first place, so if you didn't like it, you know where to send your complaint. My good friend, fellow historian, and a personal hero, Tom Grace, assisted in proofreading the manuscript—an invaluable gesture on his part and one I won't soon forget.

Then there are Lisa Frank and Andrew Fialka. In an intellectual sense, no one was closer to me while I wrote this book, but they each approached the manuscript from very different angles. Andrew, who read these chapters as they were completed, spurred me on. He constantly pushed me to think more creatively about the subject. Sometimes I felt like he was the only other person with me as I disappeared into the snowy Rockies or tracked a killer through those shadowy bottomlands of Civil War Missouri. For her part, Lisa reined me in. She went through the manuscript line by line, cleaned up my stylistic excesses, and got me back on track when I wandered off the path. I can't thank the two of you enough.

My wife's family lives around us. With a few exceptions, these were the only people we saw and spent that time with during the pandemic. During the summer, we spent at least one day a week and sometimes more at the family cottage on Lake Erie. We visited with my in-laws, played in the water, and took walks to great-grandpa's cottage just down the beach. It was an important outlet for us. We are lucky to live close to family.

My mother-in-law deserves special recognition. She watches our kids a few days a week, and we could not have gotten through the pandemic without her. Really, none of us would have made it. She also takes care of our nephews and does a million small and large things behind the scenes to keep my wife's family on course. Thank you, Pauline.

Sadly, we did not get to spend much time with my family during the pandemic. My parents made one trip relatively early in the pandemic to see us and meet their granddaughter. They snuck into New York under the vigilant eye of Governor Cuomo. Like a couple of Missouri bushwhackers throwing on Union uniforms to avoid detection, they swapped out cars in Erie, Pennsylvania, with our cousin David Niland (thanks David!) so that those Show Me State plates wouldn't be scrutinized at the border. It was great to see them and great that they got to see their granddaughters. We have since seen my parents, my sister and brother-in-law, and my four nieces and nephews a few times, but it still isn't enough. We miss you and love you.

In the bunker with me are Rachel and our three incredible daughters (and Dublin the dog and two chickens). It is impossible to find the words to describe the amount inspiration my daughters provide on a daily basis. I love all three of you more than you know. For her part, Rachel is probably sick of me and for good reason. It's an endless cycle of bad jokes, terrible dance moves, weird music, and nearly incoherent rants about the St. Louis Cardinals' front office or the Buffalo Bills' offensive line. She is also suspicious of the writing process. When I disappear into our back room for hours at a time to write, only to emerge rejuvenated and excited, I'm pretty sure she thinks I'm just drinking beer and listening to music (and I've done little to dissuade her of this notion). On a serious note, though, despite my wife's skepticism, she's supportive of my endeavors. She's built a great career for herself as a speech pathologist and clinical supervisor, she's an amazing mother, she's my best friend, and she's there when I need her. This one's for you, Rachel.

NOTES

PREFACE

1. Connelley, *Quantrill and the Border Wars*, 226.

2. Abraham Ellis to W. W. Scott, January 5, 1879, Ellis to Scott, January 18, 1879, transcribed in Connelley, *Quantrill and the Border Wars*, 227–230. The Ellis letters can also be found transcribed in full in Edwards, *Suppressed Evidence*, 89–96. While I disagree with Edwards's take on Quantrill, the letters are faithfully transcribed here. Edwards was also kind enough to share copies of the transcribed letters that he acquired from a collector named George Hart. Hart purchased transcribed versions of the letters from the widow of another collector who acquired them from William E. Connelley's daughter. Both the copies now in my possession and the letters presented in Edwards's volume match the versions that appear in Connelley's *Quantrill and the Border Wars*. Ellis erroneously said he and Quantrill met in the winter of 1858–1859, but Quantrill was in the Utah Territory and Pikes Peak during that time. They most likely met after Quantrill returned to eastern Kansas in 1859. "Ellis, Abraham (Bullet Hole)."

3. Ellis to Scott, January 5, 1879, in Connelley, *Quantrill and the Border Wars*, 227–229.

4. Ellis to Scott, January 5, 1879, January 18, 1879, in Connelley, *Quantrill and the Border Wars*, 227–230.

5. Ellis to Scott, January 5, 1879, January 18, 1879, in Connelley, *Quantrill and the Border Wars*.

6. Portis, *True Grit*; *True Grit* (1969); *True Grit* (2010).

7. Quantrill's Letters, William Elsey Connelley Papers, Denver Public Library, Denver, Colo.

8. Rotundo, *American Manhood*.

9. Rotundo, *American Manhood*.

10. Sutherland, "Sideshow No Longer"; Sutherland, *Savage Conflict*.

11. Matthew C. Hulbert argues that "movers and shakers of the commemorative camps" of post–Civil War America re-remembered the guerrillas "into another cultural place and its corresponding geographic space: the Wild West of the American imagination." Quantrill's story does not refute this idea—the guerrilla war was re-remembered as different from the "real" Civil War—but it does show that the partisan chief was a proto-gunfighter and that his men were inspired by these distinctly western archetypes. In that sense, the guerrillas were always of the West. See Hulbert, *Ghosts of Guerrilla Memory*, 11.

For important works exploring the relationship between the West and the Civil War, see Nelson, *Three-Cornered War*; Nelson, *Saving Yellowstone*; Kelman, *Misplaced Massacre*; Richardson, *West from Appomattox*.

216   NOTES TO PREFACE AND INTRODUCTION

12. Ellis to Scott, January 5, 1879, in Connelley, *Quantrill and the Border Wars*, 227–229, italics for emphasis added; Mark Twain, *How to Tell a Story*.

13. Ellis to Scott, January 5, 1879, January 18, 1879, in Connelley, *Quantrill and the Border Wars*, 227–230; "Ellis, Abraham (Bullet Hole)." For an excellent study of the many ways in which the war obliterated men's bodies, as well as a fascinating discussion of the Army and Navy Medical Museum, see Handley-Cousins, *Bodies in Blue*.

14. Ellis to Scott, January 5, 1879, January 18, 1879, in Connelley, *Quantrill and the Border Wars*, 227–230; Handley-Cousins, *Bodies in Blue*.

INTRODUCTION. *Prey*

1. James H. Wakefield to W. W. Scott, June 13, 1888, RH MS 75, box 2, folder 21, William Clarke Quantrill Correspondence, Spencer Research Library, University of Kansas, Lawrence.

2. Ibid.; Andrew Johnson, "Proclamation 132, Ordering the Arrest of Insurgent Cruisers, May 10, 1865," The American Presidency Project, University of California, Santa Barbara, https://www.presidency.ucsb.edu/documents/proclamation-132-ordering-the-arrest-insurgent-cruisers (italics for emphasis added); Connelley, *Quantrill and the Border Wars*, 471–479.

3. Wakefield to Scott, June 13, 1888, William Clarke Quantrill Correspondence, Spencer Research Library, University of Kansas, Lawrence; Andrew Johnson, "Proclamation 132, Ordering the Arrest of Insurgent Cruisers, May 10, 1865," The American Presidency Project (italics for emphasis added); Connelley, *Quantrill and the Border Wars*, 471–479; White, *Midnight in America*, 101–120.

4. John Langford to W. W. Scott, September 28, 1888, box 1, folder 3, William Elsey Connelley Papers, Western History Collection, Denver Public Library, Denver, Colo.; Connelley, *Quantrill and the Border Wars*, 471–479. To visualize the evolution of the war in Kentucky into a full-blown guerrilla war, see Fialka, "Federal Eyes," 6–25.

5. Jacobs's name should always be associated with Quantrill's biography, even though no lines are attributed to him and whatever words he uttered were forgotten. His voice has been wiped clean from the record, replaced then (and now) by white men whose black-lettered words on a white page pale in comparison to that muscular sable arm directing Terrell and his men down the lane. The story of the blacksmith appears without a name being attributed to the man in Connelley, *Quantrill and the Border Wars*, 471. Besides a brief mention, Jacobs's name does not appear in a Quantrill biography. Thomas Shelby Watson tracked down the blacksmith's name. To Watson's great credit it appears in his well-researched book. See Watson, *Confederate Guerrilla Sue Mundy*, 181–183. Also see Taylor, *Embattled Freedom*, 221–222. According to the website Mapping Occupation, maintained by scholars Gregory P. Downs and Scott Nesbit, "Historians estimate that perhaps 2.8 million of the nation's four million slaves remained in bondage at surrender." See Mapping Occupation, http://mappingoccupation.org/.

6. Langford to Scott, September 28, 1888, William Elsey Connelley Papers, Western History Collection, Denver Public Library, Denver, Colo. For insight into Union soldiers' view of race and loyalty, see Fellman, *Inside War*, 66–67. Lorien Foote, in her watershed study of the great Union prison break of 1864–1865, notes throughout her work that the escapees knew that they could trust the enslaved populace of the Deep South. See Foote, *Yankee Plague*, 21–26.

7. Langford to Scott, September 28, 1888, William Elsey Connelley Papers, Western History Collection, Denver Public Library, Denver, Colo.

8. Ibid.

NOTES TO INTRODUCTION   217

9. Ibid.

10. Ibid.

11. Ibid.

12. Ibid.; Wakefield to Scott June 13, 1888, William Clarke Quantrill Correspondence, Spencer Research Library, University of Kansas, Lawrence. General Order 100—the so-called Lieber Code—outlawed guerrillas and advised Union officers to execute them upon capture. See Lieber, General Orders No. 100, Instructions for the Government of Armies of the United States in the Field, April 24, 1863.

13. Langford to Scott, September 28, 1888, William Elsey Connelley Papers, Western History Collection, Denver Public Library, Denver, Colo.; Wakefield to Scott, June 13, 1888, William Clarke Quantrill Correspondence, Spencer Research Library, University of Kansas, Lawrence. A few reports that mention this prodigious guerrilla were collected and published in *War of the Rebellion: A Compilation of the Official Records* (hereafter cited as *O.R.*), offering a glimpse into his activities and a fleeting sense of the man himself. See *O.R.*, series 1, vol. 49, part 1, pp. 18, 34, 612, 635, 684, 698.

14. Langford to Scott, September 28, 1888, William Elsey Connelley Papers, Western History Collection, Denver Public Library, Denver, Colo.; Wakefield to Scott, June 13, 1888, William Clarke Quantrill Correspondence, Spencer Research Library, University of Kansas, Lawrence; *O.R.*, series 1, vol. 49, part 1, pp. 18, 34, 612, 635, 684, 698.

15. Langford to Scott, September 28, 1888, William Elsey Connelley Papers, Western History Collection, Denver Public Library, Denver, Colo.; Wakefield to Scott, June 13, 1888, William Clarke Quantrill Correspondence, Spencer Research Library, University of Kansas, Lawrence; *O.R.*, series 1, vol. 49, part 1, pp. 18, 34, 612, 635, 684, 698; *O.R.*, series 1, vol. 41, part 3, pp. 202–203. See Fellman, *Inside War*, 166.

16. "The Strange Romance of Quantrill's Bride," *Kansas City (Mo.) Star*, May 23, 1926; Hoftiezer and Beck, *Kate King, in Fact and Fiction*, 281; John N. Edwards, *Noted Guerrillas*, frontispiece; Connelley, *Quantrill and the Border Wars*, frontispiece, 421; Castel, *William Clarke Quantrill*, photo appears between 122–123; Schultz, *Quantrill's War*; Leslie, *Devil Knows How to Ride*; Petersen, *Quantrill of Missouri*; Petersen, *Quantrill in Texas*.

17. "Strange Romance of Quantrill's Bride," *Kansas City (Mo.) Star*, May 23, 1926; Hoftiezer and Beck, *Kate King, in Fact and Fiction*, 281; John N. Edwards, *Noted Guerrillas*, frontispiece; Connelley, *Quantrill and the Border Wars*, frontispiece, 421; Castel, *William Clarke Quantrill*, photo appears between 122–123; Schultz, *Quantrill's War*; Leslie, *Devil Knows How to Ride*; Petersen, *Quantrill of Missouri*; Petersen, *Quantrill in Texas*.

18. For a brief exchange between Union commanders regarding a prisoner captured in Indiana in 1864 who was thought to be Quantrill, see *O.R.*, series 1, vol. 41, part 3, pp. 202–203. Several newspapers also reported the death or capture of Quantrill. For instance, under the headline "Quantrell Killed," the *Holmes County Republican* reported, "We learn by the Leavenworth Times that Quantrell, the notorious guerrilla, and the terror of the southeastern border of Kansas, is dead." The story described a fight in which the Union troopers "set fire to [the house], and two of the rebel party were killed and five surrendered. The prisoners said Quantrell was in the house and badly wounded. He, with three others perished in the flames." See the *Holmes County Republican* (Millersburg, Ohio), April, 3, 1862. Another example comes from the *Chicago Daily Tribune*, which ran the lede "Probable Death of Quantrell, the Guerrilla." The *Tribune* reprinted a story from the *St. Louis Republican* that reported, "The following dispatch was received at Headquarters this morning. The information is important, and leads to the belief that Quantrell has been killed." The report described a skirmish in which a guerrilla was killed, stating, "Papers on the man killed were invoices from Capt. H. S. Heaton, A.A.Q.M, to Col. P. C. Quantrell. The Man answered the description of Quantrel. I have no doubt [that] he is the noted chief of guerillas. He

218 NOTES TO INTRODUCTION

fought with his bowie-knife after being brought low by a pistol shot." See "Probable Death of Quantrell, the Guerrilla," *Chicago Daily Tribune*, May 21, 1864, Chicago, Illinois. For an example of his supposed capture, see *Alexandria (Va.) Gazette*, September 13, 1864. We cannot know how many times these stories were picked up by other papers across the country, but we might assume that a juicy tidbit like the death or capture of Quantrill was probably repeated, and that the practice of reprinting stories amplified these rumors.

To get a sense of the universal qualities of the tactical, psychological, and emotional challenges of fighting guerrillas throughout history, see Boot, *Invisible Armies*.

19. *Harper's Weekly*, September, 5, 1863; File on William Clarke Quantrill, Union Provost Marshals' File of Papers Relating to Individual Citizens, War Department Collection of Confederate Records, Record Group 109, National Archives and Records Administration, Washington, D.C., accessed at Ancestry.com.

20. "Who Quantrile Is," *Republican Intelligencer* (Charles City, Iowa), November 5, 1863. Connelley asserted that one of Quantrill's uncles was a rogue who assumed many aliases, one of which was Dr. Hayne. It is difficult to understand how a scoundrel in his fifties was confused for a spry bushwhacker in his twenties, but there was so much confusion surrounding Quantrill that adding this anecdote hardly seems to make it worse. See Connelley, *Quantrill and the Border Wars*, 21.

21. Hulbert, "Rise and Fall of Edwin Terrell," 42–61.

22. Ibid., 57; Utley, *Billy the Kid*.

23. "Who Is Quantrell," *Independent* (Oskaloosa, Kans.), November 28, 1863.

24. Connelley, *Quantrill and the Border Wars*.

25. John N. Edwards, *Noted Guerrillas*; Connelley, *Quantrill and the Border Wars*; Castel, *William Clarke Quantrill*; Petersen, *Quantrill of Missouri*.

26. John N. Edwards, *Noted Guerrillas*; Connelley, *Quantrill and the Border Wars*; Castel, *William Clarke Quantrill*; Petersen, *Quantrill of Missouri*.

27. John N. Edwards, *Noted Guerrillas*; Connelley, *Quantrill and the Border Wars*; Castel, *William Clarke Quantrill*; Petersen, *Quantrill of Missouri*.

28. Wakefield to Scott, June 13, 1888, William Clarke Quantrill Correspondence, Spencer Research Library, University of Kansas, Lawrence; Connelley, *Quantrill and the Border Wars*, 471–479.

29. Wakefield to Scott, June 13, 1888, William Clarke Quantrill Correspondence, Spencer Research Library, University of Kansas, Lawrence; Connelley, *Quantrill and the Border Wars*, 471–479. Dick Glasscock and Clark Hockensmith were the only two guerrillas killed outright at the Wakefield farm.

30. Beilein, *Bushwhackers*, 131.

31. Wakefield to Scott June 13, 1888, William Clarke Quantrill Correspondence, Spencer Research Library, University of Kansas, Lawrence.

32. Several archives contain significant collections of Quantrill-related documents: Denver Public Library, Denver, Colo.; McCain Library and Archives, University of Southern Mississippi, Hattiesburg; Spencer Research Library, University of Kansas, Lawrence. Many of the letters, notes, and transcriptions in these three depositories were created or collected by the biographer Connelley, or by W. W. Scott—a childhood friend of Quantrill's who died before he could write a book about his old schoolmate. I visited the Denver Public Library and the Spencer Research Library, and I received copies from the holdings at the McCain Library from LeeAnn Whites.

33. Denver Public Library, Denver, Colo.; McCain Library and Archives, University of Southern Mississippi, Hattiesburg; Spencer Research Library, University of Kansas, Lawrence; *O.R.*; Union Provost Marshals' File of Papers Relating to Individual Civilians, War Department Collection of Confederate Records, National Archives and Records Adminis-

NOTES TO INTRODUCTION AND CHAPTER ONE 219

tration, Washington, D.C.; 1840, 1850, 1860 Federal Manuscript Census, National Archives and Records Administration, Washington, D.C.

34. Wakefield to Scott, June 13, 1888, William Clarke Quantrill Correspondence, Spencer Research Library, University of Kansas, Lawrence; Langford to Scott, September 28, 1888, William Elsey Connelley Papers, Western History Collection, Denver Public Library, Denver, Colo.

35. Ibid.

36. Walker, *Recollections of Quantrill's Guerrillas*, 2; Connelley, *Quantrill and the Border Wars*, 43.

37. Wakefield to Scott, June 13, 1888, William Clarke Quantrill Correspondence, Spencer Research Library, University of Kansas, Lawrence.

38. Butler, "Performative Acts and Gender Constitution," 519–531.

39. Wakefield to Scott, June 13, 1888, William Clarke Quantrill Correspondence, Spencer Research Library, University of Kansas, Lawrence; Hulbert, "Rise and Fall of Edwin Terrell," 42–61.

40. Wakefield to Scott, June 13, 1888, William Clarke Quantrill Correspondence, Spencer Research Library, University of Kansas, Lawrence; Hulbert, "Rise and Fall of Edwin Terrell," 42–61; Connelley, *Quantrill and the Border Wars*, 481.

41. Langford to Scott, September 28, 1888, William Elsey Connelley Papers, Western History Collection, Denver Public Library, Denver, Colo. The interaction between Quantrill and the doctor was described and the conversation transcribed from a letter from Marshall's widow that appears in Connelley, *Quantrill and the Border Wars*, 480.

42. Connelley, *Quantrill and the Border Wars*, 480–481.

43. *Louisville (Ky.) Daily Courier*, May 14, 1865; *Louisville (Ky.) Daily Democrat*, May 14, 1865; "Quantrill," May 15, 1865; *Louisville (Ky.) Daily Union Press*, May 16, 1865.

44. *Louisville (Ky.) Daily Courier*, May 14, 1865; *Louisville (Ky.) Daily Democrat*, May 14, 1865.

45. Notes of W. W. Scott regarding his first trip to Louisville to find Quantrill's grave, RH MS 75, box 2, folder 62, William Clarke Quantrill Correspondence Spencer Research Library, University of Kansas, Lawrence; Connelley, *Quantrill and the Border Wars*, 482.

46. Watson, *Confederate Guerrilla Sue Mundy*, 172. At over 130 pages' worth of transgressions and insights into the war, Magruder's published confession makes for an excellent recounting of the war in Kentucky. Magruder was accepted into the Catholic faith, assured that his soul would live on after he finished dancing that desperate jig in the air.

47. Notes of W. W. Scott regarding his first trip to Louisville to find Quantrill's grave, William Clarke Quantrill Correspondence, Spencer Research Library, University of Kansas, Lawrence; Connelley, *Quantrill and the Border Wars*, 482.

48. *Louisville (Ky.) Daily Union Press*, May 16, 1865.

49. Ibid.

50. Greenaway, *Language of Flowers*.

51. Ibid.

CHAPTER 1. *Student*

1. Connelley, *Quantrill and the Border Wars*, 42.

2. Rotundo describes this process as inarticulate and almost accidental. Further, he contends that the actual milestones of growth and the moment of transition were far from universal or uniform, especially as the artisanal system disappeared, and with it the apprenticeships that marked the growth of a boy to a man in a structural, socioeconomic sense. See *American Manhood*, 21–22, 53–55, 56–74. Many historians suggest that boys *learned* to

220 NOTES TO CHAPTER ONE

become men. See especially Wyatt-Brown, *Southern Honor*, 149–174; Berry, *All That Makes a Man*; Broomall, *Private Confederacies*, 12–31.

3. Rotundo, *American Manhood*, 21–22, 53–55, 56–74. See especially Wyatt-Brown, *Southern Honor*, 149–174; Berry, *All That Makes a Man*; Broomall, *Private Confederacies*, 12–31.

4. *Louisville (Ky.) Courier-Journal*, Louisville, Kentucky, May 13, 1888.

5. *Harper's Weekly: A Journal of Civilization*, 1857–1916; *Godey's Lady's Book*, 1830–1878.

6. *Louisville (Ky.) Courier-Journal*, May 13, 1888; Pierson, *Free Hearts and Free Homes*.

7. *History of Tuscarawas County, Ohio*, 464.

8. Connelley, *Quantrill and the Border Wars*, 32.

9. Ibid., 31–41.

10. Viewing Caroline Quantrill through the chauvinistic lens so many men applied to women in the early twentieth century, Connelley actually called her much worse than overbearing. For example, he said that she had "a catlike manner which left the impression that her character was based upon treachery and cruelty." See *Quantrill and the Border Wars*, 32, 31–41; Ryan, *Cradle of the Middle Class*. My observations regarding Quantrill's birth order are anecdotal and speculative. Plenty of research has been done in regard to birth order and intelligence, personality, political views, and just about everything else. According to Julia M. Rohrer, Boris Egloff, and Stefan C. Schmukle, scholars tend to agree that the oldest children score higher on intelligence tests, but the question of personality is more contentious. For their part, Rohrer, Egloff, and Schmukle conclude that birth order does not have a lasting effect on one's personality. See Rohrer, Egloff, and Schmukle, "Examining the Effects of Birth Order," 14224–14229.

11. Hand-transcribed copies of Quantrill's letters can be found in William Clarke Quantrill Letters, William Elsey Connelley Papers, Denver Public Library, Denver, Colo., and the correspondence has also been published in numerous places. Recently, a collection of the letters between William and his mother was transcribed and edited by Kelly D. Mezurek and published in *Dear Mother: The Letters of William C. Quantrill to His Mother Caroline, 1855–1860*.

Apparently Quantrill demonstrated poor form when he questioned his mother's willingness to respond. According to William Merrill Decker, "However desperate for a reply, however despairing of the post's capacity to convey it, a letter writer must resist questioning the partner's will to requite epistolary attentions, for the exchange economy of the correspondence is founded on a transcendent belief in the mutuality of the will to correspond." Decker, *Epistolary Practices*, 58–59. Also see Lystra, *Searching the Heart*, 12–27.

12. Decker, *Epistolary Practices*.

13. William Quantrill to Caroline Quantrill, November 17, 1855, February 8, 1860, William Elsey Connelley Papers, Denver Public Library, Denver, Colo.

14. Connelley, *Quantrill and the Border Wars*, 23.

15. 1850 Federal Manuscript Census, Tuscarawas County, Ohio, National Archives and Records Administration, Washington, D.C.; Quantrill, *Mechanic's Calculator and Tinman's Guide*. The book, which is difficult to find these days, is nevertheless still included in the bibliographies of tinsmithing associations and museums dedicated to the preindustrial crafts. It was a notable publication for the time period. See the Winterthur Museum website, http://tinware.winterthur.org/notes-references.

16. Johnson, *Shopkeeper's Millennium*.

17. *History of Tuscarawas County, Ohio*, 370, 388, 535–537.

18. Scott, *Reminiscences of Dover*, 34–38.

19. Ibid. The 1850 Census lacks a good record of manufactures, but the 1860 Manufacturing Census sheds some light on the type of production in Tuscarawas County. Built on a strong agricultural base, the county had twenty-three flour mills by 1860. There were also

four cooperages in the county; these establishments built the barrels in which the flour was transported. Apparently ample livestock provided hides for the nearly twenty tanneries in Tuscarawas County. Moreover, forty lumber mills popped up to take advantage of the densely timbered countryside that surrounded towns like Canal Dover and New Philadelphia. Finally, the county was home to shoe factories, pottery kilns, saddlemakers, and metal shops. See *Manufactures of the United States in 1860* (Washington, D.C.: Government Printing Office, 1865), 478; *History of Tuscarawas County, Ohio*, 388.

20. 1850 Federal Manuscript Census, Tuscarawas County, Ohio, National Archives and Records Administration, Washington, D.C.; *History of Tuscarawas County, Ohio*, 537; Connelley, *Quantrill and the Border Wars*, 29, 44.

21. *History of Tuscarawas County, Ohio*, 368–369. While the county history has no record of the 1848 election, the election results were as follows: Taylor—2,662 (47.5 percent); Cass—2,553 (47.5 percent); Van Buren—164 (3.0 percent). Dubin, *United States Presidential Elections*, 109–110.

22. Abraham Ellis interview, *Topeka (Kans.) Weekly Capital*, February 3, 1882; Connelley, *Quantrill and the Border Wars*, 29.

23. Sellers, *Market Revolution: Jacksonian America*. For a history of men who were left behind by economic changes, see Sandage, *Born Losers*.

24. Johnson, *Shopkeeper's Millennium*, 56–61.

25. Graham, *Lecture to Young Men on Chastity*, 23. Graham influenced J. H. Kellogg, who took his teachings to their next (il)logical steps. We have Kellogg and his brother to thank for cornflakes cereal. See Kellogg, *Man, the Masterpiece*.

26. Graham, *Lecture to Young Men on Chastity*, 23; Kellogg, *Man, the Masterpiece*.

27. Graham, *Lecture to Young Men on Chastity*, 114–115, 185.

28. Beilein, "Whiskey, Wild Men, and Missouri's Guerrilla War," 243–244, 236–259; Giesberg, *Sex and the Civil War*, 63–65; Lowry, *Story the Soldiers Wouldn't Tell*, 21–24; ibid., 185.

29. Connelley, *Quantrill and the Border Wars*, 18; 1850 Federal Manuscript Census, Stark County, Ohio, National Archives and Records Administration, Washington, D.C.

30. Connelley, *Quantrill and the Border Wars*, 34, 44, 53, 63–64.

31. Ibid., 28.

32. Ibid., 28, 54.

33. *History of Tuscarawas County, Ohio*, 537.

34. Ibid.; Connelley, *Quantrill and the Border Wars*, 44, 87–88; Castel, *William Clarke Quantrill*, 24–25.

35. 1850 Federal Manuscript Census, Tuscarawas County, Ohio, National Archives and Records Administration, Washington, D.C.; Roediger, *Wages of Whiteness*, 6–11; Fields, "Ideology and Race in American History," 150, 143–177; Fields, "Slavery, Race and Ideology," 109–110, 95–118.

36. Ibid; *History of Tuscarawas County, Ohio*, 135; Finkleman, "Strange Career of Race Discrimination," 373–408. Ohio was not anomalous in its racial segregation. Despite the popular recollection of the modern civil rights movement, segregation in schools did not start in the South after Reconstruction. It originated in the antebellum North. This segregation was not exclusive to rural backwaters or the states that made up the Middle West, but rather took its defining shape in the urban centers of the Northeast. Boston, for instance, segregated its schools, creating a situation in which a Black child walked past several white public schools on her way to reaching a school designated for children "of colored parentage." These situations were challenged in the courts, the most notable lawsuit being that of *Sarah C. Roberts vs. The City of Boston*. Attorneys Robert Morris and Charles Sumner—the future senator—argued that equality under the law forbade segregation based on race. The Massa-

222 NOTES TO CHAPTERS ONE AND TWO

chusetts Supreme Court ruled against Roberts and ironically laid the legal foundation for the "separate but equal" ruling of *Plessy vs. Ferguson* nearly half a century later. Due to the persistent efforts of the Black community in Boston, though, and the rising tide of antislavery politicians elected to office in the 1850s, in 1855 the state passed a law forbidding segregation in schools. See *Sarah C. Roberts vs. The City of Boston*, 59 Mass. 198, 5 Cush. 198 (1849); Kendrick and Kendrick, *Sarah's Long Walk*; Archer, *Jim Crow North*.

37. *History of Tuscarawas County, Ohio*, 135; Finkleman, "Strange Career of Race Discrimination," 373–408; *Sarah C. Roberts vs. The City of Boston*, 59 Mass. 198, 5 Cush. 198 (1849); Kendrick and Kendrick, *Sarah's Long Walk*; Archer, *Jim Crow North*. The first version of the textbook was Willard, *History of the United States* (New York: White, Gallaher and White, 1828). Updated versions were printed every couple of years, including small changes and new events. Willard, *Abridged History of the United States*, 46. As most scholars know, these people of African descent were brought into the community as indentured servants, not slaves, and "negro slavery" did not come about in its mature form until decades later.

38. Christopher Phillips, *Rivers Ran Backward*, 47–48.

39. *History of Tuscarawas County, Ohio*, 463, 537.

40. For historical perspective of the evolving challenges of teaching, see Goldstein, *Teacher Wars*.

41. 1850 Federal Manuscript Census, Tuscarawas County, Ohio, National Archives and Records Administration, Washington, D.C.; Connelley, *Quantrill and the Border Wars*, 44.

CHAPTER 2. *Teacher*

1. William Clarke Quantrill to Caroline Quantrill, November 17, 1855, William Elsey Connelley Papers, Denver Public Library, Denver, Colo.

2. Connelley, *Quantrill and the Border Wars*, 49.

3. Rotundo, *American Manhood*, 21–22.

4. William Quantrill to Caroline Quantrill, February, 21, 1856, William Elsey Connelley Papers, Denver Public Library, Denver, Colo.

5. William Quantrill to Caroline Quantrill, August 8, 1855, William Elsey Connelley Papers, Denver Public Library, Denver, Colo.; Connelley, *Quantrill and the Border Wars*, 45.

6. William Quantrill to Caroline Quantrill, August 8, 1855.

7. Baldwin, *History of LaSalle County, Illinois*, 479.

8. William Quantrill to Caroline Quantrill, September 18, 1855; William Elsey Connelley Papers, Denver Public Library, Denver, Colo.

9. *History of Tuscarawas County, Ohio*, 537; Connelley, *Quantrill and the Border Wars*, 44, 87–88; Castel, *William Clarke Quantrill*, 24–25.

10. Irving, "Legend of Sleepy Hollow," 275. From Connecticut, Crane is an outsider to the community of Sleepy Hollow, New York, and like many outsiders in rural America he is both the source of some intrigue and derision. He puts off the farm boys who sit in his classroom. However, he sees the young ladies of his classroom, especially those from good families, as potential mates. A striver, Crane seeks the hand of Katrina Van Tassel, who is also the object of local roughneck Abraham Van Brunt's affections. Crane seeks Van Tassel while Van Brunt plays pranks on the schoolmaster. After Van Tassel rejects Crane, the teacher rides back to his quarters and is set upon by a headless horseman, whom he takes to be the ghost of a Hessian soldier decapitated by a cannonball during the American War for Independence. The fright runs the superstitious schoolmaster off. Van Brunt marries Van Tassel, and no one feels sympathy for Crane. In his article on the image of schoolmasters in popular literature, George W. Crandall states that the iconic depiction of the teacher in those days was "of the emperor wielding a birch or hickory scepter . . . within the con-

NOTES TO CHAPTERS TWO AND THREE   223

fines of a small, one-room schoolhouse, his little empire." See Crandall, "Emperors and Little Empires," 51.

11. Irving, "Legend of Sleepy Hollow," 275; Connelley, *Quantrill and the Border Wars*, 43–44.

12. Clifford, *Those Good Gertrudes*.

13. William Quantrill to Caroline Quantrill, September 18, 1855.

14. Ibid.; Quantrill, *Mechanic's Calculator and Tinman's Guide*.

15. William Quantrill to Caroline Quantrill, September 18, 1855; William Quantrill to Edward T. Kellam, October 2, 1855, William Elsey Connelley Papers, Denver Public Library, Denver, Colo.; Connelley, *Quantrill and the Border Wars*, 44.

16. William Quantrill to Caroline Quantrill, September 18, 1855; William Quantrill to Edward T. Kellam, October 2, 1855; Connelley, *Quantrill and the Border Wars*, 44.

17. William Quantrill to Caroline Quantrill, September 18, 1855; William Quantrill to Edward T. Kellam, October 2, 1855; William Quantrill to Caroline Quantrill, November 17, 1855, William Elsey Connelley Papers, Denver Public Library, Denver, Colo.

18. William Quantrill to Caroline Quantrill, September 18, 1855; William Quantrill to Edward T. Kellam, October 2, 1855; William Quantrill to Caroline Quantrill, November 17, 1855.

19. William Quantrill to Caroline Quantrill, February 21, 1856, William Elsey Connelley Papers, Denver Public Library, Denver, Colo.

20. Ibid.; Connelley, *Quantrill and the Border Wars*, 51–52.

21. Connelley, *Quantrill and the Border Wars*, 41; Castel, *William Clarke Quantrill*, 24.

22. William Quantrill to Caroline Quantrill, February 21, 1856.

23. Connelley, *Quantrill and the Border Wars*, 52.

24. William Quantrill to Caroline Quantrill, September 18, 1855, November 17, 1855.

CHAPTER 3. *Dunce*

1. "A Woman Hanged," *Daily American Organ* (Washington, D.C.), January 19, 1856.

2. "A Man Killed and Burned by His Slave," *Glasgow (Mo.) Weekly Times*, July 5, 1855.

3. Ibid.; "Woman Hanged," *Daily American Organ* (Washington, D.C.), January 19, 1856.

4. McLaurin, *Celia, a Slave*, 24, 24–37.

5. Ibid., 30.

6. Ibid., 36–37.

7. Wilson-Kleekamp, "Descendants of Celia and Robert Newsom Speak," 1–21; King, *Stolen Childhood*.

8. Pierson, *Free Hearts and Free Homes*.

9. Charles E. Johnson Jr., *Nonvoting Americans*, 2. For the latest scholarship on black voter participation, limited though it was by outright restriction or property qualification, see Gosse, *The First Reconstruction*, 151, 160, 196, 204, 283, 482, 500, 503–504, 509–510, and passim. For turnout in northern states from 1840 to 1860, see Gienapp, "Politics Seem to Enter into Everything," 14–69.

10. Ibid.; Winkle, "Social Analysis of Voter Turnout in Ohio," 411–435.

11. Woods, *Bleeding Kansas*, 19–23.

12. Oertel, *Bleeding Borders*, 33–57.

13. "Interesting News from Kansas," *New York Herald*, January 9, 1856.

14. Woods, *Bleeding Kansas*, 46, 42–46.

15. Sumner, *Crime against Kansas*, 9–14.

16. Ibid., 9.

17. Stephen Douglas as quoted in Freeman, *Field of Blood*, 219.

224   NOTES TO CHAPTERS THREE AND FOUR

18. 1850 Slave Schedule, Edgefield, South Carolina, National Archives and Records Administration, Washington, D.C. Paul Quigley is currently working on a biography of Preston Brooks, and he says that, despite the lack of conclusive proof that Brooks raped his slaves or the slaves of his father, it is possible and perhaps even probable that he did so. Quigley, *Man behind the Cane*, forthcoming. Stephen Berry and James Hill Welborn III make a strong argument that Brooks was driven to attack Sumner by a few forces. He did want to defend his cousin's honor, but he might have taken a more moderate approach had his fellow congressman Laurence Keitt not pushed him to act. Brooks was also so consumed by the apparent need to do something that he did not sleep for two days and might have started drinking again, a behavior he had put to bed at least four years earlier. In other words, Brooks was coming apart, and in the absence of good judgment, his conscience was hijacked by the meddling Keitt. See Berry and Welborn, "Cane of His Existence," 5–21; Freeman, *The Field of Blood*, 217–230.

CHAPTER 4. *Roustabout*

1. Connelley, *Quantrill and the Border Wars*, 58–63.

2. Connelley, *Quantrill and the Border Wars*, 58–63; Hildt, "Diary of George H. Hildt," 265, 260–298.

3. Connelley, *Quantrill and the Border Wars*, 58–63; Hildt, "Diary of George H. Hildt," 265, 260–298; Federal Land Patent, William C. Quantrill, Kansas Trust Lands, Certificate No. 325, October 1, 1858, Bureau of Land Management, Washington, D.C. Quantrill's plot was located at the 6th PM, Township 017S, Range 021E, NE ¼, section 21, Franklin County, Kansas. See Bureau of Land Management, accession number, KS4180___.325.

4. William Quantrill to his Caroline Quantrill, May 16, 1857, William Elsey Connelly Letters, Denver Public Library, Denver, Colo.; Connelley, *Quantrill and the Border Wars*, 64–65.

5. Hildt, "Diary of George H. Hildt," 265.

6. Connelley, *Quantrill and the Border Wars*, 63–64.

7. Ibid.

8. Ibid.

9. Ibid.

10. Ibid. The language of the Quantrill-Beeson story brings to mind another controversial nineteenth-century recollection. A couple of letters from Thomas J. Withers to James Henry Hammond written in 1826 describe sexual intimacy between the two men. Withers and Hammond were roommates and perhaps bedmates during law school, and they related to each other in a way that twenty-first century observers are inclined to categorize as homosexual—although that category and the thought that sex is an identity rather than an act were alien to men of that era. In one letter, Withers asked Hammond, "[Have you had] the extravagant delight of poking and punching a writhing Bedfellow with your long fleshen pole—the exquisite touches of which I have often had the honor of feeling?" Additionally, Withers described Hammonds's "furious lunges," and "the crushing force of a Battering Ram" that he endured.

Historian Craig T. Friend argues that the Withers-Hammond episode is best understood in the context of power and masculinity. Friend notes that "male sexuality was supposedly boundless" in the minds of men like Hammond, and sex could be a performance of power, not just over women—white and Black—but over men as well. As Friend concludes, "Hammond's sexual interactions with his wife, nieces, slaves, and Withers demonstrate how sex was one device employed by white men in the incessant contest of seeming and becoming, providing a way to establish power over others . . . and ultimately, to

NOTES TO CHAPTERS FOUR AND FIVE   225

demonstrate manliness." Friend, "Sex, Self, and the Performance of Patriarchal Manhood," 257, 258, 259, 261.

11. William Quantrill to Caroline Quantrill, August 23, 1857, William Elsey Connelly Letters, Denver Public Library, Denver, Colo.

12. Connelley, *Quantrill and the Border Wars*, 66–68; Hildt, "Diary of George H. Hildt," 265, 260–298.

13. Hildt, "Diary of George H. Hildt," 295.

14. William Quantrill to W. W. Scott, January 22, 1858, William Elsey Connelly Letters, Denver Public Library, Denver, Colo.; Connelley, *Quantrill and the Border Wars*, 73; Etcheson, *Bleeding Kansas*, 139–167.

15. Quantrill to Scott, January 22, 1858, William Elsey Connelly Letters, Denver Public Library, Denver, Colo.; Connelley, *Quantrill and the Border Wars*, 73; Etcheson, *Bleeding Kansas*, 139–167; Oertel, *Bleeding Borders*.

16. Quantrill to Scott, January 22, 1858, William Elsey Connelly Letters, Denver Public Library, Denver, Colo.; Connelley, *Quantrill and the Border Wars*, 73.

17. Amy S. Greenberg, *Manifest Manhood*, 112–128.

18. Deborah Gray White, *Ar'n't I a Woman?*, 27–61; McLaurin, *Celia, a Slave*; Silber, *Gender and the Sectional Conflict*; Whites, *Civil War as a Crisis in Gender*; Whites and Long, *Occupied Women*; Frank and Whites, *Household War*; Giesberg, *Sex and the Civil War*; Pierson, *Free Hearts and Free Homes*.

19. Quantrill to Scott, January 22, 1858, William Elsey Connelly Letters, Denver Public Library, Denver, Colo.; Connelley, *Quantrill and the Border Wars*, 73.

20. Connelley, *Quantrill and the Border Wars*, 74–75. The portion of George Hildt's diary that was transcribed and published goes silent before Bill's departure.

21. William Quantrill to Caroline Quantrill, October 15, 1858, William Elsey Connelly Letters, Denver Public Library, Denver, Colo.; Moorman and Sessions, *Camp Floyd and the Mormons*.

22. William Quantrill to Caroline Quantrill, October 15, 1858, William Elsey Connelly Letters, Denver Public Library, Denver, Colo.; Connelley, *Quantrill and the Border Wars*, 77–78; Rarick, *Desperate Passage*.

23. William Quantrill to Caroline Quantrill, October 15, 1858, William Elsey Connelly Letters, Denver Public Library, Denver, Colo.; Connelley, *Quantrill and the Border Wars*, 77–78; Rarick, *Desperate Passage*.

24. William Quantrill to Caroline Quantrill, October 15, 1858, January 9, 1859, William Elsey Connelly Letters, Denver Public Library, Denver, Colo.

25. William Quantrill to Caroline Quantrill, October 15, 1858, December 1, 1858, William Elsey Connelly Letters, Denver Public Library, Denver, Colo.

26. William Quantrill to Caroline Quantrill, October 15, 1858, December 1, 1858, January 9, 1859, William Elsey Connelly Letters, Denver Public Library, Denver, Colo.

27. Connelley, *Quantrill and the Border Wars*, 80–82.

28. Coleman, *Here Lies Hugh Glass*, 19–63.

29. Susan Lee Johnson, *Roaring Camp*, 71–76.

CHAPTER 5. *Hunter*

1. William Quantrill to Caroline Quantrill, July 30, 1859, William Quantrill to Mary Quantrill, March 23, 1860, William Elsey Connelley Papers, Denver Public Library, Denver, Colo.

2. William Quantrill to his sister, March 23, 1860, italics for emphasis added; Connelley, *Quantrill and the Border Wars*, 97–98.

NOTES TO CHAPTER FIVE

3. William Quantrill to his sister, March 23, 1860, italics for emphasis added; Connelley, *Quantrill and the Border Wars*, 97–98.

4. See Coleman, *Here Lies Hugh Glass*; Dolan, *Fur, Fortune, and Empire*, 223–254; Hafen, *Mountain Men and Fur Traders*; Slotkin, *Regeneration through Violence*; Slotkin, *Fatal Environment*; Utley, *Life Wild and Perilous*. As an activity, hunting is an important historical topic. See Bruce, *Violence and Culture in the Antebellum South*, 196–211; Herman, *Hunting and the American Imagination*; Jones, *Epiphany in the Wilderness*; Proctor, *Bathed in Blood*.

5. *History of Tuscarawas County, Ohio*, 464. Across antebellum Ohio, many boys like Quantrill developed a love for the woods and for hunting. See Grant, *Personal Memoirs of U. S. Grant*, 2–8; Sherman, *Memoirs of General William T. Sherman*, 19–20; Sheridan, *Personal Memoirs of P.H. Sheridan*, 352–354; Custer, *My Life on the Plains*, 49–52; Connell, *Son of the Morning Star*, 141–142.

6. Walker, *Recollections of Quantrill's Guerrillas*, 2; John N. Edwards, *Noted Guerrillas*, 439–440; Connelley, *Quantrill and the Border Wars*, 318. There was not a consensus that Bill was a real-life Leatherstocking. Holland Wheeler, a longtime citizen of Lawrence, Kansas, said he knew Bill and "frequently went down on the river bank to practice pistol shooting" with him. Wheeler was not impressed with what he saw. "He [Quantrill] was somewhat of a horseman," he recalled, but "only a fair shot." Bill was probably a novice with a revolver—a very different kind of shooting than the riflery he had learned in his youth—but through practice like that down by the Kansas River he became a skilled pistoleer. It is possible, too, that Wheeler was just the type of man who was hard to impress or was still embittered by what his onetime shooting companion did during the war. It hardly matters. Wheeler was in the minority camp when considering Bill's marksmanship. See Wheeler, "Quantrill a Suspicious Loafer," 225, 226.

7. Franklin, *Militant South, 1800–1861*, 18.

8. Rosa, *Wild Bill Hickok*, 16.

9. Connelley, *Wild Bill and His Era*, 13; ibid.

10. Connelley, *Wild Bill and His Era*.

11. Ibid.

12. Ibid.

13. Jones, *Epiphany in the Wilderness*, 79.

14. Ibid.

15. Turner, "The Significance of the Frontier in American History;" Slotkin, *Fatal Environment*, 11, 15–16, 64–68.

16. Johnson, *Shopkeeper's Millennium*.

17. William Quantrill to Mary Quantrill, March 23, 1860; Connelley, *Quantrill and the Border Wars*, 97–98.

18. Quantrill's Powder Horn, Reeves Victorian Home and Carriage House Museum, Dover, Ohio. It is said that this powder horn was once owned by Bill Quantrill. There is no record of its donation or of its acquisition, raising questions about its provenance. It would almost be more surprising if a documented connection to the infamous guerrilla accompanied this beautiful remnant of frontier life. Grancsay, *American Engraved Powder Horns*.

19. Quantrill's Powder Horn, Reeves Victorian Home and Carriage House Museum, Dover, Ohio; Grancsay, *American Engraved Powder Horns*.

20. Beilein, *Bushwhackers*, 1–13.

21. Fellman, *Inside War*, 14.

22. Ibid.

23. Gladstone, *Englishman in Kansas*, 252; Jason Phillips, *Looming Civil War*, 28, 27–30.

24. Berry, *All That Makes a Man*, 34. Berry asserts, "In the North, boys were encouraged to pattern themselves after what might be called civilized manhood." In other words,

NOTES TO CHAPTER FIVE 227

it was central to the maturation process of northern boys to learn restraint and abstinence. In *Manifest Manhood*, Amy Greenberg describes this difference between northern manhood and southern manhood as restrained manhood versus martial manhood.

25. Christopher Phillips, "Crime against Missouri," 78.

26. See Rarick, *Desperate Passage*.

27. William Quantrill to Caroline Quantrill, July 30, 1859, William Elsey Connelley Papers, Denver Public Library, Denver, Colo.

28. Ibid.

29. Chauncey, *Gay New York*. The list of named men with whom Quantrill slept includes Richard and Harmon Beeson, Abraham Ellis, Holland Wheeler, the jayhawking reverend Captain John E. Stewart, and George Todd. Other nineteenth-century men alluded to close bonds with other men without fully disclosing the nature of those relationships. In 1926, Carl Sandburg wrote that he sensed something similar to Quantrill's anonymous partnerships in the missives of Abraham Lincoln. Sandburg, who authored the single most substantial and influential biography of the sixteenth president, asserts in the preface of the first two volumes of that work that when he was reading Abraham Lincoln's letters and past accounts of his life, he felt the presence of "invisible companionships that surprised" him. While he left the veils over these companionships, Sandburg thought Lincoln's close relationships with other men possible, stating, "Perhaps a few of these presences lurk and murmur in this book." It is difficult to decipher exactly what Sandburg means in this passage because he says no more about these "invisible companionships." In fact, a new edition of the biography printed in 1954 omits any mention of these relationships. Apparently, in the 1920s Sandburg was unsure about how he might articulate the presences he sensed, but in 1950s America they were wholly unspeakable. See Sandburg, *Abraham Lincoln: The Prairie Years*, 1:xii.

30. Tripp, *Intimate World of Abraham Lincoln*; Guelzo, "Lincoln Bedroom"; Susan Lee Johnson, *Roaring Camp*, 173–174.

31. Susan Lee Johnson, *Roaring Camp*, 174; D'Emilio and Freedman, *Intimate Matters*, 121–130; Chauncey, *Gay New York*, 99–130. Historian Craig T. Friend suggests that "we should not overlook . . . sex as power among men." See Friend, "Sex, Self, and the Performance of Patriarchal Manhood," 257.

32. Bill's letters reveal that during this period in his life he began to seek out quiet moments like this one to process and understand his memories. Quantrill's thoughts have been extracted from his correspondence dating from around this time.

33. Quantrill to Caroline Quantrill, July 30, 1859, William Elsey Connelley Papers, Denver Public Library, Denver, Colo.

34. Ibid.

35. Ibid.

36. A scan of newspapers from the Kansas Territory during the summer of 1859 available through the Library of Congress did not turn up any stories about this specific raid. However, a great deal of reporting concerned real and rumored raids by Kaw, Osage, and Comanche warriors.

37. 1860 Federal Manuscript Census, Wyandotte Township, Wyandotte County, Kansas Territory, 38, National Archives and Records Administration, Washington, D.C.; Connelley, *Quantrill and the Border Wars*, 168–170; 530. For important analysis of interactions between Native Americans and whites in the Kansas Territory, see Oertel, *Bleeding Borders*.

38. Connelley, *Quantrill and the Border Wars*, 168–170, 530. Italics for emphasis are mine.

39. 1860 Federal Manuscript Census, Wyandotte Township, Wyandotte County, Kansas Territory, 38, National Archives and Records Administration, Washington, D.C.; Connelley, *Quantrill and the Border Wars*, 168–170; 530; Oertel, *Bleeding Borders*.

228   NOTES TO CHAPTERS FIVE, SIX, AND SEVEN

40. 1860 Federal Manuscript Census, Wyandotte Township, Wyandotte County, Kansas Territory, 38, National Archives and Records Administration, Washington, D.C.; Connelley, *Quantrill and the Border Wars*, 168–170, 530; Oertel, *Bleeding Borders*.

41. 1860 Federal Manuscript Census, Wyandotte Township, Wyandotte County, Kansas Territory, 38, National Archives and Records Administration, Washington, D.C.; Connelley, *Quantrill and the Border Wars*, 168–170, 530; Oertel, *Bleeding Borders*; Frank, *Creeks and Southerners*, 46–60.

42. 1860 Federal Manuscript Census, Wyandotte Township, Wyandotte County, Kansas Territory, 38, National Archives and Records Administration, Washington, D.C.; Connelley, *Quantrill and the Border Wars*, 168–170, 530; Oertel, *Bleeding Borders*.

43. William Quantrill to Caroline Quantrill, July 30, 1859, William Elsey Connelley Papers, Denver Public Library, Denver, Colo.

44. Ibid.

45. Ibid.

46. Connelley, *Quantrill and the Border Wars*, 87–88.

47. Ibid.

48. Ibid.

49. William Quantrill to Caroline Quantrill, January 26, 1860, William Elsey Connelley Papers, Denver Public Library, Denver, Colo.

50. Ibid.

51. William Quantrill to Caroline Quantrill, March 25, 1860, William Elsey Connelley Papers, Denver Public Library, Denver, Colo.; Fellman, *Inside War*, 141.

CHAPTER 6. *Jailbird*

1. Wheeler, "Quantrill a Suspicious Loafer," 225. Wheeler's account seems reliable, but he possibly confused this arrest and imprisonment with one that occurred the following year.

2. Ibid.

3. William Quantrill to Caroline Quantrill, February 8, 1860, William Elsey Connelley Papers, Denver Public Library, Denver, Colo.

4. Ibid.; William Quantrill to Caroline Quantrill, January 26, 1860, William Elsey Connelley Papers, Denver Public Library, Denver, Colo; Etcheson, *Bleeding Kansas*, 190–218.

5. William Quantrill to Caroline Quantrill, February 8, 1860, January 26, 1860, William Elsey Connelley Papers, Denver Public Library, Denver, Colo.; Etcheson, *Bleeding Kansas*, 190–218.

6. Campbell, "Lochiel's Warning," lines 84–87.

7. Ibid.

8. McPherson, *Battle Cry of Freedom*, 213–216.

9. Ibid., 216–221; Lincoln, "Speech at Leavenworth, Kansas," 502.

10. Wheeler, "Quantrill a Suspicious Loafer," 225.

CHAPTER 7. *Charley Hart*

1. Wheeler, "Quantrill a Suspicious Loafer," 224.

2. Woods, *Bleeding Kansas*, 32; 1860 Federal Manuscript Census, Lawrence, Douglas County, Kansas Territory, National Archives and Records Administration, Washington, D.C. A scan of the census for the town reveals the social strata and economic hierarchy. The census taker began on the wealthiest block of the city and then worked his way down Mas-

sachusetts Street, eventually getting to the droves of teamsters, ferrymen, laborers, and those without professions.

3. Woods, *Bleeding Kansas*, 32; 1860 Federal Manuscript Census, Lawrence, Douglas County, Kansas Territory, National Archives and Records Administration, Washington, D.C.

4. Dorsey, *Reforming Men & Women*.

5. Beecher, *Seven Lectures to Young Men*, 78, 101, 77–101. Karen Halttunen's book *Confidence Men and Painted Women* serves as the benchmark historical study of the phenomenon. Using advice manuals and fashion magazines, Halttunen contends that middle-class Americans were deeply concerned about men and women who took advantage of the increasingly anonymous urban society to pass as upright individuals, exploiting the trust of well-meaning young men and women for their own gain. Echoing Beecher's fear, it was believed not only that a confidence man might swindle a youth of his pocket watch or billfold, but also that he might plunder the young man's soul. "The fear of hypocrisy expressed in mid-nineteenth century conduct manuals ran deep," says Halttunen, adding, "These archetypal hypocrites threatened ultimately, by undermining social confidence among men and women, to reduce the American republic to social chaos." For middle-class Americans, a man who assumed a name, passed as someone else, or otherwise sought to pull one over on the innocent was indeed the enemy of society itself. Halttunen, *Confidence Men and Painted Women*, xv.

6. "'The Confidence Man' on a Large Scale," *New York Herald*, July 11, 1849. Reading the column in the *Herald* makes it evident that New Yorkers' disdain for "the Confidence Man of the Tombs" only slightly exceeded their disdain for the men of Wall Street he was grifting. On December 5, 1849, the *Herald* also referred to William Thompson as Samuel Thompson and Samuel Williams, but he might very well have been an altogether different confidence man. "Police Intelligence. Confidence Man No. 2," *New York Herald*, August 5, 1849; Halttunen, *Confidence Men and Painted Women*, 6–7; Melville, *Confidence-Man: His Masquerade*, xv–xvi.

7. Kenney, *Raise the Wind*, 1803; Poe, "Diddling."

8. Melville, *Confidence-Man*, xv–xvi.

9. Ibid.

10. Halttunen, *Confidence Men and Painted Women*, 33–55.

11. *Collections of the Kansas State Historical Society*, 212–229.

12. Wheeler, "Quantrill a Suspicious Loafer," 225; Herd, "Always under an Alias," 227.

13. W. A. Johnson, "Early Life of Quantrill in Kansas," 213; Riggs, "Outlaw When He Took to the Bush," 224; Wheeler, "Quantrill a Suspicious Loafer," 225; Herd, "Always under an Alias," 227; Connelley, *Quantrill and the Border Wars*, 129.

14. John Dean to W. W. Scott, January 26, 1879, in Connelley, *Quantrill and the Border Wars*, 133–134.

15. Wheeler, "Quantrill a Suspicious Loafer," 225.

16. Ibid.; Farley, "Delaware Indians in Kansas, 1829–1867," 13–14.

17. Clarke, "W. C. Quantrill in 1858," 219.

18. Wheeler, "Quantrill a Suspicious Loafer," 225.

19. Clarke, "W. C. Quantrill in 1858," 219.

20. Kenneth S. Greenberg, *Honor & Slavery*, 51–86. For an excellent analysis of the varied forms of personal combat across class and race in antebellum America, see Bruce, *Violence and Culture in the Antebellum South*. Credit for the first quick-draw contest went to Quantrill's doppelganger "Wild Bill" Hickok when he squared off with Arkansan Davis K. "Dave" Tutt, or "Little Dave," in Springfield, Missouri, in 1865. The origin of this dis-

230 NOTES TO CHAPTERS SEVEN AND EIGHT

pute related to Hickok's gambling debt owed to Tutt, and Tutt's flaunting of Hickok's watch given (or perhaps taken) as collateral. On the afternoon of Friday, July 21, 1865, there were talks, drinks, and more talks as friends tried to intervene between the men; it seemed that no one wanted a fight. Then, after the two men happened on each other, entering the town square from opposite sides, words were shouted, and Tutt pulled a pistol from under his duster. Hickok grabbed his pistol, and both men fired simultaneously at each other across the square at a distance of perhaps one hundred paces or more. Tutt's ball missed, but Hickok's did not, hitting Tutt in the heart. It was quite the shot with a Colt Navy at that distance. This story served as the template for duels thereafter. See Rosa, *Wild Bill Hickok*, 116–123.

21. Clarke, "W. C. Quantrill in 1858," 219.

22. 1860 Federal Manuscript Census, Douglas County, Kansas Territory, 34, National Archives and Records Administration, Washington, D.C. Robert C. Kenzer offers an insightful description of the peculiarities of the local census taker's pattern of movement throughout a rural southern community. No doubt the census taker in Lawrence made his way up and down the blocks based on his own individual sense of the town, but the layout of the town in a grid might have focused his movement in a more geometric fashion. See Kenzer, *Kinship and Neighborhood in a Southern Community*, 155–160.

23. 1860 Federal Manuscript Census, Douglas County, Kansas Territory, 34, National Archives and Records Administration, Washington, D.C.

24. Wheeler, "Quantrill a Suspicious Loafer," 224–225.

25. Halttunen, *Confidence Men and Painted Women*, 33–55.

26. Melville, *Confidence-Man*, 42.

27. Ibid., xiv-xxv; Kenneth S. Greenberg, *Honor & Slavery*, 3–23.

28. Dutton, *Charlemagne's Mustache*.

CHAPTER 8. *Detective*

1. W. L. Potter to W. W. Scott, November 9, 1895. William E. Connelley collected Potter's letters to W. W. Scott and transcribed much of what Potter wrote in *Quantrill and the Border Wars*, 149–151, 187–191, 440–448. The letters can also be found in Edwards, *Suppressed Evidence*, 15–86. I also acquired the copies of Connelley's transcriptions of the originals from Edwards.

2. Potter to Scott, January 20, 1896, in Edwards, *Suppressed Evidence*, 27–31. Also see Connelley, *Quantrill and the Border Wars*, 187–188.

3. Ibid.

4. Woods, *Bleeding Kansas*, 33.

5. Phillips, *Looming Civil War*, 30–31.

6. Phillips, *Looming Civil War*, 30; Oertel, *Bleeding Borders*, 49–52.

7. Kenneth S. Greenberg, *Honor & Slavery*, 33–50; Wyatt-Brown, "Mask of Obedience."

8. Hobbs, *Chosen Exile*, 28–70.

9. Wheeler, "Quantrill a Suspicious Loafer," 224–225.

10. William Quantrill to Caroline Quantrill, June 23, 1860, William Elsey Connelley Papers, Denver Public Library, Denver, Colo.; Connelley, *Quantrill and the Border Wars*, 122–127.

11. William Quantrill to Caroline Quantrill, June 23, 1860, William Elsey Connelley Papers, Denver Public Library, Denver, Colo.; Connelley, *Quantrill and the Border Wars*, 122–127.

12. William Quantrill to Caroline Quantrill, June 23, 1860, William Elsey Connelley

NOTES TO CHAPTER EIGHT   231

Papers, Denver Public Library, Denver, Colo.; Connelley, *Quantrill and the Border Wars*, 122–127.

13. William Quantrill to Caroline Quantrill, June 23, 1860, William Elsey Connelley Papers, Denver Public Library, Denver, Colo.; Connelley, *Quantrill and the Border Wars*, 122–127.

14. Potter to Scott, November 9, 1895, January 20, 1896, in Edwards, *Suppressed Evidence*, 15–20, 27–31.

15. Connelley, *Quantrill and the Border Wars*, 111, 113–114; Beilein, introduction to Gregg, *William Gregg's Civil War*.

16. Connelley, *Quantrill and the Border Wars*, 111, 113–114; Beilein, introduction to Gregg, *William Gregg's Civil War*.

17. Potter to Scott, November 9, 1895, January 22, 1896, both in Edwards, *Suppressed Evidence*, 15–20, 31–52. Also see Connelley, *Quantrill and the Border wars*, 188–191.

18. Potter to Scott, November 9, 1895, January 22, 1896, in Edwards, *Suppressed Evidence*, 15–20, 31–52.

19. Ibid.; "B. J. Sheridan's Collection, Stories of a Kansas, 1030–31, The Western Spirit," found at "Paola Kansas: A 150 Year History in Detail."

20. Potter to Scott, November 9, 1895, January 22, 1896; "B. J. Sheridan's Collection, Stories of a Kansas, 1030–31, The Western Spirit," found at "Paola Kansas: A 150 Year History in Detail."

21. Potter to Scott, November 9, 1895, in Edwards, *Suppressed Evidence*, 15–20.

22. John Dean to Colonel Samuel Walker, July 31, 1879, in Connelley, *Quantrill and the Border Wars*, 161; Walker, *Recollections of Quantrill's Guerrillas*, 2.

23. John Dean to Colonel Samuel Walker, July 31, 1879, in Connelley, *Quantrill and the Border Wars*, 161; Walker, *Recollections of Quantrill's Guerrillas*, 2.

24. Walker, *Recollections of Quantrill's Guerrillas*, 2. William H. Gregg, a man who fought beside Quantrill as a guerrilla, wrote that Quantrill told him, "[I] joined Montgomery's band, under the name of Charley Hart. I soon found I had the confidence of Montgomery, his officers and men." The partisan chief continued, "[I[obtained the names of all the men who had, taken part in the killing of my brother[, and] . . . I at once went to work in a systematic way to get revenge for the wrongs heaped upon me and my Brother." See Gregg, *William Gregg's Civil War*, 47–48. Most of Quantrill's followers who left an account knew that he called himself by a different name. His first biographer—John N. Edwards—even mistook Charles for Quantrill's God-given name. See John N. Edwards, *Noted Guerrillas*, frontispiece.

25. Walker, *Recollections of Quantrill's Guerrillas*, 2–4. In the popular culture of the age, a revenge story was often framed as a masquerade. It was no accident that Edgar Allen Poe set "The Cask of Amontillado" in Italy during carnival, when men and women traditionally wore masks. Behind these masks, real and symbolic, people hid their true selves and obscured their intentions. The vengeful hero in Alexandre Dumas's *The Count of Monte Cristo* also makes an appearance in Italy during carnival, participating in a complex charade to veil his real motives and win the confidence of a stranger. Furthermore, the protagonist, Edmund Dantes, takes on an assumed identity—the Count of Monte Cristo. This alias serves as the title for the work, as if the modern publishers sought to further cloak the entire narrative in a mask. Throughout the story, Dantes–cum–Monte Cristo is unrecognizable to his enemies even though he appears to them most often without an actual mask. Looking through a veil of guilt, the count's foes cannot see the man they once betrayed; in this crowd of backstabbers and deceivers, he wears a mask of authenticity. When he reveals his true identity as Dantes, the veil is lifted: his enemies see him and understand their own cor-

232 NOTES TO CHAPTERS EIGHT AND NINE

ruption. Dantes's vengeance unmasks his enemies. See Poe, "Cask of Amontillado"; Dumas, *Count of Monte Cristo*, 1845.

26. John Dean to Col. Samuel Walker, July 31, 1879, in Connelley, *Quantrill and the Border Wars*, 161.

27. Beecher, *Seven Lectures to Young Men*, 78; Connelley, *Quantrill and the Border Wars*, 140–151.

28. Phillips, *Looming Civil War*, 31.

29. Kenneth S. Greenberg, *Honor & Slavery*, 3–23.

30. Walker, *Recollections of Quantrill's Guerrillas*, 4.

31. Ibid., 5.

32. Ibid., 4, 9. Connelley pushed the idea that Quantrill fell in love with Morgan Walker's daughter, and that he orchestrated the December 1860 raid on her father's farm and the bushwhacking of his traveling companions to impress her. This was quite the scheme to gain the attention of someone Quantrill probably never met. Not surprisingly, there is no evidence that the attack was a bloody attention grab. Connelley repeated this canard to explain why the guerrilla chief came back to the Walker farm in the fall of 1861: he just needed to see Anna Walker. See Connelley, *Quantrill and the Border Wars*, 197–198; Castel, *William Clarke Quantrill*, 64.

33. Walker, *Recollections of Quantrill's Guerrillas*, 9.

CHAPTER 9. *Overseer*

1. Scarborough, *Overseer*; Stubbs, *Masters of Violence*, 2–4; McMurtry-Chubb, *Race Unequals*, xi–xxi. Even Quantrill's most critical biographers ignore the significance of whiteness to Quantrill's identity and shift toward proslavery politics. See Connelley, *Quantrill and the Border Wars*; Castel, *William Clarke Quantrill*.

2. Scarborough, *Overseer*, 10; Vlach, *Back of the Big House*, 234; McMurtry-Chubb, *Race Unequals*, xi–xxi.

3. Stubbs, *Masters of Violence*, xiii–xv, 142–143.

4. 1860 Slave Schedule, Jackson County, Missouri, 13, National Archives and Records Administration, Washington, D.C.; King, *Stolen Childhood*. Almost certainly, Mary Gill saw her husband's face in those light-skinned children. She was probably pleased to see them driven away, far from her sight, but she never forgot the way in which they originated. Mrs. Gill knew well what the abolitionist senator Charles Sumner was talking about when he recovered from the beating he received from Preston Brooks and returned to Congress in 1860. There, on the floor of the Senate, he proclaimed that the systemic rape of Black women by their owners was "recorded in the tell-tale faces of children, glowing with their master's blood, but doomed for their mother's skin." See Sumner, *Barbarism of Slavery*, 14.

5. McPherson, *Battle Cry of Freedom*, 234–307; Connelley, *Quantrill and the Border Wars*, 191–195.

6. W. L. Potter to W. W. Scott, January 20, 1896, in Edwards, *Suppressed Evidence*, 27–31; Connelley, *Quantrill and the Border Wars*, 182–195. It is not clear how the jayhawkers living in and around Stanton discovered Hart's true identity (or Quantrill's assumed name).

7. Thomas Roberts to H. V. Beeson, May 16, 1881, RH MS 75, Box 2, Folder 59, William Clarke Quantrill Correspondence, Spencer Research Library, University of Kansas, Lawrence.

8. Matthew M. Stith provides a good account of the ways in which news of the war came to the border region of the Kansas and Indian Territories, Arkansas, and Missouri, and of that news's reception by Unionists, Confederates, and Native Americans. See Stith, *Extreme Civil War*, 27–32; McPherson, *Battle Cry of Freedom*, 308–338.

NOTES TO CHAPTERS NINE AND TEN   233

9. Although there was no documentation of Mayes's enlistment until September 1862, the original rolls including his name quite possibly disappeared, if they existed in the first place. Huston, "Quantrill's Raiders"; Castel, *William Clarke Quantrill*; Campbell, "Lochiel's Warning."

10. Walker, *Recollections of Quantrill's Guerrillas*, 10; Piston and Hatcher, *Wilson's Creek*.

11. Walker, *Recollections of Quantrill's Guerrillas*, 10; Geary, "Letter to Editor George W. Martin," 11:284; Stiles, *Jesse James*, 62–67.

12. Sutherland, *Savage Conflict*, 9–40; Fellman, *Inside War*, vi, 132–136, 176.

13. Piston and Hatcher, *Wilson's Creek*.

14. Shea and Hess, *Pea Ridge*.

15. Walker, *Recollections of Quantrill's Guerrillas*, 10; Connelley, *Quantrill and the Border Wars*; Castel, *William Clarke Quantrill*.

16. Beilein, *Bushwhackers*, 14–38.

17. Ibid.

18. Sutherland, *Savage Conflict*, 46.

CHAPTER 10. *Killer*

1. Walker, *Recollections of Quantrill's Guerrillas*, 13–14.

2. Ibid.

3. John N. Edwards, *Noted Guerrillas*; Connelley, *Quantrill and the Border Wars*; Castel, *William Clarke Quantrill*; Schultz, *Quantrill's War*; Leslie, *Devil Knows How to Ride*; Petersen, *Quantrill of Missouri*; Petersen, *Quantrill in Texas*. For modern studies of the guerrilla war in Missouri that look at the effect of killing on the human psyche, see Fellman, *Inside War*; Stiles, *Jesse James*.

4. Connelley, *Quantrill and the Border Wars*, 42.

5. Hogarth, *Engravings by Hogarth: 101 Prints*, plates 77–80; Connelley, *Quantrill and the Border Wars*, 42. Modern studies of serial killers confirm that many men (and it is typically, but not always, men) who become disturbingly violent perform acts of violence on small animals. See Ressler, et al., "Murderers Who Rape and Mutilate," 273–287; Lockwood, "Animal Cruelty and Violence against Humans," 81–87.

6. "Quantrill's Mother," *Louisville (Ky.) Courier-Journal*, March 20, 1898. Occasionally it is necessary to evoke common sense, which suggests that it would be nearly impossible for any man to shoot a living pig through one ear. It would certainly be impossible to shoot a writhing, running, squealing pig in the second ear after hitting it in the first one from a distance of 250 yards with a muzzle-loaded rifle.

7. Connelley, *Quantrill and the Border Wars*, 49, 51–52.

8. Walker, *Recollections of Quantrill's Guerrillas*, 3–9; John N. Edwards, *Noted Guerrillas*, 39–40.

9. Walker, *Recollections of Quantrill's Guerrillas*, 3–9.

10. Besides W. W. Scott, who died before he could write and publish his biography of Quantrill, Connelley was the first to uncover and document these lies. See Connelley, *Quantrill and the Border Wars*, 166–173.

11. Dumas, *Count of Monte Cristo*; Poe, "Cask of Amontillado;" Scott, *Ivanhoe: A Romance*; Coleman, *Here Lies Hugh Glass*. The story of Hugh Glass is still told with as much potency as ever, an indication that vengeance remains a fantasy among Americans. See the film *The Revenant*.

12. Walker, *Recollections of Quantrill's Guerrillas*, 3–9.

13. Ibid., 1.

14. Clifford Geertz's watershed work offers a starting point for this type of deep cultural

234 NOTES TO CHAPTERS TEN AND ELEVEN

study. See Geertz, "Deep Play: Notes on the Balinese Cockfight," 1–37. See also Lepore, *Name of War*, x. Historian Jill Lepore notes in her remarkable cultural study of King Philip's War, "War is a contest of injuries and of interpretation." Her book models so well the possibilities of reading actions as a text. *Name of War* illustrates the ways in which wartime violence, contemporary explanations for those bloody and destructive deeds, and later historical interpretations relate to one another and become intertwined and tangled.

15. Walker, *Recollections of Quantrill's Guerrillas*, 14–15, 16.

16. *War of the Rebellion: A Compilation of the Official Records*, series 1, vol. 8, pp. 57–58.

17. Walker, *Recollections of Quantrill's Guerrillas*, 17.

18. Interview with William H. Gregg, July 14, 1916, RH MS 2, box 1, William E. Connelley Collection, Spencer Research Library, University of Kansas, Lawrence; Gregg, *William Gregg's Civil War*, 83–84.

19. Gregg, *William Gregg's Civil War*, 49. According to a few reports, Quantrill and his men acted in ways that transgressed this general code in February and March 1862, but these accounts are vague and cannot be corroborated. For examples of these reports, see *Wyandotte Commercial Gazette* (Kansas City, Kans.), February 8, 1862; *Olathe (Kans.) Mirror*, March 20, 1862.

20. Connelley, *Quantrill and the Border Wars*, 225–230.

21. Ibid. For photograph of Abraham Ellis, see B Ellis, Abraham *1, DaRT ID: 208531, Kansas Historical Society, Topeka. Also see "Ellis, Abraham (Bullet Hole)."

22. Guerrilla George Maddox noted, "The first Federal soldier killed in Jackson County was killed by Quantrill." See Maddox Testimony, folder 38, William Elsey Connelley Papers, Denver Public Library, Denver, Colo. Most of the literature surrounding killers focuses on murder and murderers in peacetime. There are a few mentions of killing in war in these books, though, stating that war absolves killers: Davis, *Homicide in American Fiction, 1798–1860*; Halttunen, *Murder Most Foul*. There exists another body of literature about violence and killing in war. While these studies focus on and emphasize different elements of the phenomenon, the basic conceit is that men are expected to kill in war. Of note here are Grossman, *On Killing*; Keegan, *Face of Battle*.

CHAPTER 11. *Captain*

1. Dalton, *Under the Black Flag*, 100–101; John N. Edwards, *Noted Guerrillas*, 296; McCorkle, *Three Years with Quantrill*, 164; Trow, *Charles W. Quantrell*, 176–177, 180; Younger, *Story of Cole Younger, by Himself*, 58; Beilein and Hulbert, *Civil War Guerrilla*, 1–11. A few guerrillas thought it was necessary to assert that the black flags did not exist, which speaks to the popularity of the notion of such flags regardless of the lack of evidence concerning them. Andrew Walker said, "Quantrill's men never carried a flag, black or otherwise, except on the march southward in the fall of '63, when a Confederate and a Federal flag (Jim Lane's) both were used," in Walker, *Recollections of Quantrill's Guerrillas*, 23.

2. Fellman, *Inside War*; Sutherland, *Savage Conflict*; Mackey, *Uncivil War*; Myers, *Executing Daniel Bright*.

3. Fellman, *Inside War*; Sutherland, *Savage Conflict*; Mackey, *Uncivil War*; Myers, *Executing Daniel Bright*; Dalton, *Under the Black Flag*, 100–101; John N. Edwards, *Noted Guerrillas*, 296; McCorkle, *Three Years with Quantrell*, 164; Trow, *Chas. W. Quantrell*, 176–177, 180; Walker, *Recollections of Quantrill's Guerrillas*, 23; Younger, *Story of Cole Younger, by Himself*, 58; Beilein and Hulbert, *Civil War Guerrilla*, 1–11.

4. *War of the Rebellion: A Compilation of the Official Records* (hereafter cited as *O.R.*), series 1, vol. 8, part 1, pp. 611–612; *O.R.*, series 3, vol. 2, part 1, pp. 301–309.

NOTES TO CHAPTER ELEVEN   235

5. *O.R.*, series 1, vol. 8, part 1, pp. 611–612; *O.R.*, series 3, vol. 2, part 1, pp. 301–309;; *O.R.*, series 1, vol. 8, part 1, pp. 463–464.

6. *O.R.*, series 3, vol. 2, part 1, pp. 301–309. John Pope and John C. Frémont, both officers in Missouri early in the Civil War, also emphasized the problem of the guerrillas' disruption of the railroads and the movements of Union troops without mention of indiscriminate killing. While there is an implication that violence was extending beyond troops to "Unionists," little detail was given. See John Pope to John C. Frémont, August 25, 1861, in *O.R.*, series 2, vol. 1, pp. 215–216.

7. *O.R.*, series 3, vol. 2, part 1, pp. 301–309; *O.R.*, series 2, vol. 1, pp. 215–216. Recent literature reveals that Lieber's generalization continues to be misread as an assessment of the events on the ground. Historians and writers engaging with the Lieber Code tend to transpose some of the loose, ungrounded descriptions of guerrilla warfare onto the actual fighting in Missouri early in the war. A few scholars either neglect to investigate beyond the correspondence between Lieber and Halleck or, worse, read Halleck and Lieber and then view the guerrilla war through the lenses of these intellectual counterinsurgents. See Grimsley, *Hard Hand of War*, 148–151; Witt, *Lincoln's Code*, 188, 193–196.

8. Gregg, *William Gregg's Civil War*, 56; Foote, *Rites of Retaliation*, 3.

9. Walker, *Recollections of Quantrill's Guerrillas*, 19; Gregg, *William Gregg's Civil War*, 49–50.

10. Buel, *Border Bandits*, 16; Buel, *Border Outlaws*, 40–43, 254.

11. Gregg, *William Gregg's Civil War*, 49–50; Buel, *Border Outlaws*, 42–43, 254.

12. William Quantrill to Caroline Quantrill, February 8, 1860, William Elsey Connelley Letters, Denver Public Library, Denver, Colo.; Berry, *All That Makes a Man*, 12.

13. *Brooklyn (N.Y.) Evening Star*, May 1, 1862; *Daily Milwaukee (Wisc.) News*, August 6, 1862. Perry Hoy was tried for the murder of the "citizen Allison," and for the death of a Union soldier who was killed in a different fight later that day. It was odd that Hoy was held responsible for two of the three men killed that day, rather than all three. In particular, the charges leveled against Hoy left no one responsible for the killing of the soldier at the bridge—that is, unless Allison was the "Dutch sergeant" at the bridge.

14. McCorkle, *Three Years with Quantrill*, 39, 40–41.

15. Ibid.; Walker, *Recollections of Quantrill's Guerrillas*, 20.

16. *O.R.*, ser. 1, vol. 5, pp. 346–347; *Wyandotte Commercial Gazette* (Kansas City, Kans.), March 29, 1862; *Smoky Hill and Republican Union* (Junction City, Kans.), April 3, 1862.

17. Walker, *Recollections of Quantrill's Guerrillas*, 19; Gregg, *William Gregg's Civil War*, 9–10; *Brooklyn (N.Y.) Evening Star*, May 1, 1862; *Daily Milwaukee (Wisc.) News*, August 6, 1862; *O.R.*, ser. 1, vol. 5, pp. 346–347; *Wyandotte Commercial Gazette* (Kansas City, Kans.), March 29, 1862; *Smoky Hill and Republican Union* (Junction City, Kans.), April 3, 1862.

18. Gregg, *William Gregg's Civil War*, 49–50, 57.

19. Ibid., 56.

20. Ibid., 57.

21. Ibid., 57–58; *O.R.*, series 1, vol. 13, p. 803; *O.R.*, series 2, vol. 4, p. 721; Connelley, *Quantrill and the Border Wars*, 270–273.

22. Foote, *Rites of Retaliation*, 8.

23. Ibid., 2–8.

24. Quantrill's Flag, KSHS Identifier, 1930.29.0, Kansas Historical Society, Topeka. Also visible at their website: https://www.kshs.org/kansapedia/.

25. Charles Dew makes clear the centrality of slavery and white supremacy to the secession movement and the formation of the Confederacy in *Apostles of Disunion*.

26. Ibid.; Beilein, *Bushwhackers*, 101–122. For detailed descriptions of a scene that was re-

236 NOTES TO CHAPTERS ELEVEN AND TWELVE

peated across the country, North and South, in which the women of a community made the regimental flag for the unit in which their boys served, see Wiley, *Life of Billy Yank*, 28–31; Wiley, *Life of Johnny Reb*, 21–22.

27. Gregg, *William Gregg's Civil War*, 57.

28. Walker, *Recollections of Quantrill's Guerrillas*, 31–38.

29. McCorkle, *Three Years with Quantrill*, 102–104.

30. Ibid.

31. Walker, *Recollections of Quantrill's Guerrillas*, 31–38.

32. "Quantrile's General Orders?," *Emporia (Kans.) News*, August 23, 1862.

33. Ibid.; William Quantrill to Caroline Quantrill, January 26, 1860, William Elsey Connelley Letters, Denver Public Library, Denver, Colo.; Beilein, *Bushwhackers*, 20–21.

34. "Quantrile's General Orders?," *Emporia (Kans.) News*, August 23, 1862; William Quantrill to Caroline Quantrill, January 26, 1860, William Elsey Connelley Letters, Denver Public Library, Denver, Colo.; Beilein, *Bushwhackers*, 20–21; ; *O.R.*, series 1, vol. 8, part 1, pp. 611–612; *O.R.*, series 3, vol. 2, part 1, pp. 301–309.

35. "Quantrile's General Orders?," *Emporia (Kans.) News*, August 23, 1862; William Quantrill to Caroline Quantrill, January 26, 1860, William Elsey Connelley Letters, Denver Public Library, Denver, Colo.; Beilein, *Bushwhackers*, 20–21; *O.R.*, series 1, vol. 8, part 1, pp. 611–612; *O.R.*, series 3, vol. 2, part 1, pp. 301–309. Historians dismiss the guerrillas' attempts at official policy as farce. Fellman describes them as "boyish pretense" and "infantile narcissism." See Fellman, *Inside War*, 136–139.

36. John N. Edwards, *Noted Guerrillas*; Connelley, *Quantrill and the Border Wars*; Brownlee, *Gray Ghosts of the Confederacy*; Castel, *William Clarke Quantrill*; Fellman, *Inside War*, 265.

37. Dalton, *Under the Black Flag*, 100–101; John N. Edwards, *Noted Guerrillas*, 296; McCorkle, *Three Years with Quantrill*, 164; Trow, *Charles W. Quantrell*, 176–177, 180; Walker, *Recollections of Quantrill's Guerrillas*, 23; Younger, *Story of Cole Younger, by Himself*, 58; Beilein and Hulbert, *Civil War Guerrilla*, 1–11.

38. Buel, *Border Bandits*, 16; Buel, *Border Outlaws*, 42–43, 254.

CHAPTER 12. *Partisan Ranger*

1. Connelley, *Quantrill and the Border Wars*, 278–283.

2. Grace and Richardson, "Forced to the Cannon's Mouth."

3. McPherson, *Ordeal by Fire*, 283–288, 303–305.

4. The Emancipation Proclamation, September 22, 1862, The American Presidency Project, University of California, Santa Barbara, https://www.presidency.ucsb.edu/documents/proclamation-95-regarding-the-status-slaves-states-engaged-rebellion-against-the-united.

5. John N. Edwards suggested that it was the rank of colonel that Quantrill sought. *Noted Guerrillas*, 156. See also McPherson, *Battle Cry of Freedom*, 328–329.

6. "Act to Organize Bands of Partisan Rangers," 48; Beilein, "Householder and General," 35–54; Lee, *Memoirs of the War*.

7. "Act to Organize Bands of Partisan Rangers," 48.

8. Myers, "Partisan Ranger Petitions," 18–19.

9. Ibid., 13–35.

10. Sutherland, *Savage Conflict*, 26–29. Even knowing how things escalated over the first year of the war in western Missouri, those events were nothing compared to the soldiering other men from that area found themselves doing as a part of the Confederate army. Pea Ridge confirmed that. For several days in early March, Earl Van Dorn led thousands of men on a forced march through snow, sleet, and rain. The troops were allowed no rest or food. Then, that vainglorious lothario led a risky march around the Union lines that turned di-

NOTES TO CHAPTERS TWELVE AND THIRTEEN   237

sastrous on day one of the battle. Day two was a meat grinder: Missourians were blasted to bits by Union artillery until they were forced to retreat. See Shea and Hess, *Pea Ridge*.

11. John N. Edwards, *Noted Guerrillas*, 156–158.

12. Ibid.

13. *Sentinel* (Richmond, Va.), March 14, 1863; Connelley, *Quantrill and the Border Wars*, 278–283.

14. *Sentinel* (Richmond, Va.), March 14, 1863; Connelley, *Quantrill and the Border Wars*, 278–283.

CHAPTER 13. *Colonel*

1. Walker, *Recollections of Quantrill's Guerrillas*, 51–52.

2. Fellman, *Inside War*, v.

3. Wyatt-Brown, *Southern Honor*, 352–361; Bruce, *Violence and Culture in the Antebellum South*, 1; Steward, *Duels and the Roots of Violence*.

4. Walker, *Recollections of Quantrill's Guerrillas*, 51–52. A similar democratic culture governed piracy. On a pirate ship manliness, violence, authority, and democracy made for a unique sociopolitical structure, but it was more empowering than any other in the world at the time. See Woodard, *Republic of Pirates*.

5. Gregg, *William Gregg's Civil War*, 62.

6. Ibid.

7. Ibid.; McCorkle, *Three Years with Quantrill*, 63, 97, 104, 124, 129; Walker, *Recollections of Quantrill's Guerrillas*, 21, 41, 50; *O.R.*, series 1, vol. 13, p. 125; *O.R.* vol. 34, part 1, pp. 861–862, part 2, pp. 532, 604–605; *O.R.*, vol. 34, part 3, p. 51.

8. Gregg, *William Gregg's Civil War*, 54–55; Beilein, "Whiskey, Wild Men, and Missouri's Guerrilla War," 236–259.

9. Younger, *Story of Cole Younger, by Himself*; Bowen, "Quantrill, James, Younger, et al.," 42–48.

10. Gregg, *William Gregg's Civil War*.

11. Castel and Goodrich, *Bloody Bill Anderson*, 12–18.

12. Ibid., 24; Fellman, *Inside War*, 136.

13. 1860 Federal Manuscript Census, Jackson County, Missouri, National Archives and Records Administration, Washington, D.C.; Geary, "Letter to Editor George W. Martin," 11:284.

14. To view the unpublished portrait of George Todd, see Fletcher, "Backdrop Connected to Portraits"; Beilein, *Bushwhackers*, 75; Gregg, *William Gregg's Civil War*, 52–53. Younger claimed that he, too, went along, but no one else recalled that. Younger's account, which was colorful and helpful, was likely told to him by Todd or Quantrill and then repeated in the first person. See Younger, *Story of Cole Younger, by Himself*, 19.

15. Younger, *Story of Cole Younger, by Himself*, 19.

16. Ibid.

17. Ibid.; Beilein, *Bushwhackers*, 101–122.

18. Gregg, *William Gregg's Civil War*, 61.

19. "The Sam Gaty Boarded and Plundered—the Murder of Two White Men and Fifteen Negroes," *Smoky Hill and Republican Union* (Junction City, Kans.), April 4, 1863; *O.R.*, series 1, vol. 22, part 1, pp. 245–246; *O.R.*, part 2, pp. 183, 195, 203.

20. "Sam Gaty Boarded and Plundered—the Murder of Two White Men and Fifteen Negroes," *Smoky Hill and Republican Union* (Junction City, Kans.), April 4, 1863; *O.R.*, series 1, vol. 22, part 1, pp. 245–246; *O.R.*, part 2, pp. 183, 195, 203.

21. "Sam Gaty Boarded and Plundered—the Murder of Two White Men and Fifteen Ne-

238 NOTES TO CHAPTERS THIRTEEN AND FOURTEEN

groes," *Smoky Hill and Republican Union* (Junction City, Kans.), April 4, 1863; *O.R.*, series 1, vol. 22, part 1, pp. 245–246; *O.R.*, part 2, pp. 183, 195, 203. Another controversy emerged concerning the bushwhacking of the *Sam Gaty*. Years after the war, Gregg claimed he was responsible for the attack. "Lieutenant Gregg's operations were limited until March, when with eleven men he captured the government steamer Sam Gaty near Sibley, destroying half a million dollars in sugar, coffee, flour, bacon, et cetera," but that was not all. He and his men also killed "some fourteen soldiers of Penick's command." Gregg's memoir of the war is typically reliable. It is possible that he took down the *Gaty* and that he omitted the atrocity—or just added the number of Black men, women, and children killed to the two white soldiers killed. It is also possible that he was still bitter about Todd's impudence. See Gregg, *William Gregg's Civil War*, 62.

22. Walker, *Recollections of Quantrill's Guerrillas*, 49.

23. Ibid.

24. Ibid., 50–51.

25. Ibid.

26. Ibid., 52–53; Gregg, *William Gregg's Civil War*, 62.

27. Walker, *Recollections of Quantrill's Guerrillas*, 52–53; Gregg, *William Gregg's Civil War*, 62.

28. Gregg, *William Gregg's Civil War*, 62.

29. Ibid.; Walker, *Recollections of Quantrill's Guerrillas*, 53.

30. In Quantrill's geographic partitioning of the border and his understanding of the local populace, it is possible to see the faint outlines of what Charles Lee imagined as "zones of resistance." This concept would define the strategy of Continental militiamen against the British Army in New York and New Jersey. See Shy, *People Numerous and Armed*, 151, 133–162.

31. Walker, *Recollections of Quantrill's Guerrillas*, 22, 25–26; Beilein, *Bushwhackers*, 101–122.

32. Melville, *Confidence-Man*; Beilein, *Bushwhackers*, 114.

33. To view the unpublished portrait of George Todd, see Fletcher, "Backdrop Connected to Portraits."

34. *O.R.*, series 1, vol. 22, part 2, pp. 428–429; Gregg, *William Gregg's Civil War*, 9–10, 50–51; Castel, *William Clarke Quantrill*, 116.

35. *O.R.*, series 1, vol. 22, part 2, pp. 428–429; Gregg, *William Gregg's Civil War*, 9–10, 50–51; Castel, *William Clarke Quantrill*, 116.

CHAPTER 14. *Gambler*

1. Gregg, *William Gregg's Civil War*, 46–48.

2. Ibid.; Whites, "Forty Shirts and a Wagonload of Wheat," 56–78.

3. Foote, *Rites of Retaliation*, 49–112.

4. There must have been some cursing about abolitionists and Black men. Perhaps Quantrill enticed his men by telling them what he saw there: Black men and women walking free after having run away from slavery in Missouri. These African Americans were mixing, talking, and even laughing with whites miles from the brutality of war, all while the fighting took its toll on the guerrillas' families. While most of the actual words used during this conversation are lost, Anderson, Todd, and Quantrill likely used language laced with racial epithets and punctuated with vulgarities. It is difficult to imagine the partisans speaking any other way. Their world was in peril, and their words must have reflected their desperation and bigoted hatred. See "The Sam Gaty Boarded and Plundered—the Murder of Two White Men and Fifteen Negroes," *Smoky Hill and Republican Union* (Junction City, Kans.), April 4, 1863; *O.R.*, series 1, vol. 22, part 1, pp. 245–246; *O.R.*, series 1, vol. 22, part 2, pp. 183, 195, 203; Gregg, *William Gregg's Civil War*, 46–48. In his memoir, Harrison Trow claimed that when debating whether they would go to Lawrence, one of the guerrilla cap-

tains said, "Lawrence. I know it of old; 'niggers' and white men are just the same there." See Trow, *Charles W. Quantrell*, 143.

5. Gregg, *William Gregg's Civil War*, 46–48.

6. *O.R.*, series 1, vol. 22, part 2, pp. 460–461.

7. Ibid., pp. 428–429, 460–461. In his August 3 report, Ewing offered the earliest hint at his recasting of Union strategy along the border. Proposing a sketch of what became General Orders Nos. 10 and 11, Ewing said, "I think that the families of several hundred of the worst of these men should be sent, with their clothes and bedding, to some rebel district south." It was a costly plan, as Ewing estimated: "About one-half of them could take with them no provisions or money or any consequence, and would have to be temporarily supplied by Government." However, this was a much cheaper alternative to waging the war as the Federals were. "I can see no prospect of an early and complete end to the war on the border," Ewing worried, "without a great increase of troops, so long as those families remain there." Banishing the families cut the guerrilla supply line and also removed one reason for fighting.

8. *O.R.*, series 1, vol. 22, part 2, pp. 428, 460–461. General Order No. 10 came out on August 18, 1863, but the subsequent passage of the more radical General Order No. 11 on August 25 would make it null and void. See *O.R.*, series 1, vol. 22, part 2, p. 473. Also see Harris, "Catalyst for Terror," 290–306. For more about the Union process of targeting, arresting, and imprisoning women, see Curran, *Women Making War*.

9. McCorkle, *Three Years with Quantrill*, 125; Gregg, *William Gregg's Civil War*, 59. For the views of a guerrilla toward Black soldiers, see Trow, *Charles W. Quantrell*, 57–58.

10. Woods, *Bleeding Kansas*, 109. This racial violence fit so well with the social and political beliefs of the guerrillas and white southerners in general at this moment in the war. Black units were now in the field for the Union army—a part of a strategy to boost northern manpower at the expense of the labor available to the South—but southerners considered this move a gambit by Black Republicans. It was an insult and taunt, and the Confederate army responded. Lee invaded the North in the summer of 1863 and sent one of his legions—Jenkins's Cavalry Brigade—to round up African Americans in Pennsylvania and drive them back into Virginia, where they would be enslaved. See Jefferson Davis's address to the Confederate Congress delivered on January 14, 1863, which offered a pointed response to the Emancipation Proclamation. *Journal of the Congress of the Confederate States*, 3:13–14; Creighton, *Colors of Courage*, 126–132. Race also shaped the way that the killing at Lawrence is remembered. Like the Slave Schedule, Black men—Black victims—were anonymous, a nameless heap of bodies. Like the reports of the *Sam Gaty*—"Meyers and Henry, of Company E, killed others escaped. Twenty negroes killed"—names were only important for the white men brought low by a bushwhacker bullet. Like the houses burned, the property destroyed, the horses rustled, these men warrant a tally, a notch for each "negro" or "contraband," even in the Kansans's recollection of the attack on Lawrence. See 1860 Slave Schedule, United States Government, National Archives and Records Administration, Washington, D.C.; "Sam Gaty Boarded and Plundered—the Murder of Two White Men and Fifteen Negroes," *Smoky Hill and Republican Union* (Junction City, Kans.), April 4, 1863; *O.R.*, series 1, vol. 22, part 1, pp. 245–246; *O.R.*, series 1, vol. 22, part 2, pp. 183, 195, 203.

11. Castel, *William Clarke Quantrill*, 122–141.

12. Ibid., 128–129.

13. Ibid., 122–141.

14. McCorkle, *Three Years with Quantrill*, 123–124.

15. Castel and Goodrich, *Bloody Bill Anderson*, 29.

16. Gregg, *William Gregg's Civil War*, 79–81.

17. *O.R.*, series 1, vol. 22, part 1, pp. 688–690.

240 NOTES TO CHAPTERS FOURTEEN AND FIFTEEN

18. Ibid.; McCorkle, *Three Years with Quantrill*, 136.

19. *O.R.*, series 1, vol. 22, part 1, pp. 688–690; McCorkle, *Three Years with Quantrill*, 136.

20. *O.R.*, series 1, vol. 22, part 1, pp. 688–690; McCorkle, *Three Years with Quantrill*, 136.

21. Connelley, *Quantrill and the Border Wars*, 421–434; Stith, *Extreme Civil War*, 112–115; Quantrill, *Mechanic's Calculator and Tinman's Guide*; Morrison, *"Best School in the World:"*, 87–101.

22. *O.R.*, series 1, vol. 22, part 1, p. 701; Gregg, *William Gregg's Civil War*, 74–75; Connelley, *Quantrill and the Border Wars*, 434.

23. *O.R.*, series 1, vol. 32, part 1, pp. 520–521.

24. Ibid.

25. *O.R.*, series 1, vol. 22, part 1, p. 701; Gregg, *William Gregg's Civil War*, 74–75; Connelley, *Quantrill and the Border Wars*, 434. Forrest certainly seemed to embody the racial antipathy of the white South. His entire biography paints a picture of a white man who despised Black women and men; he was a slave trader before the war, commander of the Confederate troops during the massacre at Fort Pillow, and a leader of the first iteration of the Reconstruction-era Ku Klux Klan. No man worked harder to reject the reality of the changing world than Forrest. See Wills, *Battle from the Start*.

26. Connelley, *Quantrill and the Border Wars*, 440–441; Beilein, "Whiskey, Wild Men, and Missouri's Guerrilla War," 236–259.

27. Connelley, *Quantrill and the Border Wars*, 440–441; Beilein, "Whiskey, Wild Men, and Missouri's Guerrilla War," 236–259.

28. Fletch Taylor to W. W. Scott, 1879 and undated, William Elsey Connelley Papers, Denver Public Library, Denver, Colo.

29. "William Quantrill: Some Facts Concerning His Life and Death," *St. Louis (Mo.) Daily Globe-Democrat*, March 29, 1881.

30. Taylor to Scott, 1879 and undated, William Elsey Connelley Papers, Denver Public Library, Denver, Colo.

31. Ibid.

32. Connelley, *Quantrill and the Border Wars*, 440–441.

33. Ibid.

34. Ibid., 448.

35. Smith, "Original Frank Smith Manuscript," 16; Leslie, *Devil Knows How to Ride*, 300–301.

36. Smith, "Original Frank Smith Manuscript," 16; Leslie, *Devil Knows How to Ride*, 300–301.

CHAPTER 15. *Outcast*

1. Gregg, *William Gregg's Civil War*, 76.

2. 1860 Federal Manuscript Census, Sni-A-Bar Township, Jackson County, Missouri, National Archives and Records Administration, Washington, D.C.; 1860 Slave Schedule, Jackson County, Missouri, National Archives and Records Administration, Washington, D.C. See Whites, "Tale of Three Kates," 73–94.

3. "The Strange Romance of Quantrill's Bride," *Kansas City (Mo.) Star*, May 23, 1926.

4. Ibid.; Hoftiezer and Beck, *Kate King, in Fact and Fiction*, 275.

5. "Strange Romance of Quantrill's Bride," *Kansas City (Mo.) Star*, May 23, 1926; Hoftiezer and Beck, *Kate King, in Fact and Fiction*, 276.

6. "Strange Romance of Quantrill's Bride," *Kansas City (Mo.) Star*, May 23, 1926; Hoftiezer and Beck, *Kate King, in Fact and Fiction*, 276.

7. "Strange Romance of Quantrill's Bride," *Kansas City (Mo.) Star*, May 23, 1926; Hoftiezer and Beck, *Kate King, in Fact and Fiction*, 276.

NOTES TO CHAPTERS FIFTEEN AND SIXTEEN   241

8. Fletch Taylor to W. W. Scott, 1879, William Elsey Connelley Papers, Denver Public Library, Denver, Colo.

9. "Strange Romance of Quantrill's Bride," *Kansas City (Mo.) Star*, May 23, 1926; Hoftiezer and Beck, *Kate King, in Fact and Fiction*, 278.

10. "Strange Romance of Quantrill's Bride, *Kansas City (Mo.) Star*, May 23, 1926"; Hoftiezer and Beck, *Kate King, in Fact and Fiction*, 278.

11. "Strange Romance of Quantrill's Bride," *Kansas City (Mo.) Star*, May 23, 1926; Hoftiezer and Beck, *Kate King, in Fact and Fiction*, 278.; Hoftiezer and Beck, *Kate King, in Fact and Fiction*, 280.

12. "Strange Romance of Quantrill's Bride," *Kansas City (Mo.) Star*, May 23, 1926; Hoftiezer and Beck, *Kate King, in Fact and Fiction*, 278.

13. Case against Robert Louden, Union Provost Marshals' File of Papers Relating to Individual Civilians, 1861–1867, War Department Collection of Confederate Records, Record Group 109, accessed at Ancestry.com, http://www.ancestry.com.

14. "Strange Romance of Quantrill's Bride," *Kansas City (Mo.) Star*, May 23, 1926.

15. Connelley, *Quantrill and the Border Wars*, 282–283.

16. "Strange Romance of Quantrill's Bride," *Kansas City (Mo.) Star*, May 23, 1926; Hoftiezer and Beck, *Kate King, in Fact and Fiction*, 276.

17. Gregg, *William Gregg's Civil War*, 76; McCorkle, *Three Years with Quantrill*, 103–104.

18. Gregg, *William Gregg's Civil War*, 76.

19. Rhea, *In the Footsteps of Grant and Lee*; McPherson, *Battle Cry of Freedom*, 774–775; Thomas, *John Hunt Morgan and His Raiders*, 94–112; Beilein, *Bushwhackers*, 51–59.

20. Gregg, *William Gregg's Civil War*, 76.

CHAPTER 16. *Vagabond*

1. McCorkle, *Three Years with Quantrill*, 160.

2. Ibid.

3. Ibid., 161–162.

4. Beilein, "1864 Invasion of Missouri," 520–533.

5. Beilein, *Bushwhackers*, 184–187.

6. Beilein, "1864 Invasion of Missouri," 531.

7. Beilein, *Bushwhackers*, 101–102.

8. McCorkle, *Three Years with Quantrill*, 180.

9. "The Strange Romance of Quantrill's Bride," *Kansas City (Mo.) Star*, May 23, 1926; Hoftiezer and Beck, *Kate King, in Fact and Fiction*, 281.

10. Connelley, *Quantrill and the Border Wars*, 456.

11. Union general Stephen G. Burbridge, who was commander of Union forces in Kentucky, issued the infamous General Order No. 59 on July 16, 1864. This directive threatened to kill four guerrilla prisoners for each unarmed Union civilian killed by guerrillas. As dark as it was, the order probably did little to deter Quantrill and his men, who were operating under conditions in which being taken prisoner at all was a luxury. See *O.R.*, series 1, vol. 39, part 2, p. 174.

12. *O.R.*, ser. 1, vol., 44, part 1, p. 688.

13. Beilein, "Terror of Kentucky," 157–181.

14. Ibid.

15. Ibid.

16. Ibid.

17. Dawson Family Collection, Spencer Research Library, University of Kansas, Lawrence; Watson, *Confederate Guerrilla Sue Mundy*, 155–157.

18. Dawson Family Collection, Spencer Research Library, University of Kansas, Law-

242 NOTES TO CHAPTERS SIXTEEN AND SEVENTEEN

rence. In his highly detailed book on the life of Jerome Clarke, Thomas Shelby Watson transcribes another piece of poetry attributed to Quantrill and notes that the Dawson family possesses several others. These works are not included here because the author has not seen the originals or copies of the originals. See Watson, *Confederate Guerrilla Sue Mundy*, 155–157.

19. Dawson Family Collection, Spencer Research Library, University of Kansas, Lawrence; Byron, "To Thomas Moore."; Watson, *Confederate Guerrilla Sue Mundy*, 155–157.

20. Connelley, *Quantrill and the Border Wars*, 474–476.

21. Ibid., 476.

22. John N. Edwards, *Noted Guerrillas*, 437.

23. Byron, "Love and Death," lines 20–24.

CHAPTER 17. *Quarry*

1. Notes of W. W. Scott regarding his first trip to Louisville to find Quantrill's grave, William Clarke Quantrill Correspondence RH MS 75, box 2, folder 62, Spencer Research Library, University of Kansas, Lawrence.

2. Levi Filson Club Address, April 5, 1909, Filson Historical Society, Louisville, Ky.

3. "The Strange Romance of Quantrill's Bride," *Kansas City (Mo.) Star*, May 23, 1926.

4. Levi Filson Club Address, April 5, 1909, Filson Historical Society, Louisville, Ky.

5. Faust, *Republic of Suffering*, 146–170.

6. W. W. Scott notes on the back of letter from Rev. Dues to Rev. Brady. William Clarke Quantrill Correspondence, RH MS 75 box 2, folder 62, Spencer Research Library, University of Kansas, Lawrence.

7. Leslie, *Devil Knows How to Ride*, 408.

8. Ibid.

9. Beilein, *Bushwhackers*, 189–194.

10. Ibid.

11. William Robbins, "Guerrilla's Bones Get a Confederate Soldier's Funeral," *New York Times*, October 25, 1992.

12. Ibid.

13. Ibid.

14. Ibid.; "Replica Head of Confederate Raider Quantrill," Roadside America, https://www.roadsideamerica.com/story/10054. Nixon's relationship to Quantrill's memory and his bones was refreshing. For Nixon, it must have been difficult to understand others' impulse to possess some part of the long-dead bushwhacker. Perhaps owning some piece of Quantrill gave these individuals the power to explain what he symbolized, proclaim who his people were and what he stood for, tell the world what the war was really about. See Hulbert, *Ghosts of Guerrilla Memory*, 248–264. There is a large body of literature devoted to the study of the way that groups like the UDC and SCV use commemoration and memorial sites to promote a vision of the past rooted in the Lost Cause. For a couple of examples, see Cox, *Dixie's Daughters*; Janney, *Burying the Dead but Not the Past*.

15. The Quantrill's Guerrillas website offers a description of the event, in which a few of its members participated. See Patrick R. Marquis, "The Memorial Stone Dedication Which Took 143 Years: Highlights from October 25, 2008," 2008, http://quantrillsguerrillas.com /en/articles/148-the-memorial-stone-dedication-which-took-143-years-highlights-from -october-25–2008-article.html.

16. Marquis, "Memorial Stone Dedication."

17. "Quantrill, 'the Terror,'" *Louisville (Ky.) Courier Journal*, May 13, 1888.

BIBLIOGRAPHY

PRIMARY SOURCES

Unpublished Materials

Bureau of Land Management, Washington, D.C.

Federal Land Patent, Kansas Trust Lands

Denver Public Library, Denver, Colo.

William Elsey Connelley Papers

Ellis Library and State Historical Society of Missouri, Columbia

George, B. James, (1896–1975). Collection, 1887–1975. (C3564)
Gregg, William H. "A Little Dab of History Without Embellishment" [1906]. (C>1113)

Filson Historical Society, Louisville, Ky.

Levi Filson Club Addresses

Kansas Historical Society, Topeka

Photograph of Abraham Ellis (208531)
Quantrill's Flag (1930.29.0)

McCain Library and Archives, University of Southern Mississippi, Hattiesburg

Quantrill Collection

National Archives and Records Administration, Washington, D.C.

Agricultural Census, 1850, 1860
Federal Manuscript Census, 1850, 1860, 1870, 2010
Manufacturing Census, 1850, 1860
Slave Schedule, 1850, 1860
Union Provost Marshals' File of Papers Relating to Individual Civilians, 1861–1867. War Department Collection of Confederate Records, Record Group 109. Accessed at Ancestry.com. http://www.ancestry.com.

Reeves Victorian Home and Carriage House Museum, Dover, Ohio

William Clarke Quantrill Collection

244 BIBLIOGRAPHY

Spencer Research Library, University of Kansas, Lawrence

Dawson Family Collection
William Clarke Quantrill Correspondence
William E. Connelley Collection

Newspapers

Alexandria (Va.) Gazette, 1864
Brooklyn (N.Y.) Evening Star, 1862
Chicago Daily Tribune, 1864
Daily American Organ (Washington, D.C.), 1856
Daily Milwaukee (Wisc.) News, 1862
Emporia (Kans.) News, 1862
Glasgow (Mo.) Weekly Times, 1856
Godey's Lady's Book, 1830–1878
Harper's Weekly: A Journal of Civilization, 1863
Holmes County Republican (Millersburg, Ohio), 1862
Independent (Oskaloosa, Kans.), 1863
Kansas City (Mo.) Star, 1926
Louisville (Ky.) Courier-Journal, 1888, 1898
Louisville (Ky.) Daily Courier, 1865
Louisville (Ky.) Daily Democrat, 1865
Louisville (Ky.) Daily Union Press, 1865
New York Herald, 1849, 1856
New York Times, 1992
Olathe (Kans.) Mirror, 1862
Republican Intelligencer (Charles City, Iowa), 1863
Sentinel (Richmond, Va.), 1863
Smoky Hill and Republican Union (Junction City, Kans.), 1862
St. Louis (Mo.) Daily Globe-Democrat, 1881
Topeka (Kans.) Weekly Capital, 1882
Wyandotte Commercial Gazette (Kansas City, Kans.), 1862

Published Memoirs, Early Histories, and Literature

"An Act to Organize Bands of Partisan Rangers." In *Public Laws of the Confederate States of America, Passed at the First Session of the First Congress, 1862*, edited by James M. Matthews, 48. Richmond, Va.: R. M. Smith, Printer to Congress, 1862.

Baldwin, Elmer. *History of LaSalle County, Illinois*. Chicago: Rand McNally, 1877.

Beecher, Henry Ward. *Seven Lectures to Young Men on Various Important Subjects: Delivered before the Young Men of Indianapolis, Indiana during the Winter of 1843–44*. Indianapolis: Thomas B. Culter, 1844.

Buel, J. W. *The Border Bandits: An Authentic and Telling History of the Noted Outlaws, Jesse and Frank James*. St. Louis, Mo.: Historical Publishing, 1881.

———. *The Border Outlaws*. Cincinnati, Ohio: Forshee and McMakin, 1882.

Byron, Lord George Gordon. "Love and Death." 1824. Poetry Foundation. https://www.poetryfoundation.org/poems/49266/love-and-death.

———. *The Major Works*. London: Oxford University Press, 1986.

———. "To Thomas Moore." N.d. Poets.org. https://poets.org/poem/thomas-moore.

Campbell, Thomas. "Lochiel's Warning." 1801. PoemHunter.com. https://www.poemhunter.com/poem/lochiel-s-warning/.

BIBLIOGRAPHY 245

Clarke, Henry S. "W. C. Quantrill in 1858." *Collections of the Kansas State Historical Society* 7 (1902): 218–223.

Collections of the Kansas State Historical Society 7 (1902): 212–229.

Connelley, William Elsey. *James Henry Lane: The "Grim Chieftain" of Kansas*. Topeka, Kans.: Crane, 1899.

————. *John Brown*. Topeka, Kans.: Crane and Company, 1900.

————. *Quantrill and the Border Wars*. Cedar Rapids, Iowa: Torch, 1910.

————. *Wild Bill and His Era: The Life and Adventures of James Butler Hickok*. 1933. Reprint, New York: Cooper Square, 1972.

————. *Wyandot Folk-Lore*. Topeka, Kans.: Crane, 1899.

Cummings, James. *Jim Cummins, the Guerrilla*. Excelsior Springs. Mo.: Daily Journal, 1908.

Custer, George Armstrong. *My Life on the Plains, or Personal Experiences with Indians*. 1874. Reprint, Norman: University of Oklahoma Press, 1962.

Dalton, Kit. *Under the Black Flag*. Memphis, Tenn.: L. J. Tobert, 1995.

Duke, Basil W. *The History of Morgan's Cavalry*. Cincinnati, Ohio: Miami Printing and Publishing, 1867.

Dumas, Alexandre. *The Count of Monte Cristo*. New York: Oxford University Press, 2008. Originally serialized 1844–1846.

"Early Life of Quantrill in Kansas." *Collections of the Kansas State Historical Society* 7 (1902): 212–229.

Edwards, James C, ed. *Suppressed Evidence: Neglected Information about Confederate Colonel William Clarke Quantrill; The Letters of W. L. Potter and Abraham Ellis*. Harrisonville, Mo.: Burnt District, 2021.

Edwards, John N. *Noted Guerrillas, or The Warfare of the Border*. St. Louis, Mo.: H. W. Brand, 1879.

Geary, Daniel. "Letter to Editor George W. Martin." In *Collections of the Kansas State Historical Society: 1909–1910*, 11:284. Topeka, Kans.: State Printing Office, 1910.

Gladstone, T. H. *The Englishman in Kansas: Or, Squatter Life and Border Warfare*. New York: Miller, 1857.

Graham, Sylvester. *A Lecture to Young Men on Chastity: Intended Also for the Serious Consideration of Parents and Guardians*. 2nd ed. Boston: Light and Stearns, Crocker and Brewster, 1837.

Grant, Ulysses S. *Personal Memoirs of U. S. Grant*. New York: Charles L. Webster, 1885.

Greenaway, Kate. *Language of Flowers*. London: George Routledge and Sons, 1884.

Gregg, William H. *William Gregg's Civil War: The Battle to Shape the History of Guerrilla Warfare*. Edited by Joseph M. Beilein Jr. Athens: University of Georgia Press, 2019.

Herd, Sydney S. "Always under an Alias, and without Visible Means of Support." *Collections of the Kansas State Historical Society* 7 (1902): 226–228.

Hildt, George H. "The Diary of George H. Hildt." *Kansas Historical Quarterly* 10 (August 1941): 260–298.

The History of Tuscarawas County, Ohio. Chicago: Warner, Beers, 1884.

Hogarth, William. *Engravings by Hogarth: 101 Prints*. Edited by Sean Shesgreen. New York: Dover, 1973.

Irving, Washington. "The Legend of Sleepy Hollow." In *The Sketch Book of Geoffrey Crayon, Gent*, edited by Haskell Springer, no pages. 1820. Reprint, Boston: Twayne, 1978.

Johnson, W. A. "Early Life of Quantrill in Kansas." *Collections of the Kansas State Historical Society* 7 (1902): 212–214.

Journal of the Congress of the Confederate States of America, 1861–1865. Vol. 3. Washington, D.C.: Government Printing Office, 1904.

Kellogg, J. H. *Man, the Masterpiece*. Battle Creek, Mich.: Modern Medicine, 1894.

BIBLIOGRAPHY

Kenney, James. *Raise the Wind.* N.p., 1803.

Lee, Henry. *Memoirs of the War in the Southern Department of the United States.* New York: University Publishing, 1869.

Lieber, Francis. General Orders No. 100, Instructions for the Government of Armies of the United States in the Field. April 24, 1863. The Avalon Project: Documents in Law, History and Diplomacy. https://avalon.law.yale.edu/19th_century/lieber.asp.

Lincoln, Abraham. "Speech at Leavenworth, Kansas," December 3, 1859. In *Collected Works of Abraham Lincoln*, edited by Roy P. Basler, 3:497–502. New Brunswick, N.J.: Rutgers University Press, 1953.

Manufactures of the United States in 1860. Washington, D.C.: Government Printing Office, 1865.

Melville, Herman. *The Confidence-Man: His Masquerade.* 1857. Reprint, edited by Stephen Matterson. New York: Penguin Books, 1990.

McCorkle, John. *Three Years with Quantrill: A True Story.* Written by O. S. Barton. Notes by Albert Castel. Norman: University of Oklahoma Press, 1992.

Poe, Edgar Allan. "The Cask of Amontillado." *Godey's Lady's Book.* November 1846.

——. "Diddling: Considered as One of the Exact Sciences." 1835. The Edgar Allen Poe Society of Baltimore. https://www.eapoe.org/works/tales/diddlnga.htm.

Public Laws of the Confederate States of America, Passed at the First Session of the First Congress, 1862. Edited by James M. Matthews. Richmond, Va.: R. M. Smith, Printer to Congress, 1862.

Quantrill, Thomas H. *The Mechanic's Calculator and Tinman's Guide.* Washington, D.C., 1847.

Quantrill, William Clarke. *Dear Mother: The Letters of William C. Quantrill to His Mother Caroline, 1855–1860.* Edited by Kelly D. Mezurek. Dover, Ohio: Dover Historical Society, 2017.

Riggs, Samuel A. "An Outlaw When He Took to the Bush." *Collections of the Kansas State Historical Society* 7 (1902): 223–224.

Sarah C. Roberts vs. The City of Boston. 59 Mass. 198, 5 Cush. 198 (1849).

Scott, Sir Walter. *Ivanhoe: A Romance.* 1820. Reprint, New York: Houghton Mifflin, 1913.

Scott, William W. *Reminiscences of Dover.* Canal Dover, Ohio: Iron Valley Reporter Newspaper, Book and Job Office, 1879.

Shakespeare, William. *As You Like It.* In *First Folio*, 185–207. London: William and Isaac Jaggard and Edward Blount, 1623.

Sheridan, Philip. *Personal Memoirs of P. H. Sheridan. General United States Army.* Vol. 2. New York: Charles L. Webster, 1888.

Sherman, William T. *Memoirs of General William T. Sherman.* 1875. Reprint, Bloomington: Indiana University Press, 1957.

Smith, Frank. "The Original Frank Smith Manuscript." Undated transcribed copy in possession of the author (and others).

Sumner, Charles. *The Barbarism of Slavery.* New York: Young Men's Republican Union, 1862.

——. *The Crime against Kansas.* Boston, Mass.: John P. Jewett, 1856.

Trow, Harrison. *Charles W. Quantrell: A True History of his Guerrilla Warfare on the Missouri and Kansas Border during the Civil War of 1861 to 1865.* Edited and written by J. P. Burch. Vega, Tex.: J. P. Burch, 1923.

Turner, Frederick Jackson. "The Significance of the Frontier in American History." Delivered at the American Historical Association Meeting, Chicago, July 12, 1893. American Historical Association. https://www.historians.org/about-aha-and-membership/ah a-history-and-archives/historical-archives/the-significance-of-the-frontier-in-american -history-(1893).

Walker, A. J. *Recollections of Quantrill's Guerrillas: As Told by A. J. Walker of Weatherford, Texas to Victor E. Martin in 1910.* 1910. Reprint, edited by Joanne Chiles Eakin. Independence, Mo.: Two Trails, 1996.

The War of the Rebellion: A Compilation of the Official Records of the Union and Confederate Armies. 128 vols. Washington, D.C.: GPO 1880–1902.

Watts, Hamp B. *The Babe of the Company: An Unfolded Leaf from the Forest of Never-to-Be Forgotten Years.* Fayette, Mo.: Democrat-Leader Press, 1913.

Wheeler, Holland. "Quantrill a Suspicious Loafer." *Collections of the Kansas State Historical Society* 7 (1902): 224–226.

Willard, Emma. *Abridged History of the United States, Republic of America.* New York: Pratt, Woodford, 1844.

——. *History of the United States.* New York: White, Gallaher and White, 1828.

Younger, Thomas Coleman. *The Story of Cole Younger, by Himself.* Chicago: Henneberry, 1903.

SECONDARY MATERIALS
Books, Articles, Theses, Presentations, and Dissertations

Archer, Richard. *Jim Crow North: The Struggle for Equal Rights in Antebellum New England.* New York: Oxford University Press, 2017.

Beilein, Joseph M., Jr. *Bushwhackers: Guerrilla Warfare, Manhood, and the Household in Civil War Missouri.* Kent, Ohio: Kent State University Press, 2016.

——. "The 1864 Invasion of Missouri." In *The Oxford Handbook of the American Civil War*, edited by Lorien Foote and Earl J. Hess, 520–533. New York: Oxford University Press, 2021.

——. "The Guerrilla Shirt: A Labor of Love and the Style of Rebellion in Civil War Missouri." *Civil War History* 58, no. 2 (June 2012): 151–179.

——. "Householder and General: Lee's War as a Household War." In *Household War: How Americans Lived and Fought the Civil War.* Edited by Lisa Tendrich Frank and LeeAnn Whites, 35–54. Athens: University of Georgia Press, 2020.

——. Introduction to *William Gregg's Civil War: The Battle to Shape the History of Guerrilla Warfare*, by William Gregg, edited by Joseph M. Beilein Jr., 1–42. Athens: University of Georgia Press, 2019.

——. "The Terror of Kentucky: Sue Mundy's Highly Gendered War against Convention." *Register of the Kentucky Historical Society* 116 (Spring 2018): 157–181.

——."Whiskey, Wild Men, and Missouri's Guerrilla War." In *The Guerrilla Hunters: Irregular Conflicts during the Civil War*, edited by Brian D. McKnight and Barton A. Myers, 236–259. Baton Rouge: Louisiana State University Press, 2017.

Beilein, Joseph M., Jr., and Matthew C. Hulbert, eds. *The Civil War Guerrilla: Unfolding the Black Flag in History, Memory, and Myth.* Lexington: University of Kentucky Press, 2015.

Benedict, Bryce D. *Jayhawkers: The Civil War Brigade of James Henry Lane.* Norman: University of Oklahoma Press, 2009.

Berger, Thomas. *Little Big Man.* New York: Dial, 1964.

Berry, Stephen, and James Hill Welborn III. "The Cane of His Existence: Depression, Damage, and the Brooks-Sumner Affair." *Southern Cultures* 20 (Winter 2014): 5–21.

Berry, Stephen W. *All That Makes a Man: Love and Ambition in the Civil War South.* New York: Oxford University Press, 2003.

——, ed. *Weirding the War: Stories from the Civil War's Ragged Edges.* Athens: University of Georgia Press, 2011.

Blight, David W. *Race and Reunion: The Civil War in American Memory.* Cambridge, Mass.: Harvard University Press, 2001.

Boer, Charles. *Varmint Q.* Chicago: Swallow, 1972.

Boot, Max. *Invisible Armies: An Epic History of Guerrilla Warfare from Ancient Times to the Present*. New York: Liveright, 2013.

Bowen, Don R. "Counterrevolutionary Guerrilla War: Missouri, 1861–1865." *Conflict* 8 (1988): 69–78.

———. "Guerrilla War in Western Missouri, 1862–1865: Historical Extensions of the Relative Deprivation Hypothesis." *Comparative Studies in Society and History* 19 (January 1977): 30–51.

———. "Quantrill, James, Younger, et al.: Leadership in a Guerrilla Movement, Missouri, 1861–1865." *Military Affairs* 41 (February 1977): 42–48.

Broomall, James J. *Private Confederacies: The Emotional Worlds of Southern Men as Citizens and Soldiers*. Chapel Hill: University of North Carolina Press, 2019.

Brownlee, Richard S. *Gray Ghosts of the Confederacy: Guerrilla Warfare in the West, 1861–1865*. Baton Rouge: Louisiana State University Press, 1958.

Brown, Thomas J. *Civil War Monuments and the Militarization of America*. Chapel Hill: University of North Carolina Press, 2019.

Bruce, Dickson D., Jr. *Violence and Culture in the Antebellum South*. Austin: University of Texas Press, 1979.

Butler, Judith. "Performative Acts and Gender Constitution: An Essay in Phenomenology and Feminist Theory." *Theatre Journal* 40 (December 1988): 519–531.

Castel, Albert E. *Civil War Kansas: Reaping the Whirlwind*. Lawrence: University Press of Kansas, 1997.

———. "Quantrill's Bushwhackers: A Case Study in Partisan Warfare." *Civil War History* 13 (March 1967): 40–50.

———. *William Clarke Quantrill: His Life and Times*. New York: F. Fell, 1962.

Castel, Albert E., and Thomas Goodrich. *Bloody Bill Anderson: The Short, Savage Life of a Civil War Guerrilla*. Lawrence: University Press of Kansas, 1998.

Chauncey, George. *Gay New York: Gender, Urban Culture, and the Making of the Gay Male World, 1890–1940*. New York: Basic Books, 1994.

Clifford, Geraldine J. *Those Good Gertrudes: A Social History of Women Teachers in America*. Baltimore: Johns Hopkins University Press, 2014.

Clinton, Catherine, and Nina Silber, eds. *Divided Houses: Gender and the Civil War*. New York: Oxford University Press, 1992.

Coleman, Jon T. *Here Lies Hugh Glass: A Mountain Man, a Bear, and the Rise of the American Nation*. New York: Hill and Wang, 2012.

Connell, Evan S. *Son of the Morning Star: Custer and the Little Bighorn*. New York: North Point, 1984.

Cordley, Richard. *A History of Lawrence, Kansas: From the Earliest Settlement to the Close of the Rebellion*. Lawrence, Kans.: E. F. Cardwell, 1895.

Cox, Karen L. *Dixie's Daughters: The United Daughters of the Confederacy and the Preservation of Confederate Culture*. Gainesville: University Press of Florida, 2003.

Crandall, George W. "Emperors and Little Empires: The Schoolmaster in Nineteenth-Century American Literature." *Studies in American Humor* 5 (Spring 1986): 51–61.

Creighton, Margaret S. *The Colors of Courage: Gettysburg's Forgotten History; Immigrants, Women, and African Americans in the Civil War's Defining Battle*. New York: Basic Books, 2005.

Curran, Thomas F. *Women Making War: Female Confederate Prisoners and Union Military Justice*. Carbondale: Southern Illinois University Press, 2020.

Davis, David Brion. *Homicide in American Fiction, 1798–1860: A Study in Social Values*. Ithaca, N.Y.: Cornell University Press, 1957.

Decker, William Merrill. *Epistolary Practices: Letter Writing in America Before Telecommunications*. Chapel Hill: University of North Carolina Press, 1998.

D'Emilio, John, and Estelle B. Freedman. *Intimate Matters: A History of Sexuality in America*. 2nd ed. Chicago: University of Chicago Press, 1997.

Dew, Charles B. *Apostles of Disunion: Southern Secession Commissioners and the Causes of the Civil War*. Charlottesville: University of Virginia Press, 2017.

Dolan, Eric Jay. *Fur, Fortune, and Empire: The Epic History of the Fur Trade in America*. New York: W. W. Norton, 2010.

Domby, Adam. *The False Cause: Fraud, Fabrication, and White Supremacy in Confederate Memory*. Charlottesville: University of Virginia Press, 2020.

Dorsey, Bruce. *Reforming Men & Women: Gender in the Antebellum City*. Ithaca, N.Y.: Cornell University Press, 2002.

Dubin, Michael J. *United States Presidential Elections, 1788–1860*. Jefferson, N.C.: McFarland & Company Publishers, 2002.

Duncan, Russell. *Where Death and Glory Meet: Colonel Robert Gould Shaw and the 54th Massachusetts Infantry*. Athens: University of Georgia Press, 1999.

Dutton, Paul Edward. *Charlemagne's Mustache and Other Cultural Clusters of a Dark Age*. New York: Palgrave Macmillan, 2004.

Earle, Jonathan H., and Diane Mutti Burke. *Bleeding Kansas, Bleeding Missouri: The Long Civil War on the Border*. Lawrence: University of Kansas Press, 2013.

Etcheson, Nicole. *Bleeding Kansas: Contested Liberty in the Civil War Era*. Lawrence: University Press of Kansas, 2004.

Farley, Alan W. "Delaware Indians in Kansas, 1829–1867." Paper delivered to Kansas City Posse of the Westerners (historical group), Grinter House, May 14, 1955.

Faust, Drew Gilpin. *The Republic of Suffering: Death and the American Civil War*. New York: Alfred A. Knopf, 2008.

Fellman, Michael. *Inside War: The Guerrilla Conflict in Missouri during the American Civil War*. Oxford: Oxford University Press, 1990.

Fialka, Andrew. "Federal Eyes: How the Union Saw Kentucky's War." *Ohio Valley History* 18 (Fall 2018): 6–25.

Fields, Barbara J. "Ideology and Race in American History." In *Region, Race, and Reconstruction: Essays in Honor of C. Vann Woodward*, edited by J. Morgan Kousser and James M. McPherson, 143–177. New York: Oxford University Press, 1982.

——. "Slavery, Race and Ideology in the United States of America." *New Left Review* 181 (May–June 1990): 95–118.

Finkleman, Paul. "The Strange Career of Race Discrimination in Antebellum Ohio." *Case Western Reserve Law Review* 55, no. 2 (2004): 373–408.

Foote, Lorien. *The Gentlemen and the Roughs: Violence, Honor, and Manhood in the Union Army*. New York: New York University Press, 2010.

——. *Rites of Retaliation: Civilization, Soldiers, and Campaigns in the American Civil War*. Chapel Hill: University of North Carolina Press, 2021.

——. *The Yankee Plague: Escaped Union Prisoners and the Collapse of the Confederacy*. Chapel Hill: University of North Carolina Press, 2016.

Fox-Genovese, Elizabeth. *Within the Plantation Household: Black and White Women of the Old South*. Chapel Hill: University of North Carolina Press, 1988.

Frank, Andrew, K. *Creeks and Southerners: Biculturalism on the Early American Frontier*. Lincoln: University of Nebraska Press, 2005.

Franklin, John Hope. *The Militant South, 1800–1861*. Urbana: University of Illinois Press, 1956.

Frank, Lisa Tendrich, and LeeAnn Whites. *Household War: How Americans Lived and Fought the Civil War*. Athens: University of Georgia Press, 2020.

Freeman, Joanne B. *The Field of Blood: Violence in Congress and the Road to Civil War*. New York: Farrar, Straus and Giroux, 2018.

Friend, Craig T. "Sex, Self, and the Performance of Patriarchal Manhood in the Old South." In *The Old South's Modern Worlds: Slavery, Region, and Nation in the Age of Progress*, edited by L. Diane Barnes, Brian Schoen, and Frank Towers, 246–265. New York: Oxford University Press.

Gallagher, Gary W. *The Confederate War*. Cambridge, Mass.: Harvard University Press, 1997.

Geertz, Clifford. "Deep Play: Notes on the Balinese Cockfight." "Myth, Symbol, and Culture," special issue, *Daedalus* 101, no. 1 (Winter 1972): 1–37.

Geiger, Mark W. *Financial Fraud and Guerrilla Violence in Missouri's Civil War, 1861–1865*. New Haven, Conn.: Yale University Press, 2010.

Gerteis, Louis S. *The Civil War in Missouri: A Military History*. Columbia: University of Missouri Press, 2012.

——. *Civil War St. Louis*. Lawrence: University of Kansas Press, 2001.

Gienapp, William E. "'Politics Seem to Enter into Everything': Political Culture in the North, 1840–1860." In *Essays on American Antebellum Politics, 1840–1860*, edited by Stephen E. Maizlish and John J. Kushma, 14–69. College Station: Texas A&M University Press, 1982.

Giesberg, Judith. *Sex and the Civil War: Soldiers, Pornography, and the Making of American Morality*. Chapel Hill: University of North Carolina Press, 2017.

Goldstein, Dana. *The Teacher Wars: A History of America's Most Embattled Profession*. New York: Anchor Books, 2014.

Goodrich, Thomas. *Black Flag: Guerrilla Warfare on the Western Border, 1861–1865*. Bloomington: Indiana University Press, 1999.

Gosse, Van. *The First Reconstruction: Black Politics in America from the Revolution to the Civil War*. Chapel Hill: University of North Carolina Press, 2021.

Grace, Thomas M., and Allen F. Richardson. "'Forced to the Cannon's Mouth': An Ohio Regiment's Desperate Venture from Perryville to the War's End." *America's Civil War* 30 (January 2018): 30–39.

Grancsay, Stephen V. *American Engraved Powder Horns: A Study Based on the J. H. Grenville Gilbert Collection*. New York: Metropolitan Museum of Art, 1945.

Greenberg, Amy S. *Manifest Manhood and the Antebellum American Empire*. New York: Cambridge University Press, 2005.

Greenberg, Kenneth S. *Honor & Slavery*. Princeton, N.J.: Princeton University Press, 1996.

Grimsley, Mark. *The Hard Hand of War: Union Military Policy toward Southern Civilians, 1861–1865*. New York: Cambridge University Press, 1995.

Grossman, Dave. *On Killing: The Psychological Cost of Learning to Kill in War and Society*. New York: Little, Brown, 1995.

Guelzo, Allen C. "The Lincoln Bedroom: Seven Scholars Assess C. A. Tripp's *The Intimate World of Abraham Lincoln*." *Claremont Review* 5 (Summer 2005). https://claremontreview ofbooks.com/the-lincoln-bedroom/.

Hafen, Leroy R., ed. *Mountain Men and Fur Traders of the Far West*. Lincoln: University of Nebraska Press, 1965.

Halttunen, Karen. *Confidence Men and Painted Women: A Study of Middle-Class Culture in America, 1830–1870*. New Haven, Conn.: Yale University Press, 1982.

——. *Murder Most Foul: The Killer and the American Gothic Imagination*. Cambridge, Mass.: Harvard University Press, 1998.

Handley-Cousins, Sarah. *Bodies in Blue: Disability in the Civil War North*. Athens: University of Georgia Press, 2021.

Harris, Charles F. "Catalyst for Terror: The Collapse of the Women's Prison in Kansas City." *Missouri Historical Review* 83, no. 3 (April 1995): 290–306.

Herman, Daniel Justin. *Hunting and the American Imagination*. Washington, D.C.: Smithsonian Institute Press, 2001.

Hettle, Wallace. *Inventing Stonewall Jackson: A Civil War Hero in History and Memory*. Baton Rouge: Louisiana State University Press, 2011.

Hobbs, Allyson. *A Chosen Exile: A History of Racial Passing in American Life*. Cambridge, Mass.: Harvard University Press, 2016.

Hoftiezer, Virgil D., and Vicki P. Beck. *Kate King, in Fact and Fiction: The Life and Legend of Sarah Catherine King-Quantrill-Evans-Batson-Head, aka. Kate Clarke*. N.p.: Orderly Pack Rat, 2015.

Hulbert, Matthew C. "Constructing Guerrilla Memory: John Newman Edwards and Missouri's Irregular Lost Cause." *Journal of the Civil War Era* 2, no. 1 (March 2012): 58–81.

——. *The Ghosts of Guerrilla Memory: How Civil War Bushwhackers Became Gunslingers in the American West*. Athens: University of Georgia Press, 2016.

——. "Guerrilla Memory: Irregular Recollections from the Civil War Borderlands." PhD diss., University of Georgia, 2015.

——. "The Rise and Fall of Edwin Terrell, Guerrilla Hunter, U.S.A." *Ohio Valley History* 18 (Fall 2018): 42–61.

Isenberg, Andrew C. *Wyatt Earp: A Vigilante Life*. New York: Hill and Wang, 2013.

Janney, Caroline E. *Burying the Dead but Not the Past: Ladies' Memorial Association and the Lost Cause*. Chapel Hill: University of North Carolina Press, 2008.

Johnson, Charles E., Jr. *Nonvoting Americans*. Washington, D.C.: U.S. Government Printing Office, 1980.

Johnson, Paul E. *A Shopkeeper's Millennium: Society and Revivals in Rochester, New York, 1815–1837*. New York: Hill and Wang, 2004.

Johnson, Susan Lee. *Roaring Camp: The Social World of the California Gold Rush*. New York: W. W. Norton, 2000.

Jones, Karen R. *Epiphany in the Wilderness: Hunting, Nature, and Performance in the Nineteenth-Century American West*. Boulder: University Press of Colorado, 2015.

Keegan, John. *The Face of Battle: A Study of Agincourt, Waterloo, and the Somme*. New York: Penguin, 1978.

Kelman, Ari. *A Misplaced Massacre: Struggling over the Memory of Sand Creek*. Cambridge, Mass.: Harvard University Press, 2015.

Kendrick, Stephen, and Paul Kendrick. *Sarah's Long Walk: The Free Blacks of Boston and How Their Struggle for Equality Changed America*. Boston: Beacon, 2004.

Kenzer, Robert C. *Kinship and Neighborhood in a Southern Community: Orange County, North Carolina, 1849–1881*. Knoxville: University of Tennessee Press, 1987.

King, Wilma. *Stolen Childhood: Slave Youth in Nineteenth-Century America*. 2nd ed. Bloomington: Indiana University Press, 2011.

Lepore, Jill. *The Name of War: King Philip's War and the Origins of American Identity*. New York: Alfred A. Knopf, 1998.

Leslie, Edward. *The Devil Knows How to Ride: The True Story of William Clarke Quantrill and His Confederate Raiders*. New York: Da Capo, 1998.

Linderman, Gerald F. *Embattled Courage: The Experience of Combat in the American Civil War*. New York: Free Press, 1987.

Lockwood, Randall. "Animal Cruelty and Violence against Humans: Making the Connection." *Animal Law* 5, no. 81 (1999): 81–87.

Lowry, Thomas P. *The Story the Soldiers Wouldn't Tell: Sex in the Civil War.* Mechanicsburg, Pa.: Stackpole Books, 1994.

Lussana, Sergio A. *My Brother Slaves: Friendship, Masculinity, and Resistance in the Antebellum South.* Lexington: University Press of Kentucky, 2016.

Lystra, Karen. *Searching the Heart: Women, Men, and Romantic Love in Nineteenth-Century America.* New York: Oxford University Press, 1989.

Mackey, Robert R. *The Uncivil War: Irregular Warfare in the Upper South, 1861–1865.* Norman: University of Oklahoma Press, 2004.

McCarthy, Cormac. *Blood Meridian: Or the Evening Redness in the West.* New York: Random House, 1985.

McKnight, Brian D. *Confederate Outlaw: Champ Ferguson and the Civil War in Appalachia.* Baton Rouge: Louisiana State University Press, 2011.

McKnight, Brian D., and Barton A. Myers. *The Guerrilla Hunters: Irregular Conflicts during the Civil War.* Baton Rouge: Louisiana State University Press, 2017.

McLaurin, Melton A. *Celia, a Slave: A True Story.* 1991. Reprint, New York: Perennial, 2002.

McMurtry-Chubb, Teri A. *Race Unequals: Overseer Contracts, White Masculinities, and the Formation of Managerial Identity in the Plantation Economy.* New York: Lexington Books, 2021.

McPherson, James M. *Battle Cry of Freedom: The Civil War Era.* New York: Oxford University Press, 1988.

———. *For Cause and Comrades: Why Men Fought in the Civil War.* New York: Oxford University Press, 1997.

———. *Ordeal By Fire: The Civil War and Reconstruction.* New York: Alfred A. Knopf, 1982.

———. *The War That Forged a Nation: Why the Civil War Still Matters.* New York: Oxford University Press, 2015.

Miller, Brian C. *John Bell Hood and the Fight for Civil War Memory.* Knoxville: University of Tennessee Press, 2010.

Moorman, Donald R., and Gene Allred Sessions. *Camp Floyd and the Mormons: The Utah War.* Salt Lake City: University of Utah Press, 2005.

Morrison, James L., Jr. *"The Best School in the World": West Point, the Pre–Civil War Years, 1833–1866.* Kent, Ohio: Kent State University Press, 1986.

Mountcastle, Clay. *Punitive War: Confederate Guerrillas and Union Reprisals.* Lawrence: University Press of Kansas, 2009.

Mutti-Burke, Diane. *On Slavery's Border: Missouri's Small-Slaveholding Households, 1815–1865.* Athens: University of Georgia Press, 2010.

Myers, Barton A. *Executing Daniel Bright: Race, Loyalty, and Guerrilla Violence in a Coastal Carolina Community, 1861–1865.* Baton Rouge: Louisiana State University Press, 2009.

———. "Partisan Ranger Petitions and the Authorized Petite Guerre Service." In *The Guerrilla Hunters: Irregular Conflicts during the Civil War*, edited by Brian D. McKnight and Barton A. Myers, 13–36. Baton Rouge: Louisiana State University Press, 2017.

Neely, Jeremy. *The Border between Them: Violence and Reconciliation on the Kansas-Missouri Line.* Columbia: University of Missouri Press, 2007.

Nelson, Megan Kate. *Saving Yellowstone: Exploration and Preservation in Reconstruction America.* New York: Scribner, 2022.

———. *The Three-Cornered War: The Union, the Confederacy, and Native Peoples in the Fight for the West.* New York: Scribner, 2020.

Noe, Kenneth W. "Who Were the Bushwhackers? Age, Class, Kin, and Western Virginia's Confederate Guerrillas, 1861–1862." *Civil War History* 49 (2003): 5–26.

Oertel, Kristen Tegtmeier. *Bleeding Borders: Race, Gender, and Violence in Pre–Civil War Kansas*. Baton Rouge: Louisiana State University Press, 2009.

O'Flaherty, Daniel. *General Jo Shelby: Undefeated Rebel*. Chapel Hill: University of North Carolina Press, 2000.

Petersen, Paul R. *Quantrill in Texas: The Forgotten Campaign*. Nashville, Tenn.: Cumberland House, 2007.

———. *Quantrill of Missouri: The Making of a Guerrilla Warrior: The Man, the Myth, the Soldier*. Nashville, Tenn.: Cumberland House, 2003.

Phillips, Christopher. "'The Crime against Missouri': Slavery, Kansas, and the Cant of Southernness in the Border West." *Civil War History* 48, no. 1 (2002): 60–81.

———. *The Rivers Ran Backward: The Civil War and the Remaking of the American Middle Border*. New York: Oxford University Press, 2016.

Phillips, Jason. *Looming Civil War: How Nineteenth-Century Americans Imagined the Future*. New York: Oxford University Press, 2018.

Pierson, Michael D. *Free Hearts and Free Homes: Gender and American Antislavery Politics*. Chapel Hill: University of North Carolina Press, 2003.

Piston, William G., and Richard W. Hatcher III. *Wilson's Creek: Second Battle of the Civil War and the Men Who Fought It*. Chapel Hill: University of North Carolina Press, 2000.

Ponce, Pearl T. *Kansas's War: The Civil War in Documents*. Athens: Ohio University Press, 2011.

Portis, Charles. *True Grit*. New York: Overlook, 2013.

Proctor, Nicholas W. *Bathed in Blood: Hunting and Mastery in the Old South*. Charlottesville: University Press of Virginia, 2002.

Quigley, Paul. *The Man behind the Cane: Words, Violence, and the Coming of the Civil War*. New York: Oxford University Press, forthcoming.

Ramage, James A. *Rebel Raider: The Life of General John Hunt Morgan*. Lexington: University Press of Kentucky, 1996.

Rarick, Ethan. *Desperate Passage: The Donner Party's Perilous Journey West*. New York: Oxford University Press, 2008.

Ressler, Robert K., Ann W. Burgess, Carol R. Hartman, John E. Douglas, and Arlene McCormack. "Murderers Who Rape and Mutilate." *Journal of Interpersonal Violence* 1, no. 3 (1986): 273–287.

Rhea, Gordon C. *In the Footsteps of Grant and Lee: The Wilderness through Cold Harbor*. Baton Rouge: Louisiana State University Press, 2007.

Richardson, Heather Cox. *West from Appomattox: The Reconstruction of America after the Civil War*. New Haven, Conn.: Yale University Press, 2007.

Roediger, David R. *The Wages of Whiteness: Race and the Making of the American Working Class*. New York: Verso, 1991.

Rohrer, Julia M., Boris Egloff, and Stefan C. Schmukle. "Examining the Effects of Birth Order on Personality." *Proceedings of the National Academy of Sciences of the United States of America* 112 (November 17, 2015): 14224–14229.

Rosa, Joseph G. *Wild Bill Hickok: The Man and His Myth*. Lawrence: University Press of Kansas, 1996.

Rotundo, Anthony E. *American Manhood: Transformations in Masculinity from the Revolution to the Modern Era*. New York: Basic Books, 1993.

Ryan, Mary P. *Cradle of the Middle Class: The Family in Oneida County, New York, 1790–1865*. New York: Cambridge University Press, 1981.

Sandage, Scott A. *Born Losers: A History of Failure in America*. Cambridge, Mass.: Harvard University Press, 2005.

Sandburg, Carl. *Abraham Lincoln: The Prairie Years and The War Years*. New York: Dell, 1959.

—— . *Abraham Lincoln: The Prairie Years*. Vol. 1. New York: Harcourt, Brace, 1926.

Scarborough, William Kauffman. *The Overseer: Plantation Management in the Old South*. Athens: University of Georgia Press, 1984.

Schultz, Duane. *Quantrill's War: The Life and Times of William Clarke Quantrill, 1837–1865*. New York: St. Martin's, 1996.

Sellers, Charles. *The Market Revolution: Jacksonian America, 1815–1846*. New York: Oxford University Press, 1991.

Shaara, Michael. *The Killer Angels: A Novel*. New York: Ballantine Books, 1974.

Shea, William L., and Earl Hess. *Pea Ridge: Civil War Campaign in the West*. Chapel Hill: University of North Carolina Press, 1997.

Sheehan-Dean, Aaron. *Why Confederates Fought: Family and Nation in Civil War Virginia*. Chapel Hill: University of North Carolina Press, 2007.

Shy, John. *A People Numerous and Armed: Reflections on the Military Struggle for American Independence*. Rev. ed. Ann Arbor: University of Michigan Press, 1990.

Silber, Nina. *Gender and the Sectional Conflict*. Chapel Hill: University of North Carolina Press, 2008.

—— . *The Romance of Reunion: Northerners and the South, 1865–1900*. Chapel Hill: University of North Carolina Press, 1993.

Slotkin, Richard. *The Fatal Environment: The Myth of the Frontier in the Age of Industrialization, 1800–1890*. Norman: University of Oklahoma Press, 1985.

—— . *Regeneration through Violence: The Mythology of the American Frontier, 1600–1860*. Norman: University of Oklahoma Press, 1973.

Smith, W. Wayne. "An Experiment in Counterinsurgency: The Assessment of Confederate Sympathizers in Missouri." *Journal of Southern History* 35 (August 1969): 361–380.

Stanley, Matthew. *The Loyal West: Civil War and Reunion in Middle America*. Urbana: University of Illinois Press, 2017.

Steward, Dick. *Duels and the Roots of Violence in Missouri*. Columbia: University of Missouri Press, 2000.

Stiles, T. J. *Jesse James: Last Rebel of the Civil War*. New York: Vintage Books, 2003.

Stith, Matthew M. *Extreme Civil War: Guerrilla Warfare, Environment, and Race on the Trans-Mississippi Frontier*. Baton Rouge: Louisiana State University Press, 2016.

Stubbs, Tristan. *Masters of Violence: The Plantation Overseers of Eighteenth-Century Virginia, South Carolina, and Georgia*. Columbia: University of South Carolina Press, 2018.

Sutherland, Daniel E. *American Civil War Guerrillas: Changing the Rules of Warfare*. New York: Praeger, 2013.

—— . *A Savage Conflict: The Decisive Role of Guerrillas in the American Civil War*. Chapel Hill: University of North Carolina Press, 2009.

—— . "Sideshow No Longer: A Historiographical Review of the Guerrilla War." *Civil War History* 46 (March 2000): 5–23.

Taylor, Amy Murrell. *Embattled Freedom: Journeys through the Civil War's Slave Refugee Camps*. Chapel Hill: University of North Carolina Press, 2018.

Tegtmeier-Oertel, Kristen. *Bleeding Borders: Race, Gender, and Violence in Pre–Civil War Kansas*. Baton Rouge: Louisiana State University Press, 2009.

Thomas, Edison H. *John Hunt Morgan and His Raiders*. Lexington: University Press of Kentucky, 1985.

Tripp, C. A. *The Intimate World of Abraham Lincoln*. New York: Free Press, 2005.

Twain, Mark. *How to Tell a Story and Other Essays*. New York: Harper and Brothers, 1898.

Utley, Robert M. *Billy the Kid: A Short and Violent Life*. Lincoln: University of Nebraska Press, 1989.

———. *A Life Wild and Perilous: Mountain Men and the Paths to the Pacific.* New York: Henry Holt, 1997.

Vlach, John Michael. *Back of the Big House: The Architecture of Plantation Slavery.* Chapel Hill: University of North Carolina Press, 1993.

Watson, Thomas Shelby. *Confederate Guerrilla Sue Mundy: A Biography of Kentucky Soldier Jerome Clarke.* Jefferson, N.C.: McFarland, 2008.

White, Deborah Gray. *Ar'n't I a Woman? Female Slaves in the Plantation South.* New York: W. W. Norton, 1999.

White, Jonathan W. *Midnight in America: Darkness, Sleep, and Dreams during the Civil War.* Chapel Hill: University of North Carolina Press, 2017.

Whites, LeeAnn. *The Civil War as a Crisis in Gender: Augusta, Georgia, 1860–1890.* Athens: University of Georgia Press, 1995.

———. "Forty Shirts and a Wagonload of Wheat: Women, the Domestic Supply Line, and the Civil War on the Western Border." *Journal of the Civil War Era* 1 (March 2011): 56–78.

———. *Gender Matters: Civil War, Reconstruction, and the Making of the New South.* New York: Palgrave MacMillan, 2005.

———. "The Tale of Three Kates: Outlaw Women, Loyalty, and Missouri's Long Civil War." In *Weirding the War: Stories from the Civil War's Ragged Edges,* edited by Stephen W. Berry, 73–94. Athens: University of Georgia Press, 2011.

Whites, LeeAnn, and Alecia P. Long, eds. *Occupied Women: Gender, Military Occupation, and the American Civil War.* Baton Rouge: Louisiana State University Press, 2009.

Wiley, Bell Irvin. *The Life of Billy Yank: The Common Soldier of the Union.* 1952. Reprint, Baton Rouge, La.: Louisiana State University Press, 2008.

———. *The Life of Johnny Reb: The Common Soldier of the Confederacy.* 1943. Reprint, Baton Rouge: Louisiana State University Press, 2008.

Wills, Brian Steel. *A Battle from the Start: The Life of Nathan Bedford Forrest.* New York: Harper Perennial, 1993.

Wilson-Kleekamp, Traci. "Descendants of Celia and Robert Newsom Speak." *Genealogy* 4, no. 49 (April 2020): 1–21.

Winkle, Kenneth J. "A Social Analysis of Voter Turnout in Ohio, 1850–1860." *Journal of Interdisciplinary History* 13, no. 3 (Winter 1983): 411–435.

Witt, John Fabian. *Lincoln's Code: The Laws of War in American History.* New York: Free Press, 2013.

Woodard, Colin. *The Republic of Pirates: Being the True and Surprising Story of the Caribbean Pirates and the Man Who Brought Them Down.* Orlando, Fla.: Harcourt Books, 2007.

Woods, Michael E. *Bleeding Kansas: Slavery, Sectionalism, and Civil War on the Missouri-Kansas Border.* New York: Routledge, 2017.

Wyatt-Brown, Bertram. "The Mask of Obedience: Male Slave Psychology in the Old South." *American Historical Review* 93 (December 1988): 1228–1252.

———. *Southern Honor: Ethics and Behavior in the Old South.* New York: Oxford University Press, 1982.

Films

Altman, Robert, dir. *McCabe and Mrs. Miller.* Burbank, Calif.: Warner Brothers, 1971.

Coen, Ethan, dir. *True Grit.* Santa Monica, Calif.: Skydance Media, 2010.

Eastwood, Clint, dir. *High Plains Drifter.* Burbank, Calif.: Malpaso Productions, 1973.

———, dir. *The Outlaw Josey Wales.* Burbank, Calif.: Malpaso Productions, 1976.

Hathaway, Henry, dir. *True Grit.* Hollywood, Calif.: Paramount Pictures, 1969.

Iñárritu, Alejandro González, dir. *The Revenant.* Los Angeles: Regency, 2015.

256 BIBLIOGRAPHY

Lee, Ang, dir. *Ride with the Devil*. New York: Good Machine, 1999.
Zwick, Edward, dir. *Glory*. Culver City, Calif.: TriStar Pictures, 1989.

WEBSITES

The American Presidency Project. University of California, Santa Barbara. www.presidency.ucsb.edu.
Ancestry.com. http://www.ancestry.com/.
"Chronicling America: Historic American Newspapers." Library of Congress. http://chroniclingamerica.loc.gov/.
"Ellis, Abraham (Bullet Hole)." Elk City, KS, website. 2022. https://elkcityks.com/early-pioneers-of-elk-city-kansas-area/ellis-abraham-bullet-hole/.
Fletcher, Adam Ochs. "A Backdrop Connected to Portraits of Quantrill's Men." *Military Images Magazine*, May 31, 2021. www.militaryimagesmagazine-digital.com/2021/05/31/a-backdrop-connected-to-portraits-of-quantrills-men/.
Huston, James L. "Quantrill's Raiders." Oklahoma Historical Society online encyclopedia. N.d. http://okhistory.org/publications/enc/entry.php?entry=QU002.
Kansas Historical Society. http://www.kshs.org/.
Kansas Memory. http://www.kansasmemory.org/.
The Lawrence Massacre. Accessed through Kansas Collection Books website. http://www.kancoll.org/books/cordley_massacre/quantrel.raid.html.
Mapping Occupation. http://mappingoccupation.org/.
Marquis, Patrick R. "The Memorial Stone Dedication Which Took 143 Years: Highlights from October 25, 2008." Quantrillsguerrillas.com. 2008. http://quantrillsguerrillas.com/en/articles/148-the-memorial-stone-dedication-which-took-143-years-highlights-from-october-25-2008-article.html.
Missouri Secretary of State. http://www.sos.mo.gov/.
"Paola Kansas: A 150 Year History in Detail." Miami County Kansas History. N.d. http://www.thinkmiamicountyhistory.com/.
Quantrillsguerillas.com. http://quantrillsguerrillas.com/.
"Replica Head of Confederate Raider Quantrill." Roadside America. 1996. http://www.roadsideamerica.com/story/100544.
United Confederate Veterans Records, 1899–1905. Filson Historical Society. http://filsonhistorical.org/research-doc/unitedconfederateveterans/.
The War of the Rebellion: Official Records of the Civil War. Ehistory, The Ohio State University. http://ehistory.osu.edu/osu/sources/records/.
Winterthur Museum. http://tinware.winterthur.org/notes-references.

INDEX

Note: William Clarke Quantrill is abbreviated WCQ throughout the index. Italicized page numbers indicate references to illustrations.

African Americans: in American society, 32–34, 239n10; counterinsurgency and, 3; in Dover Township, 32–33; enlistment, 174, 175; in Kentucky, 2–3; masks and identity, 107–108; Second Kansas Colored Infantry, 180–181; Second South Carolina, 174; women, 60, 61
Allison, George, 142
Anderson, Bill (bushwhacker; "Bloody Bill"), 134, 162–163, 177–178, 183, 198
antebellum travels, reflections on, 62, 84–85, 86–87, 227n32
Army of Missouri, 197–198
Aubrey, Kans., xi–xii, xvi, 135–136

Ball, Charles (jayhawker), 113–115
Bascom, Henry (Delaware Indian), 98
Battle of Fort Davidson (Mo.), 197
Battle of Fredericksburg (Va.), 153
Battle of Lone Jack (Independence, Mo.), 144, 145
Battle of Perryville (Ky.), 152
bedfellows. See sleeping situations
Beecher, Henry Ward, 107, 114–115; Seven Lectures to Young Men on Various Important Subjects, 94
Beeson, Frances (m. Thompson), 30–31, 43, 57, 58
Beeson, Harmon V. and Richard, 31–32, 55–59
Bennings, John (hunter and trapper), 61–63
Berry, Sam "One-Armed," 200
black flag. See guerrillas (bushwhackers): black flag; no-quarter policy
Black people. See African Americans
Bleeding Kansas, 48–50, 52
Blue Springs, Mo. (Walker Farm), 112, 113–116, 122–123, 132, 232n32
Blunt, Andrew (bushwhacker), 161

Blunt, James G., 179
Border Outlaws, The (Buel), 141
border ruffians, 75–76, 82, 109–110, 111. See also guerrillas (bushwhackers)
border war, Kansas-Missouri, 167–170, 168, 171, 238n30
Bragg, Braxton, 152
Breckenridge, John C., 89
Brinker, John (bushwhacker), 161
Brooks, Preston, 51, 224n18
Brown, John "Osawatomie," 87
Buchanan, James, 63
Buel, James W., 140–141; The Border Outlaws, 141
Buell, Don Carlos, 152
Burbridge, Stephen G., 241n11 (chap. 16)
Burnside, Ambrose, 153
bushwhackers. See guerrillas (bushwhackers)
Butler, Andrew, 48–49, 50, 51
Byron, Lord George Gordon, xi, 202–203

Camp Floyd, Utah Territory, 64
Campbell, Thomas, 87–88
Canal Dover, Ohio: census data on, 32, 220–221n19; changing economics of, 26–27; public school in, 28, 32, 33, 221–222n36; townspeople, 27, 32–33; WCQ return to, 55
Catholicism, Quantrill's conversion to, 16
Celia ("A Woman Hanged"), 45–47
census data: Federal Manuscript Census, 81, 100–102, 101, 228–229n2, 229–230n20; production in Tuscarawas County, 32, 220–221n19; Slave Schedule, 51, 119, 189
Centralia Massacre (Mo.), 197–198
Charles City (Iowa) Republican Intelligencer, 7
Church of Latter-day Saints (Mormons), 63, 64
Cincinnati (Ohio) Enquirer, 183–184
Civil War: American West's influence on, xv, 215n11; beginning of, 119, 120; Bleeding Kansas, 48–50, 52; at border, 238n30; end of, 1–2; guerrilla versus conventional

257

258 INDEX

Civil War: (*continued*)
warfare, 155, 167–170, *168*, 171, 236–237n10. *See also specific battles*
Clapp, Mary (fellow teacher), 37–38
Clark, Captain (WCQ alias), 4–5, 10, 13–15, *14*, 15. *See also* identities and personas, Quantrill's; Quantrill, William Clarke
Clark, Kate (possible wife; née King): on physical appearances of WCQ, 5, *6*; relationship with WCQ, 183–184, 189–193; WCQ's death and, 204–205
Clark, M. Jerome ("Sue Mundy"), 16, 200
Clarke, Henry S. (friend), 98–99
Clay, Henry, 28
Clover, Seth, 106–107, 111
Colt Navies (Navy Revolvers), 75, 164
Confederate government: flag, 146–147; WCQ's alignment with, 149–151, 184–185
Confidence Man, The (Melville), 95–96
Confiscation Act (Union), 149
Confiscation Act of 1862 (U.S. Congress), 153
Connelly, William E., 8–9. *See also* historians, treatment and attitudes
correspondences: anonymous fellows in, 41–42, 65, 78, 108; letters to Kellam, 41; letters to sister, 73, 82; letters to W. W. Scott, 60–61; Potter letters to W. W. Scott, 109–113
—letters to mother: close relationship, 23–24; on Cottonwood raid, 79–81; on gold rush, 65, 77; from Kansas farm, 56, 59; last letter, 108–109; on Mendota, 42–43; money troubles, 40–41, 42; on Mormons, 64; regrets, 24–25, 36, 42, 86–87, 142
Cottonwood River (Kansas Territory), *62*, 79–82
culture, southern: guerrilla warfare and, 155, 169–170; honor-bound vengeance, 131–132, 171; violence in, 70, 159–160; WCQ as symbol, 127–128
Curtis, Samuel, 122

Daily American Organ (Washington, D.C.), 45, 46
Davis, Jefferson, 154, 239n10
Dawson, Nancy (WCQ love interest; "Nannie"), 201–202
Dean, John (jayhawker), 97, 114
Delaware tribe, 99–100, 106–107, 108–109
Democratic Party, 48, 88–89
Douglas, Stephen, 48–49, 50–51, 88–89
Dover Historical Society (Ohio), 208–209
Dover Township. *See* Canal Dover, Ohio
Dred Scott decision, 88–89

Edwards, John Newman, 6; *Noted Guerrillas*, 6; *Suppressed Evidence*, 215n2. *See also* historians, treatment and attitudes.

Ellis, Abraham (friend), xi–xii, xv–xvi, 28, 135–136, 215n2
Emancipation Proclamation, 153, 239n10
Emporia (Kans.) News, 149–150
Ewing, Thomas, 171, 175–176, 239nn7–8

Fayette, Mo., 195–196
Fickle, Annie (black flag), 140–141, *141*
flowers, language of, 17, 164
Forrest, Nathan Bedford, 181, 240n25
Fort Blair, Tex., 178–181, *182*
Fort Leavenworth, Kans., *62*, 64, 89, 144
Fort Pillow Massacre, 181, 239n10
Fort Wayne, Ind., 37, 42–43
Frederick, Maggie, 16–17
Free-Soilers, 49, 60, 84–85, 87
Fremont, James C., *62*
friendships, Quantrill's: anonymous fellows in letters, 41–42, 65, 78, 108; betrayals and desertions, 203; with Ellis, xi–xii, xv–xvi, 135–136; loyalty, 184; with men, 69, 76, 77; as motivation to fight, 123, 195–196; after separation from guerrillas, 194; with Todd, 163–164; with Walker men, 116–117
frontiersman, Quantrill as: development into, 68–69, 72–73, 82; physical appearance, 73–75, *74*, 226n18. *See also* identities and personas, Quantrill's
Fulton, Mo., 45–47

General Order No. 2 (no-quarter policy), 138, 139–140, 171
General Order No. 9, 175
General Order No. 10, 175–176, 239n7
General Order No. 11, 178, *182*, 239n8
General Order No. 21, 199
General Order No. 32, 139
General Order No. 59, 241n11 (chap. 16)
General Order No. 100 (Lieber Code), 138–139, 217n12, 235n7
Gill, Marcus (friend), 116, 118–119, 232n4
Glasgow (Mo.) Weekly Times, 45, 46
Glasscock, Dick (bushwhacker), 10, 218n29
gold rush (Pikes Peak), *62*, 65–67, 71, 72–73, 77–78
Graham, Sylvester, 29–30, 221n25
Gregg, William H. (bushwhacker): beginning of war, 133, 134–135, 162; Confederate commission, 144; no-quarter policy, 141–142, 145; power struggle, 164–165
guerrilla, Quantrill as: arrest by McCulloch, 184–185; battlefield tactics, 169–172, 178–181; captaincy, 140, 144; colonelcy, 156, 236n5; command, 123, 156, 172; desire to leave war, 166–167, 198–199; establishment of authority, 134–136, 153–154, 159, 160–161; first kill, 127–128, 132–133, 234n22; general orders

to public, 149–151; leadership philosophy, 198–199; motivations for fighting, 123, 195–196; no-quarter policy, response to, 141–144, 147–149; physical appearances, 5–7, 77; rivalries, 159, 161–165, 177–178, 183–185; separation from group, 185–186, 189, 194; as symbol, 127–128, 133. *See also* identities and personas, Quantrill's

guerrillas (bushwhackers): Army of Missouri, joint efforts, 194, 195, 197–198; black flag, 137–138, 140–141, *141*, 146–147, 151, 234n1; clothing and appearances, 1, 75, 164, 170–171; code of discipline, 134–135; dissolution of, 183–186; escalation of violence, 145–146, 148, 150, 194; formation under WCQ, 122–123, 133–134; household as central, 123–124; influence on Civil War, xv; legitimacy of, 121–122, 144; motivations for fighting, 133, 148–149, 166, 173–174, 176, 239n10; organizational structure, 160, 167–169, *168*; tactics, 10, 139, 167–170, *168*, 171, 235n6; Wild West archetypes, 215n11. *See also* border ruffians

guerrillas (jayhawkers): arrest of WCQ, 120, 232n6; horse theft, 97, 98–99, 106, 110–111; Walker Farm raid, 111–116

gunslinger myth, 69–71

Halleck, Henry, 122, 138–140, 142, 145–146, 235n7
Haller, William (bushwhacker), 144, 161
Hannibal, Mo., 144, 161
Harper's Ferry, Va., 87, 89
Harper's Weekly (magazine), 7
Hart, Charles (WCQ alias): census data on, 100–102, *101*; as confidence man, 96–97, 114, 115, 231n24; Delaware Indians and, 98–100, 108–109; employment, 97–98, 105–106, 110–111; meaning of alias, 103–104; mystery of alias, 105–106, 108–110; Walker Farm raid, 111–116; White Turkey duel, 99–100. *See also* identities and personas, Quantrill's; Quantrill, William Clarke
Hawkins, Robert L., III, 208
Hayne, J. B., 7, 218n20
Hays, Upton, 144, 150
Herd, Sydney (friend), 96–97
Hickock, James Butler "Wild Bill," 70–71, 229–230n20
Hildt, George H. (friend), 57, 59–60
historians, treatment and attitudes: guerrilla warfare, 121–122, 137; Potter letters, 109–110; sexuality and culture, 78; of WCQ, xiv, 8–10, 11, 58, 128–130
History of Tuscarawas County, Ohio, The, 33, 69
Hockensmith, Clark (bushwhacker), 10, 218n29

homosocial environments. *See* friendships, Quantrill's; sleeping situations
honor-driven violence: caning of Sumner, 51; duels and stand-offs, 99–100, 229–230n20; revenge, 131–132, 171
horse theft, 97, 98–99, 106, 110–111
Howard County, Mo., 193–194
Hoy, Perry (bushwhacker), 235n13
Hughes, John T., 144
hunter, Quantrill as: anonymous friend, 41–42; embodiment of persona, 71, 72–73, 82; in Illinois, 70–71; marksmanship skills, 69–70, 129, 226n6; Spybuck and, 79–81; transformation into, 41, 63, 69. *See also* identities and personas, Quantrill's
hunter myth, 72–73, 82

identities and personas, Quantrill's: character development, 84–85, 87; intersection of West and South, 75–76; mysterious nature of, xiii, 5–6, 102, 218n20; shapeshifting and, xii, xiii–xiv, 13, 117. *See also* frontiersman, Quantrill as; guerrilla, Quantrill as; hunter, Quantrill as; Quantrill, William Clarke
Illinois, 36–44, 70–71
Independence, Mo., 56, 144, 145
Independent (Oskaloosa, Kansas), 8
Indians. *See* Native Americans
Irving, Washington, 39, 222–223n10

Jacobs, Almstead, 2–3, 216n5
James, Frank (bushwhacker), 121, 161
jayhawkers. *See* guerrillas (jayhawkers)
Jennison (jayhawker), 110, 111, 176
Johnson, Andrew, 2
Johnson, Susan Lee, 78
Johnston, A. V. E., 197
Joplin (Mo.) Morning Herald, 129
Junction City (Kans.) Smoky Hill and Republican Union, 165–166

Kansas City Star, 190–193, 198, 203
Kansas Territory, *112*; Bleeding Kansas, 48–50; Marais des Cygnes, 55–59; politics in, 60, 87–90; population of Lawrence, 93; prairie fire, 59–60; Second Kansas Colored Infantry, 180–181; Wyandotte Constitution, 87
Kansas-Nebraska Act, 48–52
Keagan, John (bushwhacker), 148
Keitt, Laurence, 224n18
Kellam, Edward T. (boyhood friend), 41
Kellog, J. H., 221n25
Kentucky: abolishment of slavery, 2–3; Battle of Perryville, 152; Wakefield Farm, 2–7, 10–12, 13–15, 202–203, 218–219; WCQ leads friends into, 198–200

260 INDEX

Ketchum, Al (bushwhacker), 148
killing, as language, 132–133
King, Robert, 189, 190, 191

Lane, Jim (jayhawker), 60, 71
Langford, John, 3–4, 11–12
Lawrence, Kansas Territory, *62, 112, 182*;
founding and population, 106; identity
changes in, 106–107; opinions of Hart, 96–
97; politics and population of, 93, 106–107;
raid by WCQ on, 7, 173, 174–175, 176–178,
180, 239n10; Underground Railroad stations,
107; Wakarusa War, 49–50; WCQ arrival,
82–83, 93
Leavenworth (Kans.) Times, 217n18
Lecompton Constitution, 60
Lecture to Young Men on Chastity, A (Graham),
29–30, 221n25
Lee, Robert E., 1, 152, 155, 194
"Legend of Sleepy Hollow, The" (Irving), 39,
222–223n10
letters. *See* correspondences
Lieber, Francis, 138–140, 146
Lieber Code, 138–139, 217n12, 235n7
Lincoln, Abraham, xii, 89–90, 120, 194, 227n29
Lipsey, C. T. (jayhawker), 113–115
Little, Jim (bushwhacker), 196
"Lochiel's Warning" (Campbell), 87–88
lost cause, WCQ comments on, 167
Louisville Courier-Journal, 22, 129
Louisville Daily Courier, 15
Louisville Daily Democrat, 15–16
Louisville Daily Union Press, 15, 16–17
Lovell, Sallie, 16–17
Lyon, Nathaniel, 121

Maddox, George (bushwhacker), 234n22
Magruder, Henry C., 16, 200, 219n46
manhood: apprenticeships as markers of, 219–
220n2; civilization and, 76; expectations
about, 26–27, 29, 36–37, 42, 66–67; hunting
skills, importance of, 69–70, 73; killing as
test of, 136, 140; maturation into, 219–220n2,
226–227n24; philosophy of, 29–30; WCQ
education about, 21, 28–30
manliness. *See* masculinity
Marais des Cygnes, Kansas Territory, 56–59
masculinity: bowie knife as symbol for,
75–76; gold rush as proving ground, 66–67;
marksmanship and, 70; on pirate ships,
237n4; sex as power demonstration, 224–
225n10; slavery and, 46; WCQ's approach
to, xiii–xiv, 13, 142
Matilda, Sister (nun), 16
Mayes, Joel B. (friend), 120
McCorkle, John (bushwhacker), 133, 142–143,
149, 195–196

McCulloch, Ben, 122, 184–185
McGuire, Will (bushwhacker), 149
Mechanic's Calculator and Tinman's Guide, The
(T. H. Quantrill), 25–26, 31, 40–41, 42
Melville, Herman, 95–96
Mendota, Ill., 36–44
Militia Act of 1862 (U.S. Congress), 153
mining for gold. *See* gold rush
Missouri: as American West, xv, 76–77; Walker
Farm, *112*, 113–116, 122–123, 132, 232n32;
WCQ after separation from guerrillas,
193–194
Missouri State Guard (MSG), 121–122, 123–124,
163
Mitchell, Robert B., 143
money struggles and schemes: anonymous
fellow suing government, 108; detective work
(*see* Hart, Charles); manhood and, 42, 66–
67; Mendota, 40–41, 42; Salt Lake City, 65
Montgomery, James (jayhawker), 174
Mormons (Church of Latter-day Saints), 63, 64
Morning Herald (Joplin, Mo.), 129
Morris, Wila J. (Dover resident), 32
Morrison, Ed (jayhawker), 113–115
Mosby, John S., 154
mountain-man persona. *See* frontiersman,
Quantrill as
MSG. *See* Missouri State Guard
Mundy, Sue (M. Jerome Clark), 16, 200

Native Americans: ambush of WCQ's camp, *62*,
79–82; Civil War and, 120, *182*; hunter myth,
73; WCQ and Delaware, 99–100, 106–107,
108–109; women, 60, 61
Nebraska, 48–52
New England Emigrant Aid Company, 93,
106, 115
New York Herald, 49
Newsome, Robert, 45–47
Nixon, Jim, 208–209
no-quarter policy (black flag): evolution of
killing, 137–140, 144–151, 171; guerrillas'
response to, 140–144
Noted Guerrillas (Edwards), 6. *See also* historians,
treatment and attitudes
Nuby, Jeremiah (Dover resident), 32

Ohio. *See* Canal Dover, Ohio
Olathe, Kansas Territory, 145, 146, 147
Oliver, William S., 133
Oregon Trail, *62*
Osawatomie, Kansas Territory, 57, 83, 114
Oskaloosa (Kans.) Independent, 8

Palmer, John M., 13
Paola, Kansas Territory, 39, 86–90, 105, 111, *112*,
119–120

Partisan Ranger Act of 1862 (Confederate Congress), 153, 154–155
partisan soldiers. *See* guerrillas (bushwhackers)
Petersen, Paul E., 9
Pikes Peak (gold rush), *62*, 65–67, 71, 72–73, 77–78
Pilot Knob, Mo., 197
Pomeroy (Union officer), 143
Pool, Dave (bushwhacker; Francis Marion Pool), 161
popular sovereignty, 49, 88
Potter, W. L. (friend), 109–113, 120
powder horn, 73–75, *74*, 226n18
Powers, Father, 16, 204, 206
Price, Sterling, 122–124, 167, 194, 195, 197–198

Quantrill, Caroline (mother), 21, 23–25, 220n10. *See also* correspondences: letters to mother
Quantrill, Thomas Henry (father), 21, 25–26, 27–28, 31–32, 34–35; *The Mechanic's Calculator and Tinman's Guide*, 25–26, 31, 40–41, 42
Quantrill, William Clarke ("Bill"; WCQ): antebellum (*see* antebellum travels); arrests, 97, 120, 184–185; birth, 21, 220n10; childhood, 22–23, 30–31, 40, 69, 78; comparison with Mississippi boys, 76–77; education, 21, 28–30; father's death, 35, 36, 37; free-moving ways, 55, 63, 65, 90, 103–104, 166–167; friendships (*see* friendships, Quantrill's); identity and politics of, xiv–xv; identity and whiteness, 32–34, 118–119, 232n1; as man of action, 142; marksmanship skills, 69–70, 129, 226n6; physical appearances, 5–6, *6*, 7, 12, 83–84, 115–116; poetic sensibilities, xi, 201–202; political ideas, 47–49, 60, 84–85, 87–88; self-portrait, 73, 82, 130–132; slavery and race, 119, 149–150, 181; villainous origin story, 57–59. *See also* Clark, Captain; Hart, Charles; identities and personas, Quantrill's
—death of, 16–17, 202–203; bones' removal from grave, 207–209; capture at Wakefield Farm, 2–7, 10–12; grave visitors, 204–207, 210; instructions for corpse, 204; modern memorials, 209–210; transport to Louisville, 13–15, *14*
Quantrill and the Border Wars (Connelley), 8–9
Quantrill's Raiders. *See* guerrillas (bushwhackers)

race. *See* slavery; society
Randlett, Reuben A., 135
Republican Intelligencer (Charles City, Iowa), 7
Republican Party, 89
Richmond, Va., 152–156, 159, 164–165, 166–167, 236n5

Richmond (Va.) Sentinel, 156
Ridge, Pea, 236–237n10
Riggs, Samuel A., 97
Roaring Camp (S. L. Johnson), 78
Roberts, Thomas, 120
ruffians, 75–76, 82, 109–110, 111

Salt Lake City, Utah Territory, *62*, 64–66, 68
Sam Gaty (riverboat), 165–166, 237–238n21, 239n10
Sarcoxie, George (Delaware Indian), 98–99
Scott, Fernando (bushwhacker), 161
Scott, S. S., 129–130
Scott, W. W. (friend), 43, 206–207
Scully, Patrick and Bridget (sexton), 204–205, 206–207, 210
Second South Carolina (Infantry Regiment), 174
Seddon, James, 155–156
segregation, racial, 33, 221–222n36
Sentinel (Richmond, Va.), 156
"separate but equal," 221–222n36
Seven Lectures to Young Men on Various Important Subjects (Beecher), 94
shapeshifters: confidence men, 100, 102–103; guerrilla tactics, 6, 169–171, 200, 214; in Lawrence, Kans., 106–108; WCQ's identities, xii, xiii–xiv, 13, 117
Shepherd, George, 140, 141, 151
Sherman, William Tecumseh, 194
Sisters of Charity, 15, 16
slavery: abolition of, 3, 153; census data, 51, 119, 189; guerrillas' views on, 149–150; masculinity and, 46; popular sovereignty and, 88–89; racial hierarchy, 118–119; violence of, 51–52
sleeping situations, 78–79; sexual intimacy between men, 224–225n10; WCQ-Beeson conflict, 57–59; WCQ's named bedfellows, xi–xii, 97, 135, 164, 227n29
Smoky Hill and Republican Union (Junction City, Kans.), 165–166
society: changing nature of, 66; confidence men in, 94–96, 103, 229nn5–6; deception and masks, 107–108, 115, 231–232n25; gunslinger myth, 69–71; honor-driven violence, 51, 99–100, 131–132, 171, 229–230n20; hunter myth, 72–73, 75–76, 82; manhood, concepts of, 36–37, 66, 70, 219–220n2, 226–227n24; politics and voting, 47–48; racial aspects of, 32–34, 118–119; slavery's effects on, 47; teachers, archetypes of, 39–40, 222–223n10; Wild West myth, xv, 76–77, 215n11; women in, 60–61, 64, 184
Sons of the Confederate Veterans, 208, 209, 210
South Carolina, 119, 147, 174
Springfield, Mo., 121, 122, 229–230n20

262 INDEX

Spybuck, Golightly (James), 80–82, 131
squatter sovereignty, 49, 88
St. John's Catholic Cemetery (Portland, Ky.), 204, 210
St. Louis Daily Globe-Democrat, 183–184
St. Louis Republican, 140
Stanton, Kansas Territory, 59, 83–85, *112*
Stewart, John E. (jayhawker), 97
Stone, Nathan (innkeeper), 90, 98, 102, 108, 177
Sumner, Charles, 50–51, 224n18, 232n4
Suppressed Evidence (Edwards), 215n2

Tate house firefight (Mo.), 142–143
Taylor, Fletch (bushwhacker), 148, 183–184
teaching career, Quantrill's: in Canal Dover, 34; in Mendota, 37–40, 42; in Stanton, 83–85
teamster (wagon train), 63–65
Terrell, Edwin: capture of WCQ, 2–7, 10–12, 13–15, 202–203; descriptions of, 7–8, 13
Texas: antebellum travels, 116–117, 118–119; guerrillas in, 178–181, *182*, 183
Thirteenth Amendment, 3
Todd, George (bushwhacker): commission, 121, 144; death, 198; guerrilla leader, 195–198; power struggle, 159, 163–165, 185–186
Torrey, Col. Henry, 55–59, 111
tribes. *See* Native Americans
Troxel, Roxey (student), 83–84
Tuscarawas County. *See* Canal Dover, Ohio
Tutt, Davis K. ("Little Dave"), 229–230n20

Underground Railroad, 107, 174, 238–239n4
Union Provost Marshals (U.S. Army), 7, 11, 192
United Daughters of the Confederacy, 209, 210

Van Dorn, Earl, 122, 236–237n10
Vaughn, Jim (bushwhacker), 148–149
Virginia, 152–156, 159, 164–165, 166–167, 236n5

wagon train (teamster), 63–65
Wakarusa War (Kansas Territory), 48–50, 90

Wakefield Farm (Ky.): capture of WCQ, 2–7, 10–12, 13–15, 202–203; guerrillas killed at, 218n29
Walker, Andrew J. (friend, bushwhacker): joins war, 120, 121; on WCQ, 69, 113–114, 115–116
Walker, Morgan (friend), 113–114, 116–117
Walker Farm (Blue Springs, Mo.), *112*, 113–116, 122–123, 132, 232n32
Walsh, Hugh, 106–107
Washington, D.C., Daily American Organ, 45, 46
Wertz, Louis (gravedigger), 206–207
Wheeler, Holland (roommate in Lawrence), 86, 93, 97, 98, 226n6
Whig Party, 28
white people: as guerrillas, 3; hunter myth, 73, 82; masks and identity, 107–108
White Turkey (Delaware Indian), 99–100
whiteness and Quantrill's identity, 32–34, 118–119, 232n1
Whitney House Hotel (Lawrence, Kans.), 93, 96–97, 98, *101*, 177
Wigfall, Trezevant, 155
Wild West myth, xv, 76–77, 215n11
Williams, Les, 208
Willis, William and Maranda (Dover residents), 32
Wilson's Creek battle, 121, 122
Wineberry, Ann and Amanda (Dover residents), 32
Winn, Jack, 130
"Woman Hanged, A," 45–47
women: attitudes toward, 60–61, 64, 184; flowers to WCQ, 16–17, 206; guerrillas and, 123–124, 173, 175–176, 239n7; love interest, 201–202; newspaper on WCQ and, 183–184
woodsman. *See* frontiersman, Quantrill as
Wyandotte Constitution (Kansas Territory), 87. *See also* Clark, Kate

Young, Brigham, 63
Younger, Cole (bushwhacker), 133, 162

UNCIVIL WARS

Weirding the War: Stories from the Civil War's Ragged Edges
EDITED BY STEPHEN BERRY

Ruin Nation: Destruction and the American Civil War
BY MEGAN KATE NELSON

America's Corporal: James Tanner in War and Peace
BY JAMES MARTEN

*The Blue, the Gray, and the Green: Toward an
Environmental History of the Civil War*
EDITED BY BRIAN ALLEN DRAKE

Empty Sleeves: Amputation in the Civil War South
BY BRIAN CRAIG MILLER

Lens of War: Exploring Iconic Photographs of the Civil War
EDITED BY J. MATTHEW GALLMAN AND GARY W. GALLAGHER

*The Slave-Trader's Letter-Book: Charles Lamar, the Wanderer,
and Other Tales of the African Slave Trade*
BY JIM JORDAN

Driven from Home: North Carolina's Civil War Refugee Crisis
BY DAVID SILKENAT

*The Ghosts of Guerrilla Memory: How Civil War Bushwhackers
Became Gunslingers in the American West*
BY MATTHEW CHRISTOPHER HULBERT

Beyond Freedom: Disrupting the History of Emancipation
EDITED BY DAVID W. BLIGHT AND JIM DOWNS

*The Lost President: A. D. Smith and the Hidden History
of Radical Democracy in Civil War America*
BY RUTH DUNLEY

Bodies in Blue: Disability in the Civil War North
BY SARAH HANDLEY-COUSINS

Visions of Glory: The Civil War in Word and Image
EDITED BY KATHLEEN DIFFLEY AND BENJAMIN FAGAN

Household War: How Americans Lived and Fought the Civil War
EDITED BY LISA TENDRICH FRANK AND LEEANN WHITES

Buying and Selling Civil War Memory in Gilded Age America
EDITED BY JAMES MARTEN AND CAROLINE E. JANNEY

The War after the War: A New History of Reconstruction
BY JOHN PATRICK DALY

*The Families' Civil War:
Black Soldiers and the Fight for Racial Justice*
BY HOLLY A. PINHEIRO JR.

Sand, Science, and the Civil War:
Sedimentary Geology and Combat
   BY SCOTT HIPPENSTEEL
A Man by Any Other Name: William Clarke Quantrill
and the Search for American Manhood
   BY JOSEPH M. BEILEIN JR.